The Atlantic Alliance

a bibliography

Colin Gordon

Frances Pinter Ltd., London
Nichols Publishing Co., New York

© Colin Gordon 1978

First Published in Great Britain in 1978 by
Frances Pinter (Publishers) Limited
5 Dryden Street, London WC2E 9NW

Published in the U.S.A. in 1978 by
Nichols Publishing Company
Post Office Box 96
New York, N.Y. 10024

ISBN 0 903804 32 8

Printed in Great Britain by Billing & Sons Ltd, Guildford & Worcester

Library of Congress Cataloging in Publication Data

Gordon, Colin.
  The Atlantic Alliance.

  1. North Atlantic Treaty Organization—Bibliography.
  I. Title.
  Z6464.N65G67   1978   [JX1393.N67] 016.35503˙1'091821
  ISBN 0-89397-041-7   78-15540

**The
Atlantic
Alliance**

CONTENTS

Acknowledgements

Preface   9

General Bibliographical Introduction   11

Section I: The Genesis of the Alliance: 1945–1955   16

Section II: The Years of Strain and Stress: 1955–1962   37

Section III: The Search for a *modus vivendi*: 1962–1970   79

Section IV: The Onset of Detente: 1970–1977   154

ACKNOWLEDGEMENTS

The North Atlantic Treaty which created the Atlantic Alliance was signed in April 1949; the North Atlantic Treaty Organisation, which is its permanent structure, was established in its final form early in 1951. One of the outstanding features of the Alliance is thus its longevity, and throughout its existence it has been the object of enquiry, scrutiny and criticism. Over the last few years an increasing number of people — academics, journalists, politicians, serving soldiers and the like — have felt the need for a bibliography devoted to the Alliance, and it is as a partial response to their needs that this bibliography of books, reports, papers, pamphlets and articles in English has been compiled. It has been made possible by a grant generously provided by NATO; in particular, its publication would not have occurred without the interest and concern of John Vernon of the NATO Information Directorate. Andrew Murdoch, also of the Information Directorate, has been both patient and encouraging over a gestation period which proved longer than was anticipated.

Miss Olivia Freeman, formerly librarian of the Atlantic Institute for International Affairs in Paris, was to have collaborated in the project. In the event circumstances prevented this, but her advice and early help proved invaluable.

The University of Salford provided a grant in aid of publication; Mrs. Susan Ruddy overcame the problems of typing from hand-written index cards, and Dr. Frances Pinter has been a helpful and efficient publisher.

While accepting full responsibility for any deficiencies which may appear in this bibliography, I yet hope it will prove to be a valuable introduction to a rich and many-faceted subject.

Colin Gordon
University of Salford
Spring 1978.

PREFACE

When the Atlantic Alliance was formed in April 1949 there were twelve states party to the original treaty; later two further joined and in 1955 membership stabilised at fifteen with the accession of the Federal Republic of Germany. With so many adherents and of such duration the Alliance has been much written about; this bibliography of material in English covers some 3,000 references drawn from British, Canadian, U.S., Scandinavian and Soviet sources.

The material has been arranged to fall under four chronological periods, viz:
1) from the late forties to the accession of the Federal Republic of Germany in 1955
2) from 1955 to the Cuban missile crisis of October 1962
3) from 1962 to the advent of 'the era of negotiation' in 1970; and
4) from 1970 to the review of the Helsinki accords on European security and co-operation in 1977.

Each period is introduced by a brief historical outline of its main developments, and will be divided into three sections. The first is devoted to books; the second to reports, pamphlets and occasional papers; the third is devoted to articles.

The material in each section is presented under five headings: legal; economic; national and regional; politico-military; and, finally, military-strategic. While such a division can only be made by accepting broad general definitions, it seems preferable to do this rather than on the one hand to make no attempt at subject differentiation or on the other hand to adopt a multiplicity of distinctions with regard to material which often straddles several subjects.

It is hoped that the conventions adopted for the presentation of references will be found both self-evident and acceptable. Thus, author names are presented in inverted form. Where titles have been employed originally, they have been included, along with the generational designation 'Jr.'. Care has been taken to avoid confusing non-British readers with changes of title, as when Anthony Eden later wrote as Sir Anthony Eden and later as the Earl of Avon.

Proper names are written in full, with the exception of His or Her Majesty's Stationery Office (H.M.S.O.) and the United States Government Publishing Office (U.S.G.P.O.). When the Institute for Strategic Studies (I.S.S.) the Canadian Institute for International Affairs (C.I.I.A.) or the Royal Institute for International Affairs (R.I.I.A.) has acted as publisher, the abbreviated form has generally been employed.

Changes in appellation and address occur only rarely; thus the Institute for Strategic Studies became the International Institute for Strategic Studies and the Atlantic Institute the Atlantic Institute for International Affairs. The latter also moved to Paris. In these and similar instances, designations and place of publication is given as at the time of publication; the changes are noted in the general bibliographical introduction.

GENERAL BIBLIOGRAPHICAL INTRODUCTION

Much background material on the Atlantic Alliance is to be found in the following annual compilations:
ANNUAL REGISTER OF WORLD EVENTS. London: Longmans.
THE STATESMAN'S YEARBOOK. London: Macmillan.
THE UNITED STATES IN WORLD AFFAIRS. New York: Harper and Row for the Council of Foreign Relations.
THE YEARBOOK OF WORLD AFFAIRS. London: Stevens for the Institute of World Affairs.
The annual SURVEY OF INTERNATIONAL AFFAIRS. London: R.I.I.A., though not up-to-date, is invaluable for the years it covers, as is the constantly up-dated KEESINGS CONTEMPORARY ARCHIVES. Bristol: Keynsham.

Valuable material, particularly on the early years of the Alliance, is to be found in NATO LETTER, later NATO REVIEW. Brussels: NATO Information Services.

WESTERN EUROPEAN UNION: ASSEMBLY DOCUMENTS AND DEBATES. Paris: W.E.U. appear bi-annually; NATO PARLIAMENTARIANS' CONFERENCE, later NORTH ATLANTIC ASSEMBLY: ADDRESSES, REPORTS AND RECOMMENDATIONS. Brussels: North Atlantic Assembly appear annually and contain much of interest.

A useful annual survey of events relation to N.A.T.O. and W.E.U. is to be found in INTERNATIONAL ORGANISATION, the quarterly publication of the World Peace Foundation.

Documents relating to the Alliance are to be found in the following annual publications:

DOCUMENTS ON AMERICAN FOREIGN RELATIONS. New York: Harper and Row for the Council on Foreign Relations.
DOCUMENTS ON INTERNATIONAL AFFAIRS. London: R.I.I.A. Selected documents appear regularly in the bi-monthly NATO REVIEW, formerly NATO LETTER. Brussels: NATO Information Services. SURVIVAL. London: I.I.S.S. and in the ATLANTIC COMMUNITY QUARTERLY. Washington: Atlantic Council of the United States.

The German question and Berlin, so frequently at the centre of Alliance politics, has been the subject of several specific collections of documents, notably

ed. Embree, George D.	THE SOVIET UNION AND THE GERMAN QUESTION. SEPT. 1958 – JUNE 1961. The Hague: Martinus Nijhoff. 1963.
G.D.R. Foreign Ministry	DOCUMENTATION ON THE QUESTION OF WEST BERLIN. Berlin: Ministry of Foreign Affairs of the German Democratic Republic. 1964.
G.D.R. Information Office	THE GERMAN DEMOCRATIC REPUBLIC IN THE FIGHT FOR THE UNITY OF GERMANY. London: Collet's Holdings. 1953. (See review by Donald de Hirsch in INTERNATIONAL AFFAIRS. Vol. 30. No. 1. January 1954. p. 101)
ed. von der Gablentz, O.M.	DOCUMENTS ON BERLIN 1943–1963. Munich: Oldenbourg Verlag. 1963.
ed. Graf, Rudolf et al.	DOCUMENTS ON THE DIVISION OF GERMANY AND THE RELATIONS BETWEEN THE TWO GERMAN STATES. Dresden: Verlag Zeit im Bild. 1968.
ed. Hubatsch, Walther.	THE GERMAN QUESTION. New York: Herder Book Center. 1967.
ed. Ruhm von Oppen, Beate.	DOCUMENTS ON GERMANY UNDER OCCUPATION 1945–1954. London: Oxford University Press for R.I.I.A. 1955.

More general is:
CMND 6932. SELECTED DOCUMENTS RELATING TO PROBLEMS OF SECURITY AND CO-OPERATION IN EUROPE 1954–1977. London: H.M.S.O. 1977.
Indispensable for both synopses and full texts of the communiques of ministerial sessions of the North Atlantic Council, the Defence Policy Committee and the Nuclear Planning Group is
NATO FINAL COMMUNIQUES 1949–1974. Brussels: NATO Information Services. 1975. In addition, of considerable value is
NATO FACTS AND FIGURES. Brussels: NATO Information Services. 1969., as are a number of occasional pamphlets from the same source, e.g.
NATO HANDBOOK
THE EUROGROUP
THE ATLANTIC ALLIANCE AND THE WARSAW PACT
INTERNATIONAL MILITARY EXERCISES
and the more detailed
NATO GLOSSARY OF MILITARY TERMS.
To the above should be added
IN THE SERVICE OF PEACE AND SECURITY. Mons: SHAPE and Allied Command Europe.
Attention is drawn to
WESTERN CO-OPERATION: A REFERENCE HANDBOOK. London: H.M.S.O. for Central Office of Information. 1956 (C.O.I. Pamphlet No. 11).
A pioneer and annotated bibliography on all aspects of the relationships of members of the Alliance is
THE ATLANTIC COMMUNITY: AN INTRODUCTORY BIBLIOGRAPHY (2 volumes). Leyden: Sijthoff. 1961.
Less comprehensive is
NATO BIBLIOGRAPHY. Paris: NATO Information Services. 1964.
Much more specific in relation to the inception of the Alliance is
THE UNITED STATES AND EUROPE: A BIBLIOGRAPHICAL EXPRESSION OF THOUGHT IN AMERICAN PUBLICATIONS DURING 1950. Washington: Library of Congress, Card Division. 1951.
More political and extending over a much longer period is
eds. Burt, Richard and Kemp, Geoffrey. CONGRESSIONAL HEARINGS ON AMERICAN DEFENSE POLICY 1947–1971: AN

ANNOTATED BIBLIOGRAPHY. Lawrence: University of Kansas Press. 1974.

On nuclear issues, attention is drawn to:

H.Q. Department of the Army. NUCLEAR WEAPONS AND THE ATLANTIC ALLIANCE: A BIBLIOGRAPHICAL SURVEY. Washington: U.S.G.P.O. for U.S. Department of the Army. 1965. (D.A. PAM. 20–66).

and

H.Q. Department of the Army: NUCLEAR WEAPONS AND NATO: AN ANALYTICAL SURVEY OF LITERATURE. Washington: U.S.G.P.O. 1970. (DA. PAM. 50–1).

Valuable material is to be found in

Motuik, L. STRATEGIC STUDIES READING GUIDE. Ottowa: Canadian Defence Education Establishment. n.d. (CFP. 239).

and

Center for Arms Control and International Security Studies. STRATEGIC STUDIES REFERENCE GUIDE VOL. 1. Pittsburgh: University Center for International Studies, University of Pittsburgh. 1977.

While not specifically bibliographical material, the following organisations are worthy of note:

The Atlantic Treaty Association,
185 rue de la Pompe,
Paris XV1.

and its associated bodies:

The Atlantic Council of Canada,
31 Wellesley Street East,
Toronto 5,
Ontario.

The British Atlantic Committee,
RUSI Building,
Whitehall,
London,
SW1A 3ET.

The Atlantic Council of the United States,
1616H. Street, N.W.,
Washington D.C. 20006.

On all issues connected with the Atlantic Alliance and NATO assistance is invariably forthcoming from:

NATO Information Services,
NATO,
1100 Brussels.

The address of the Atlantic Institute for International Affairs, formerly the Atlantic Institute, is now:
120 rue de Longchamp,
75116 Paris.

SECTION I

THE GENESIS OF THE ALLIANCE: 1945–1955

Difficulties in the political relationship between the major allies in the struggle against Nazi Germany began to arise before the end of the war; at that time provoked by Soviet policy in Eastern Europe, they were to be exacerbated in the first few months following the defeat of Hitler's Germany. Ranging from pressure on Iran and Turkey, they included fundamentally different stances in respect of the Greek civil war, the status of Trieste, the economy of Germany and the differences between the liberal-democratic states of Western Europe and the Peoples' Democracies of the East. In 1947, following notice being served by Britain that she could no longer support her traditional stabilising role in the Eastern Mediterranean, President Truman announced the doctrine with which his name will be permanently associated; he pledged the support of the United States to all states threatened by internal or external Communist pressures. Subsequently, Secretary of State George Marshall offered the economic support of the United States to all those European countries prepared to associate themselves with the United States in an inter-governmental economic self-help association. The only East European country to express interest, Czechoslovakia, shortly after denied its support and became a country governed by a monolithic party along the lines of the other countries in the Soviet bloc. Subsequently the Berlin blockade starkly demonstrated the existence of what Winston Churchill in 1946 had described as an 'iron-curtain running from Stettin in the Baltic to Trieste in the Adriatic'.

It was in this context that the West European states of Britain,

France, Belgium, Holland and Luxembourg which had initially considered that the medium-term threat to their security might arise from the policies of a resurgent Germany began to revise their views and ultimately accept that they risked a shorter-term threat from the policies of the Soviet Union. Given their economic weakness and, in some cases, the weakness of their social and political institutions, they began the conversations which ultimately were to lead to the clamping of the military power of the United States alongside their own in a defensive alliance, created in April 1949 with the signing of the North Atlantic Treaty.

That which the United States brought to the states of Western Europe was its critical atomic monopoly, later its enormous atomic superiority. With the outbreak of the Korean war in June 1950, Western perceptions of a Soviet military threat towards Western Europe were dramatically heightened. There began the build-up of Western military forces and the anguished debates on the need for increased conventional forces in order to establish an overall Western deterrent posture, debates which were ultimately to lead to the rearming of the Federal Republic of Germany and its incorporation into the Atlantic Alliance in May 1955.

The first section of the bibliography which follows reflects these early developments, ranging from the justly celebrated enunciation of the doctrine of containment by 'X' in 1947 through the economic preoccupations of the late forties and the intense political and military issues which characterised the early fifties.

Books

Legal Aspects

Beckett, Sir W. Eric. THE NORTH ATLANTIC TREATY, THE BRUSSELS TREATY AND THE CHARTER OF THE UNITED NATIONS. London: Stevens for the London Institute of World Affairs. 1950

Economic Aspects

Price, Harry Bayard. THE MARSHALL PLAN AND ITS MEANING. Ithaca: Cornell University Press. 1955

Ward, Barbara. POLICY FOR THE WEST. Harmondsworth: Penguin Books. 1951. (See review article by F.H. Underhill. 'Policy for the West: the gospel according to The Economist'. INTERNATIONAL JOURNAL. Vol. 6. No. 2. Spring. 1951. pp. 146–150)
Ward, Barbara. THE WEST AT BAY. New York: Norton. 1948

National and Regional Aspects

Carleton, William G. THE REVOLUTION IN AMERICAN FOREIGN POLICY, 1945–1954. New York: Doubleday. 1954
Clay, Lucius D. DECISION IN GERMANY (1945–1949). Garden City: Doubleday, 1950
Clay, General Lucius D. GERMANY AND THE FIGHT FOR FREEDOM. Cambridge, Mass.: Harvard University Press. London: Oxford University Press. 1950
Davis, Lyn Etheridge. THE COLD WAR BEGINS. SOVIET-AMERICAN CONFLICT OVER EASTERN EUROPE. Princeton: Princeton University Press. 1974
Dean, Vera Micheles. THE UNITED STATES AND RUSSIA. Cambridge, Mass.: Harvard University Press. 1947
Dean, Vera Micheles. EUROPE AND THE UNITED STATES (since 1945). New York: Knopf. Toronto: McClelland and Stewart. 1950
Epstein, Leon E. BRITAIN – UNEASY ALLY. Chicago: University of Chicago Press. 1954
Hawtrey, R.G. WESTERN EUROPEAN UNION: IMPLICATIONS FOR THE UNITED KINGDOM. London and New York: Royal Institute of International Affairs. 1949
Jordan, Z. ODER-NEISSE LINE: A STUDY OF THE POLITICAL, ECNOMIC AND EUROPEAN SIGNIFICANCE OF POLAND'S WESTERN FRONTIER. London: Polish Freedom Movement 'Independence and Democracy'. 1952
Kennan, George F. REALITIES OF AMERICAN FOREIGN POLICY. Princeton: Princeton University Press. Toronto: Saunders. 1954
Morgenthau, Hans J. (ed.). GERMANY AND THE FUTURE OF EUROPE. Chicago: University of Chicago Press. 1951
Morris, Eric. BLOCKADE: BERLIN AND THE COLD WAR. London: Hamish Hamilton. 1973
Nettl, J.P. THE EASTERN ZONE AND SOVIET POLICY IN GERMANY

1945—50. New York: Oxford University Press. 1951
Osgood, Robert Endicott. IDEALS AND SELF-INTEREST IN AMERICA'S FOREIGN RELATIONS. Chicago: University of Chicago Press. 1953
Reynaud, Paul. UNITE OR PERISH: A DYNAMIC PROGRAM FOR A UNITED EUROPE. New York: Simon and Schuster. 1951
Roberts, Henry L. RUSSIA AND AMERICA: DANGERS AND PROSPECTS. New York: Harper for the Council on Foreign Relations. 1955
Storm, Walter. THE CRISIS IN CZECHOSLOVAKIA. Prague: Orbis. 1948. (A Leftist account of the take-over in Czechoslovakia by a South African journalist)
Webster, Professor Sir Charles. *et al.* UNITED KINGDOM POLICY: FOREIGN, STRATEGIC, ECONOMIC. London and New York: Royal Institute of International Affairs. 1950

Politico-Military Aspects

Acheson, Dean. POWER AND DIPLOMACY. London: Oxford University Press. 1958
Aron, Raymond. THE CENTURY OF TOTAL WAR. London: Derek Verschoyle. 1954
Baldwin, Hanson W. POWER AND POLITICS: THE FACE OF SECURITY IN AN ATOMIC AGE. Claremont, California: Claremont College; Castle Press. 1950
Blackett, P.M.S. FEAR, WAR AND THE BOMB. New York: Whittlesey House. 1949
Boyd, Andrew and Metson, William. ATLANTIC PACT, COMMON—WEALTH AND UNITED NATIONS. London: Hutchinson (for the U.N. Association). 1949 .(Origins, creation and significance of the Atlantic Pact)
Bundy, McGeorge (ed.). THE PATTERN OF RESPONSIBILITY; POLICY STATEMENTS OF DEAN ACHESON. Boston: Houghton. 1952
Byrnes, James F. SPEAKING FRANKLY. (The Beginnings of the Cold War). New York: Harper. 1947
Chatham House Study Group. DEFENCE IN THE COLD WAR: THE TASK FOR THE FREE WORLD. London and New York: Royal

Institute of International Affairs. 1950

Clemens, Diane Shaver. YALTA: A STUDY IN SOVIET-AMERICAN RELATIONS. New York: Oxford University Press. 1970. (Described in FOREIGN AFFAIRS as 'a joy to read')

Davis, Lynn Etheridge. THE COLD WAR BEGINS: SOVIET-AMERICAN CONFLICT OVER EASTERN EUROPE. Princeton: Princeton University Press. 1974

Dobney, Frederick J. (ed.). SELECTED PAPERS OF WILL CLAYTON. Baltimore: Johns Hopkins Press. 1971

Druks, Herbert. HARRY S. TRUMAN AND THE RUSSIANS. 1945–1953. New York: Robert Speller. 1967

Feis, Herbert. FROM TRUST TO TERROR: THE ONSET OF THE COLD WAR. 1945–1950. London: Anthony Blond. 1971

Finletter, Thomas K. POWER AND POLICY: U.S. FOREIGN POLICY AND MILITARY POWER IN THE HYDROGEN AGE. New York: Harcourt, Brace. 1954

Fosdick, Dorothy. COMMON SENSE AND WORLD AFFAIRS. New York: Harcourt. 1955

Freeland, Richard M. THE TRUMAN DOCTRINE AND THE ORIGINS OF McCARTHYISM. New York: Knopf. 1972

Gaddis, John Lewis. THE UNITED STATES AND THE ORIGINS OF THE COLD WAR. 1941–1947. New York: Columbia University Press. 1972

Gardner, Lloyd C., Schlesinger, Arthur. Jr., Morgenthau, Hans. J. THE ORIGINS OF THE COLD WAR. Waltham, Mass.: Ginn-Blaisdell. . 1970. (3 essays and rejoinders – a blend of revisionism and traditionalism)

Haines, C. Grove (ed.). THE THREAT OF SOVIET IMPERIALISM. Baltimore: Johns Hopkins Press. 1954

Herz, Martin. BEGINNINGS OF THE COLD WAR. Bloomington: Indiana University Press. 1966

Hoskins, Halford L. THE ATLANTIC PACT. Washington: Public Affairs Press. 1949

Howe, Quincy. ASHES OF VICTORY: WORLD WAR II AND ITS AFTERMATH. New York: Simon and Schuster. 1972

Ingram, Kenneth. HISTORY OF THE COLD WAR. London: Darwen Finlayson. New York: Philosophical Library. 1955. (See review by P.A. Reynolds; INTERNATIONAL AFFAIRS. Vol. 31 No. 4. October 1955. pp. 492–493)

Ismay, Lord. NATO – THE FIRST FIVE YEARS. Paris: NATO. 1954.

(See review by V. Repin: 'The First Five Years of NATO' in
INTERNATIONAL AFFAIRS (Moscow). 1956. No. 3. pp. 129–133)
Kaiser, Robert G. COLD WINTER, COLD WAR. New York: Stein and
Day. 1974. (The political and economic problems of Britain and the
United States from the end of the war up to the enunciation of the
Truman doctrine)
Kennan, George F. MEMOIRS: 1925–1950. Boston: Little, Brown & Co.
1967. (See review by P. Podlesny: 'History calls to account', in
INTERNATIONAL AFFAIRS (Moscow). 1969. No. 2. pp. 96–98)
Kuklick, Bruce. AMERICAN POLICY AND THE DIVISION OF
GERMANY: THE CLASH WITH RUSSIA OVER REPARATIONS.
Ithaca: Cornell University Press. 1972. (A revisionist study)
Lafeber, Walter (ed.). THE ORIGINS OF THE COLD WAR. 1941–
1947. New York: Wiley. 1971
Lippman, Walter. THE COLD WAR: A STUDY IN U.S. FOREIGN
POLICY. New York: Harper. 1947. (A critique of Kennan's
'X' article)
Lippman, Walter. ISOLATION AND ALLIANCES. Boston: Atlantic
(Little, Brown). 1952
McGeehan, Robert. THE GERMAN REARMAMENT QUESTION:
AMERICAN DIPLOMACY AND EUROPEAN DEFENCE AFTER
WORLD WAR II. Urbana: University of Illinios Press. 1971
Macmillan, Harold. TIDES OF FORTUNE 1945–1955. (The Macmillan
memoirs, Vol. 2). London: Macmillan. 1969
McLachlan, Donald (ed.). DEFENCE IN THE COLD WAR. New York:
Royal Institute for International Affairs. 1950
Maddox, Robert James. THE NEW LEFT AND THE ORIGINS OF
THE COLD WAR. Princeton: Princeton University Press. 1973
Middleton, Drew. THE DEFENCE OF WESTERN EUROPE. New York:
Appleton-Century-Crofts. London: Muller. 1952
Millis, Walter and Duffield, E.S. (eds.). THE FORRESTAL DIARIES.
New York: Viking. 1951. London: Cassell. 1952
Morgenthau, Hans J. IN DEFENCE OF THE NATIONAL INTEREST.
New York: Knopf. 1951
Morris, Eric. BLOCKADE: BERLIN AND THE COLD WAR. London:
Hamish Hamilton. 1973
Murray, John Middleton. THE FREE SOCIETY. London: Dakers. 1948
Paterson, Thomas G. (ed.). COLD WAR CRITICS: ALTERNATIVES
TO AMERICAN FOREIGN POLICY IN THE TRUMAN YEARS.
Chicago: Quadrangle Books. 1971. (A selection of the works of

revisionist historians)
Paterson, Thomas G. SOVIET-AMERICAN CONFRONTATION: POST-WAR RECONSTRUCTION AND THE ORIGINS OF THE COLD WAR. Baltimore: Johns Hopkins Press. 1973
Ross, Hugh (ed.). THE COLD WAR: CONTAINMENT AND ITS CRITICS. Chicago: Rand McNally. 1963
Sapin, Burton M. and Snyder, Richard C. THE ROLE OF THE MILITARY IN AMERICAN FOREIGN POLICY. New York: Doubleday. 1954
Shulman, Marshall D. STALIN'S FOREIGN POLICY REAPPRAISED. Cambridge, Mass.: Harvard University Press. Toronto: S.J. Reginald Saunders. London: Oxford University Press. 1963
Slessor, Marshal of the Royal Air Force Sir John. STRATEGY FOR THE WEST. London: Cassell; New York: Morrow. 1954. (See review by Roger Hilsman: 'Research in Military Affairs' in WORLD POLITICS. Vol. 7. No. 3. April 1955. pp. 490–503)
Smith, Gaddis. DEAN ACHESON. New York: Cooper Square Publishers. 1972. (A study of Acheson's four years as Secretary of State 1949–1953)
Smith, Jean Edward (ed.). THE PAPERS OF GENERAL LUCIUS D. CLAY: GERMANY 1945–1949. (2 vols.) Bloomington: Indiana University Press. 1974
Smith, Walter Bedell. MY THREE YEARS IN MOSCOW. Philadelphia: Lippincott. 1950
Smyth, J.G. (ed.). THE WESTERN DEFENCES. London: Wingate. 1951
Stevenson, Adlai E. CALL TO GREATNESS. London: Rupert Hart-Davis. 1954
Truman, Harry S. YEAR OF DECISIONS. 1945. Garden City: Doubleday London: Hodder & Stoughton. 1955. YEARS OF TRIAL AND HOPE. 1946–1953. Garden City: Doubleday; London: Hodder & Stoughton. 1956
Turner, Arthur C. BULWARK OF THE WEST: IMPLICATIONS AND PROBLEMS OF NATO. Toronto: The Ryerson Press for C.I.I.A. 1953
Vandenberg, Arthur H., Jr. THE PRIVATE PAPERS OF SENATOR VANDENBERG. London: Gollancz. 1953
Warne, Wing-Commander J.D. N.A.T.O. AND ITS PROSPECTS. New York: Praeger. 1954
Wheeler-Bennett, Sir John and Nicholls, Anthony. THE SEMBLANCE OF PEACE: THE POLITICAL SETTLEMENT AFTER THE

SECOND WORLD WAR. New York: St. Martin's Press. 1972
White, Gilbert F. *et al.* THE UNITED STATES AND THE SOVIET UNION: SOME QUAKER PROPOSALS FOR PEACE. New Haven: Yale University Press. 1949. London: Oxford University Press. 1950

Military and Strategic Aspects

Eliot, George Fielding. IF RUSSIA STRIKES. Indianapolis: Bobbs-Merrill. 1949
Ely, Colonel Louis B. THE RED ARMY TODAY. Harrisburg: Military Service Publishing Co. 1949. (An evaluation of Soviet military power and an assessment of the possible outcome of a Soviet invasion of Western Europe).
Garthoff, Raymond L. SOVIET MILITARY DOCTRINE. Glencoe, Ill.: The Free Press. 1953. (See review article by Roger Hilsman. 'Research in Military Affairs' in WORLD POLITICS. Vol. 7. No. 3. April 1955. pp. 490–503)
Kaufmann, William W. (ed.). MILITARY POLICY AND NATIONAL SECURITY. Princeton: Princeton University Press. 1956
Liddell Hart, B.J. DEFENCE OF THE WEST. New York: Morrow. 1950
Miksche, Lieut.-Col. F.O. ATOMIC WEAPONS AND ARMIES. New York: Praeger. 1955
Oliphant, M.L. *et al.* THE ATOMIC AGE. London: Allen and Unwin. 1949
Possony, Stefan T. STRATEGIC AIR POWER. Washington: Infantry Journal. 1949. (The possibilities and limitations of strategic bombardment)
Reinhardt, Colonel G.C. and Kintner, Lt. Col. W.R. ATOMIC WEAPONS IN LAND COMBAT. Harrisburg: Military Service Publishing Co. 1953
Reinhardt, Colonel George C. AMERICAN STRATEGY IN THE ATOMIC AGE. Norman: University of Oklahoma Press. 1955

Reports, Papers and Pamphlets

Economic Aspects

Salter, Sir Arthur. THE MEANING OF THE MARSHALL PLAN NOW (i.e. 1948). London: Benn. 1948

National and Regional Aspects

Amery, Julian. THE BRITISH COMMONWEALTH AND WESTERN EUROPE. London: Longmans, Green. 1952. (British Commonwealth Affairs. No. 7)

A Student of Affairs. HOW DID THE SATELLITES HAPPEN? A STUDY OF THE SOVIET SEIZURE OF EASTERN EUROPE. London: Batchworth Press. 1952

Oxford Radical Association. BRITAIN AND THE COLD WAR: THE FUTURE OF BRITISH FOREIGN POLICY. London: Westminster Press Provincial Newspapers for the Oxford Radical Association. 1952

Roberts, Henry L. and Wilson, Paul A. BRITAIN AND THE UNITED STATES: PROBLEMS IN CO-OPERATION. (Joint report of a British and an American study group.) London: Royal Institute of International Affairs; New York: Harper for the Council on Foreign Relations. 1953

Soviet News. ON THE SITUATION IN BERLIN 1948: The Soviet note on the situation in Berlin and Marshal Sokolovsky's proclamation and order on the currency reform. London: Soviet News. 1948

Politico – Military Aspects

British Society for International Understanding. NATO AND THE PEOPLES: report of the First International Study Conference on the Atlantic Community. Oxford 7–13 September 1952. London: British Society for International Understanding. 1952

Central Office of Information. ALLIANCE FOR PEACE: THE FIRST FIVE YEARS OF NATO. London: H.M.S.O. 1954

Chatham House Study Group. ATLANTIC ALLIANCE: NATO'S ROLE IN THE FREE WORLD. London and New York: Royal

Institute of International Affairs. 1952
Geiger, Theodore and Cleveland, H. van B. MAKING WESTERN EUROPE DEFENSIBLE: an appraisal of the effectiveness of U.S. policy in Western Europe. Washington: National Planning Association. 1951. (Planning Pamphlets. No. 74)
Harrison, Eric. ATLANTIC PARTNERSHIP. Toronto: Canadian Association for Adult Education with Canadian Institute of International Affairs. 1949
Institut fur Besatzungsfragen, Tubingen. OCCUPATION COSTS: ARE THEY A DEFENCE CONTRIBUTION? Tubingen: J.C.B. Mohr (Paul Siebeck). 1951
Turner, Arthur C. BULWARK OF THE WEST: IMPLICATIONS AND PROBLEMS OF NATO. Toronto: Ryerson Press for the Canadian Institute of International Affairs. 1953. (Contemporary Affairs No. 24)

Articles

Economic Aspects

H., A. ECONOMIC INTEGRATION IN THE COMMUNIST WORLD: RECENT DEVELOPMENTS ASSESSED. The World Today. Vol. 14. No. 11. November 1958. pp. 495—506

H., P.I. J. THE MARSHALL PLAN IN OPERATION. The World Today. Vol. 5. No. 10. October 1948. pp. 430—436

H., R.G. WESTERN UNION: ECONOMIC ASPECTS. The World Today. Vol. 5. No. 4 April 1949. pp. 178—183

H., R.G. THE EUROPEAN COAL AND STEEL COMMUNITY. The World Today. Vol. 7. No. 5. May 1951. pp. 197—203

K., N. EAST — WEST TRADE IN EUROPE: ECONOMIC ADVANTAGES AND POLITICAL DRAWBACKS. The World Today. Vol. 5. No. 3. March 1949. pp. 98—108

K., W. REACHING FOR THE MOON: THE SOVIET SEVEN-YEAR PLAN. The World Today. Vol. 15. No. 2. February 1959. pp. 47—58

Mackintosh, W.A. THE FISSURE IN NATO: NORTH AMERICAN AND STERLING AREA TRADE. Foreign Affairs. Vol. 31. No. 2.

January 1953. pp. 268—279
Mason, Edwards. AMERICAN SECURITY AND ACCESS TO RAW
MATERIALS. World Politics. Vol. 1. 1948—49. pp. 147—160
Moyse, Robert. NO STAR FOR THE WISE MEN: SOME FISCAL
PROBLEMS OF NATO COUNTRIES. International Journal. Vol. 7.
No. 1. Winter 1951—52. pp. 1—11
Nettl, Peter. ECONOMIC CHECKS ON GERMAN UNITY. Foreign
Affairs. Vol. 30. No. 4. July 1952. pp. 554—563
W., G.G. THE REVIVAL OF WESTERN GERMANY'S OCEAN
SHIPPING. The World Today. Vol. 7. No. 9. September 1951.
pp. 393—404
W., P. EAST — WEST TRADE. The World Today. Vol. 10. No. 1.
January 1954. pp. 19—31
Williams, John H. THE MARSHALL PLAN HALFWAY. Foreign
Affairs. Vol. 28. No. 3. April 1950. pp. 463—476
Williams, John H. END OF THE MARSHALL PLAN. Foreign Affairs.
Vol. 30. No. 4. July 1952. pp. 593—611
Z., P.V. GERMAN VIEWS ON THE SCHUMAN PLAN. The World
Today. Vol. 7. No. 7. July 1951. pp. 292—298

National and Regional Aspects

Adenauer, Konrad. GERMANY AND THE PROBLEM OF OUR
TIMES. (Address at Chatham House. 6 December 1951). International
Affairs. Vol. 28. No. 2. April 1952. pp. 156—161
Adenauer, Konrad. GERMANY AND EUROPE. Foreign Affairs. Vol. 31.
No. 3. April 1953. pp. 361—366
Adenauer, Konrad. GERMAN REUNION AND THE FUTURE OF
EUROPE. International Journal. Vol. 9. No. 3. Summer 1954.
pp. 173—176
Adenauer, Konrad. GERMANY, THE NEW PARTNER. Foreign Affairs.
Vol. 33. No. 2. January 1955. pp. 177—183
Alphand, Hervé. THE 'EUROPEAN POLICY' OF FRANCE. International
Affairs. Vol. 29. No. 2. April 1953. pp. 141—148
Anderson, Alvin T. THE SOVIETS AND NORTHERN EUROPE. World
Politics. Vol. 4. No. 4. July 1952. pp. 468—487
Armstrong, Hamilton Fish. EISENHOWER'S RIGHT FLANK. (i.e.
Greece, Turkey, Yugoslavia). Foreign Affairs. Vol. 29. No. 4. July

1951. pp. 651—663
Aron, Raymond. FRENCH PUBLIC OPINION AND THE ATLANTIC
TREATY. International Affairs. Vol. 28. No. 1. January 1952.
pp. 1—8
Attlee, Clement R. BRITAIN AND AMERICA: COMMON AIMS,
DIFFERENT OPINIONS. Foreign Affairs. Vol. 32. No. 2. January
1954. pp. 190—202
B., J. THE NORTH ATLANTIC PACT: WEST EUROPEAN REACTIONS:
A DUTCH VIEW. The World Today. Vol. 5. No. 7. July 1949. pp.
304—310
Bolles, Blair. NATO — AN AMERICAN VIEW. International Journal.
Vol. 6. No. 4. Autumn 1951. pp. 281—291
Brodie, Bernard. HOW STRONG IS BRITAIN? Foreign Affairs. Vol. 26.
No. 3. April 1948. pp. 432—449
van den Bussche, Axel. GERMAN REARMAMENT: HOPES AND
FEARS. Foreign Affairs. Vol. 32. No. 1. October 1953. pp. 68—79
Butler, Sir Harold. A NEW WORLD TAKES SHAPE (Western
Europe). Foreign Affairs. Vol. 26. No. 4 July 1948. pp. 604—615
C., I. WESTERN UNION: POLITICAL ASPECTS. The World Today.
Vol. 5. No. 4. April 1949. pp. 170—178
C., J. RELATIONS BETWEEN POLAND AND EASTERN GERMANY.
The World Today. Vol. 7. No. 9. September 1951. pp. 370—376
Clokie, H.M. *et al.* CANADA AND THE NORTH ATLANTIC TREATY.
International Journal. Vol. 4. No. 3. Summer 1949. pp. 244—249
Cobban, Alfred. SECURITY AND SOVEREIGNTY IN FRENCH
FOREIGN POLICY. International Journal. Vol. 8. No. 3. Summer
1953. pp. 172—180
D., I. BERLIN, NEW YEAR 1950. The World Today. Vol. 6. No. 3.
March 1950. pp. 101—110
Dernburg, H.J. REARMAMENT AND THE GERMAN ECONOMY.
Foreign Affairs. Vol. 33. No. 4. July 1955. pp. 648—662
Dethleffssem, Erich. THE CHIMERA OF GERMAN NEUTRALITY.
Foreign Affairs. Vol. 30. No. 3. April 1952. pp. 361—375
Dönhoff, Marion. GERMANY PUTS FREEDOM BEFORE UNITY.
Foreign Affairs. Vol. 28. No. 3. April 1950. pp. 398—411
Duchacek, Ivo. THE STRATEGY OF COMMUNIST INFILTRATION.
CZECHOSLOVAKIA. 1944—48. World Politics. Vol. 2. No. 3. April
1950. pp. 345—372
Duchacek, Ivo. THE FEBRUARY COUP IN CZECHOSLOVAKIA.
World Politics. Vol. 2. No. 4. July 1950. pp. 511—532

Earle, Edward Mead. THE AMERICAN STAKE IN EUROPE: RETROSPECT AND PROSPECT. International Affairs. Vol. 27. No. 4. October 1951. pp. 423–433

East, W. Gordon. THE MEDITERRANEAN: PIVOT OF PEACE AND WAR. Foreign Affairs. Vol. 31. No. 4. July 1953. pp. 619–633

Eden, Anthony. BRITAIN IN WORLD STRATEGY. Foreign Affairs. Vol. 29. No. 3. April 1951. pp. 341–350

Epstein, Leon D. BRITISH LABOUR'S FOREIGN POLICY. World Politics. Vol. 6. No. 1. October 1953. pp. 106–121

Fernsworth, Lawrence. SPAIN IN WESTERN DEFENSE. Foreign Affairs. Vol. 31. No. 4. July 1953. pp. 648–662

Gibson, James A. CANADIAN FOREIGN POLICY: A FORWARD VIEW. International Journal. Vol. 4. No. 2. Spring 1949. pp. 109–118

Goormaghtigh, John. FRANCE AND THE EUROPEAN DEFENCE COMMUNITY. International Journal. Vol. 9. No. 2. Spring 1954. pp. 96–106

H., A. CHANGING RELATIONSHIPS IN EASTERN EUROPE. The World Today. Vol. 14. No. 2. February 1958. pp. 54–60

H., A.H. SOME PROBLEMS FACING DENMARK. The World Today. Vol. 8. No. 10. October 1952. pp. 420–429

H., H. ALLIED ADMINISTRATION IN GERMANY. The World Today. Vol. 5. No. 4. April 1948. pp. 160–173

Hallstein, Walter. GERMANY'S DUAL AIM: UNITY AND INTEGRATION. Foreign Affairs. Vol. 31. No. 1. October 1952. pp. 58–66

Harrison, Eric. STRATEGY AND POLICY IN THE DEFENCE OF CANADA. International Journal. Vol. 4. No. 3. Summer 1949. pp. 212–243

Harrison, W.E.C. CANADIAN-AMERICAN DEFENCE. International Journal. Vol. 5. No. 3. Summer 1950. pp. 189–200

Herz, John H. GERMAN OFFICIALDOM REVISITED: POLITICAL VIEWS AND ATTITUDES OF THE WEST GERMAN CIVIL SERVICE. World Politics. Vol. 7. No. 1. October 1954. pp. 63–83

Holborn, Hugo. AMERICAN FOREIGN POLICY AND EUROPEAN INTEGRATION. World Politics. Vol. III. No. 1. October 1953. pp. 1–30

J., C.H. THE EUROPEAN DEFENCE COMMUNITY. The World Today. Vol. 10. No. 8. August 1954. pp. 326–339

J., C.N. BRITAIN AND THE EUROPEAN CONTINENT. The World

Today. Vol. III. No. 1. January 1955. pp. 20–26. (re. WEU and the revised Brussels Treaty)

Jacobi, Claus. GERMANY'S GREAT OLD MAN. Foreign Affairs. Vol. 33. No. 2. January 1955. pp. 239–249

Jaspers, Karl. THE POLITICAL VACUUM IN GERMANY. Foreign Affairs. Vol. 32. No. 4. July 1954. pp. 595–607

K., D.J. GREECE, TURKEY AND NATO. The World Today. Vol. 8. No. 4. April 1952. pp. 162–169

L., G. CZECHOSLOVAKIA UNDER COMMUNIST RULE. The World Today. Vol. 4. No. 12. December 1948. pp. 523–530

L., H.G. WESTERN GERMANY, JUNE 1947 AND NOW: IMPRESSIONS OF CONDITIONS AND OUTLOOK. The World Today. Vol. 5. No. 11. November 1949. pp. 371–377

L., H.G. GERMAN REARMAMENT: POLICIES AND OPINIONS. The World Today. Vol. 7. No. 2. February 1951. pp. 69–76

L., H.G. THE EUROPEAN DEFENCE COMMUNITY. The World Today. Vol. 8. No. 6. June 1952. pp. 236–248

L., H.G. CROSS CURRENTS IN WESTERN GERMAN OPINION. The World Today. Vol. 10. No. 7. July 1954. pp. 283–293

L., H.G. GERMAN OPINION AND THE BERLIN CONFERENCE. The World Today. Vol. 10. No. 3. March 1954. pp. 105–113

Layton, Lord. LITTLE EUROPE AND BRITAIN. (Reflections on the proposed European Defence Community and the European Political Community). International Affairs. Vol. 29. No. 3. July 1953. pp. 292–301

Lewis, Geoffrey. TURKEY: THE THORNY ROAD TO DEMOCRACY. The World Today. Vol. 18. No. 5. May 1962. pp. 182–191

Lockhart, Sir Robert Bruce. THE CZECHOSLOVAK REVOLUTION. Foreign Affairs. Vol. 26. No. 4. July 1948. pp. 632–644

Lower, Arthur. THE WEST AND WESTERN GERMANY. International Journal. Vol. 6. No. 4. Autumn 1951. pp. 300–307

McGhee, George C. TURKEY JOINS THE WEST. Foreign Affairs. Vol. 32. No. 4. June 1954. pp. 617–630

McInnis, Edgar. ADENAUER'S GERMANY: SOME POST-ELECTION IMPRESSIONS. International Journal. Vol. 9. No. 1. Winter 1954. pp. 1–7

Marshall, Andrew. PORTUGAL: A DETERMINED EMPIRE. The World Today. Vol. 17. No. 3. March 1961. pp. 95–101

Martin, Kingsley. NATO – A BRITISH VIEW. International Journal. Vol. 6. No. 4. Autumn 1951. pp. 292–299

Mayhew, Christopher. BRITISH FOREIGN POLICY SINCE 1945. International Affairs. Vol. 26. No. 4. October 1950. pp. 477–486

Mollet, Guy. FRANCE AND THE DEFENSE OF EUROPE. Foreign Affairs. Vol. 32. No. 3. April 1954. pp. 365–373

N., O. CZECHOSLOVAKIA UNDER COMMUNIST RULE. The World Today. Vol. 6. No. 1. January 1950. pp. 15–27

N., P. EASTERN GERMANY: A SURVEY OF SOVIET POLICY 1945–50. The World Today. Vol. 6. No. 7. July 1950. pp. 297–308

Onslow, C.G.D. WEST GERMAN REARMAMENT. World Politics. Vol. 3. No. 4. July 1951. pp. 450–485

P., A.N. EAST GERMANY SINCE THE RISINGS OF JUNE 1953. The World Today. Vol. 10. No. 2. February 1954. pp. 58–69

P., D.M. FRANCE'S PROBLEM AFTER THE REJECTION OF E.D.C. The World Today. Vol. 10. No. 10. October 1954. pp. 420–429

P., O. CZECHOSLOVAKIA TEN YEARS AFTER THE COUP D'ETAT. The World Today. Vol. 14. No. 3. March 1958. pp. 101–109

Pearson, Lester B. CANADA AND THE NORTH ATLANTIC ALLIANCE. Foreign Affairs. Vol. 27. No. 3. April 1949. pp. 369–378

Pearson, Lester B. THE DEVELOPMENT OF CANADIAN FOREIGN POLICY. Foreign Affairs. Vol. 30. No. 1. October 1951. pp. 17–30

Pearson, Lester B. CANADA'S NORTHERN HORIZON. Foreign Affairs. Vol. 31. No. 4. July 1953. pp. 581–591

Pearson, Lester B. WESTERN EUROPEAN UNION: IMPLICATIONS FOR CANADA AND NATO. International Journal. Vol. 10. No. 1. Winter 1954–55. pp. 1–11

Pick, Otto, and Wiseman, A. THE USSR AND HER NORTHERN NEIGHBOURS. The World Today. Vol. 15. No. 10. October 1959. pp. 387–394

R., K. FRESH LIGHT ON THE SOVIET POPULATION: RESULTS OF THE 1959 CENSUS. The World Today. Vol. 16. No. 5. May 1960. pp. 194–204

S., A.G. SCANDINAVIA FACES THE FUTURE: NEUTRALITY OR ALLIANCE. The World Today. Vol. 4. No. 5. May 1945. pp. 191–197

S., K.R. AUSTRIA: EAST OR WEST? The World Today. Vol. 4. No. 8. August 1948. pp. 346–354

S., K.R. THE SITUATION IN AUSTRIA: THE PEACE TREATY AND INTERNAL POLITICS. The World Today. Vol. 6. No. 10. October 1950. pp. 441–454

S., K.R. AUSTRIA AND THE BERLIN CONFERENCE. The World Today. Vol. 10. No. 4. April 1954. pp. 149–158

Sadak, Necmeddin. TURKEY FACES THE SOVIETS. Foreign Affairs. Vol. 27. No. 3. April 1949. pp. 449–461

Sandwell, B.K. NORTH ATLANTIC – COMMUNITY OR TREATY? International Journal. Vol. 7. No. 3. Summer 1952. pp. 169–172

Schmid, Carlo. GERMANY AND EUROPE. International Affairs. Vol. 27. No. 3. July 1951. pp. 306–311

Schmid, Carlo. GERMANY AND EUROPE: THE GERMAN SOCIAL DEMOCRATIC PROGRAM. Foreign Affairs. Vol. 30. No. 4. July 1952. pp. 531–544

Schuman, Robert. FRANCE AND EUROPE. Foreign Affairs. Vol. 31. No. 3. April 1953. pp. 349–360

Soustelle, Jacques. FRANCE, EUROPE AND PEACE. Foreign Affairs. Vol. 26. No. 3. April 1948. pp. 497–504

Soustelle, Jacques. FRANCE AND EUROPE: A GAULLIST VIEW. Foreign Affairs. Vol. 30. No. 4. July 1952. pp. 545–553

Strong, Lord. GERMANY BETWEEN EAST AND WEST. Foreign Affairs. Vol. 33. No. 3. April 1955. pp. 387–401

T., I.M. THE BENELUX COUNTRIES AND NATO. The World Today. Vol. 15. No. 5. May 1959. pp. 195–204

Vigers, Colonel T.W. THE GERMAN PEOPLE AND REARMAMENT. International Affairs. Vol. 27. No. 2. April 1951. pp. 151–155

W., A. NORWAY AND THE ATLANTIC PACT. The World Today. Vol. 5. No. 4. April 1949. pp. 154–160

W., E. NEW IDEAS VERSUS OLD IN WESTERN GERMANY. The World Today. Vol. 6. No. 8. August 1950. pp. 331–340

W., J. ICELAND: ITS IMPORTANCE IN AN AIR AGE. The World Today. Vol. 4. No. 7. July 1948. pp. 297–307

Warner, Geoffrey. PRESIDENT DE GAULLE'S FOREIGN POLICY. The World Today. Vol. 18. No. 8. August 1962. pp. 320–327

Wigforss, Harald. SWEDEN AND THE ATLANTIC PACT. International Organisation. Vol. 3. No. 3. August 1949. pp. 434–443

Williams, J. Emlyn. THE GERMAN FEDERAL REPUBLIC TODAY. International Affairs. Vol. 28. No. 4. October 1952. pp. 422–431

Wiskemann, Elizabeth. BERLIN BETWEEN EAST AND WEST. The World Today. Vol. 16. No. 11. November 1960. pp. 463–472

Zimmer, Paul E. MARXISM IN ACTION: THE SEIZURE OF POWER IN CZECHOSLOVAKIA. Foreign Affairs. Vol. 28. No. 4. July 1950. pp. 644–658

Politico – Military Aspects

A., G.L. TOWARDS AN ATLANTIC UNION. The World Today. Vol. 10. No. 7. July 1954. pp. 309–320

A., J. RADIO IN THE COLD WAR. The World Today. Vol. 10. No. 6. June 1954. pp. 245–254

Armstrong, Hamilton Fish. REGIONAL PACTS: STRONG POINTS OR STRONG CELLARS. Foreign Affairs. Vol. 27. No. 3. April 1949. pp. 351–368

Armstrong, Hamilton Fish. THE WORLD IS ROUND. Foreign Affairs. Vol. 31. No. 2. January 1953. pp. 175–199

Armstrong, Hamilton Fish. THE GRAND ALLIANCE HESITATES. (i.e. at the death of Stalin). Foreign Affairs. Vol. 32. No. 1. October 1953. pp. 48–67

Armstrong, Hamilton Fish. POSTSCRIPT TO EDC. Foreign Affairs. Vol. 33. No. 1. October 1954. pp. 17–27

B., N. PRESIDENT EISENHOWER TAKES THE INITIATIVE. The World Today. Vol. 10. No. 2. February 1954. pp. 51–58

B., U. NATO AND THE SOVEREIGN STATE. The World Today. Vol. 14. No. 1. January 1958. pp. 11–17

Baldwin, Hanson W. THE MYTH OF SECURITY. Foreign Affairs. Vol. 26. No. 2. January 1948. pp. 253–263

Baldwin, Hanson W. STRATEGY FOR TWO ATOMIC WORLDS. Foreign Affairs. Vol. 28. No. 3. April 1950. pp. 386–397

Beloff, Max. NO PEACE, NO WAR. Foreign Affairs. Vol. 27. No. 2. January 1949. pp. 215–231

Bernard, S. CHOICE IN THE WEST. World Politics. Vol. 5. No. 2. January 1953. pp. 133–167

Brodie, Bernard. THE ATOM BOMB AS POLICY MAKER. Foreign Affairs. Vol. 27. No. 1. October 1948. pp. 17–33

Bundy, McGeorge. THE TEST OF YALTA. Foreign Affairs. Vol. 27. No. 4. July 1949. pp. 618–629

D., I. REARMAMENT BUDGETS OF THE NORTH ATLANTIC POWERS. The World Today. Vol. 7. No. 3. March 1951. pp. 109–117

Dennett, Raymond. DANGER SPOTS IN THE PATTERN OF AMERICAN SECURITY. World Politics. Vol. 4. No. 4. July 1952.

pp. 447—467
Dulles, John Foster. POLICY FOR SECURITY AND PEACE. Foreign Affairs. Vol. 32. No. 3. April 1954. pp. 353—364
Eayrs, James. NEW WEAPONS IN THE COLD WAR: A STUDY OF RECENT TECHNIQUES IN INTERNATIONAL PROPAGANDA. International Journal. Vol. 7. No. 1. Winter 1951—52. pp. 36—47
Freedman, Max. THE LISBON CONFERENCE (1952). International Journal. Vol. 7. No. 2. Spring 1952. pp. 85—93
Gaddis, John Lewis. WAS THE TRUMAN DOCTRINE A REAL TURNING POINT? Foreign Affairs. Vol. 52. No. 2. January 1974. pp. 386—402
Gaitskell, Hugh. THE SEARCH FOR ANGLO-AMERICAN POLICY. Foreign Affairs. Vol. 32. No. 4. July 1954. pp. 563—576
Garthoff, Raymond L. THE CONCEPT OF THE BALANCE OF POWER IN SOVIET POLICY MAKING. World Politics. Vol. 4. No. 1. October 1951. pp. 85—111
Haas, Ernst B. THE BALANCE OF POWER: PRESCRIPTION, CONCEPT OR PROPAGANDA. World Politics. Vol. 5. No. 4. July 1953. pp. 442—477
Harrod, Roy. HANDS AND FISTS ACROSS THE SEA. Foreign Affairs. Vol. 30. No. 1. October 1951. pp. 63—76.
Hayter, Sir William. THE MEANING OF CO-EXISTENCE. Survey. No. 50. January 1954. pp. 17—22
Hoffmann, Stanley. AFTER THE CREATION, OR THE WATCH AND THE ARROW. International Journal. Vol. 18. No. 2. Spring 1973. pp. 175—184. (i.e. Kennan, Acheson and containment)
Howard, Major-General G.B. UNITED STATES DEFENCE PROCUREMENT IN CANADA. International Journal. Vol. 5. No. 4. Autumn 1950. pp. 315—324
Ismay, Lord. ATLANTIC ALLIANCE. International Journal. Vol. 9. No. 2. Spring 1954. pp. 79—86
Jessup, Philip C. THE BERLIN BLOCKADE AND THE USE OF THE UNITED NATIONS. Foreign Affairs. Vol. 50. No. 1. October 1971. pp. 163—173
Jones, Stephen B. THE POWER INVENTORY AND NATIONAL STRATEGY. World Politics. Vol. 6. No. 4. July 1954. pp. 421—452
Kaplan, Lawrence S. NATO AND ITS COMMENTATORS. International Organisation. Vol. 18. No. 4. November 1954. pp. 447—467
Kennan, George F. AMERICA AND THE RUSSIAN FUTURE. Foreign Affairs. Vol. 29. No. 3. April 1951. pp. 351—370

Kirk, Grayson. THE ATLANTIC PACT AND INTERNATIONAL SECURITY. International Organisation. Vol. 3. No. 2. May 1949. pp. 239–253

M., D. SOVIET POLICY AND THE GERMAN PROBLEM. The World Today. Vol. 15. No. 7. July 1959. pp. 269–277

Makins, Sir Roger. THE WORLD SINCE THE WAR: THE THIRD PHASE. (i.e. since Stalin's death). Foreign Affairs. Vol. 33. No. 1. October 1954. pp. 1–16

Mayo, H.B. THE WESTERN ALLIANCE – IDEOLOGICAL OR DEFENSIVE? International Journal. Vol. 9. No. 2. Spring 1954. pp. 87–95

Middleton, Drew. NATO CHANGES DIRECTION. Foreign Affairs. Vol. 31. No. 3. April 1953. pp. 427–440

Moseley, Philip E. THE KREMLIN'S FOREIGN POLICY SINCE STALIN. Foreign Affairs. Vol. 32. No. 1. October 1953. pp. 20–33

Munro, Dana G. THE FIRST YEARS OF THE COLD WAR. World Politics. Vol. 4. No. 4. July 1952. pp. 536–547. (Review article on James F. Byrnes: 'Speaking Frankly'. New York and London: Harper and Brothers. 1947; Walter Millis (ed.): 'The Forrestal Diaries'. New York: Viking Press. 1951)

H., H.G. THE NORTH ATLANTIC PACT: CONGRESS AND THE MILITARY COMMITMENT. The World Today. Vol. 5. No. 7. July 1949. pp. 296–304

Oppenheimer, J. Robert. ATOMIC WEAPONS AND AMERICAN POLICY. Foreign Affairs. Vol. 31. No. 4. July 1953. pp. 525–535

Rotvand, Georges. NATO – A FRENCH VIEW. International Journal. Vol. 7. No. 2. Spring 1952. pp. 107–115

Spaak, Paul-Henri. THE ATOM BOMB AND NATO. Foreign Affairs. Vol. 33. No. 3. April 1955. pp. 353–359

Spofford, Charles M. TOWARDS ATLANTIC SECURITY. International Affairs. Vol. 27. No. 4. October 1951. pp. 434–439

Spofford, Charles M. NATO'S GROWING PAINS. Foreign Affairs. Vol. 31. No. 1. October 1952. pp. 95–105

Stueck, William. THE SOVIET UNION AND THE ORIGINS OF THE KOREAN WAR. World Politics. Vol. 28. No. 4. July 1976. pp. 622–635

T., J.P. SOVIET STRENGTHS AND WEAKNESSES: THE SATELLITE CONTRIBUTION. The World Today. Vol. 7. No. 4. April 1951. pp. 163–174

Vagts, Alfred. THE BALANCE OF POWER: GROWTH OF AN IDEA.

World Politics. Vol. 1. No. 1. October 1948. pp. 82–101

Vlekke, B.H.M. A DUTCH VIEW OF THE WORLD SITUATION. International Affairs. Vol. 28. No. 4. October 1952. pp. 413

W., J.E. and L., H.G. THE BREAKDOWN OF FOUR-POWER RULE IN BERLIN. The World Today. Vol. 4. No. 8. August 1948. pp. 322–331

W., J.F.A. THE WEST AS PORTRAYED BY COMMUNIST PROPAGANDA. The World Today. Vol. 10. No. 12. December 1954. pp. 532–541

W., P.J.D. THE PURSUIT OF DISENGAGEMENT: AN ANALYSIS OF RISKS. The World Today. Vol. 15. No. 4. April 1959. pp. 156–168

Warner, Geoffrey. THE UNITED STATES AND THE ORIGINS OF THE COLD WAR. International Affairs. Vol. 46. No. 3. July 1970. pp. 529–544

Willetts, H.T. PAVLOV OR KHRUSHCHEV? SOVIET METHOD IN POLITICAL WARFARE. The World Today. Vol. 16. No. 10. October 1960. pp. 426–435

Wright, Quincy. AMERICAN POLICY TOWARDS RUSSIA. World Politics. Vol. 2. No. 4. July 1950. pp. 463–481. (A critique of reliance upon military strength)

X. (i.e. George Kennan) THE SOURCES OF SOVIET CONDUCT. Foreign Affairs. Vol. 25. No. 4. July 1947. pp. 566–582 (see also Samuel P. Huntington and Warren D. Marshall, ' "X" plus 25: interview with George Kennan' in FOREIGN POLICY. No. 7. Summer 1972. pp. 3–21

Zinner, Paul E. THE IDEOLOGICAL BASES OF SOVIET FOREIGN POLICY. World Politics. Vol. 4. No. 4. July 1952. pp. 488–511

Military and Strategic Aspects

Baldwin, Hanson W. THE SOVIET NAVY. Foreign Affairs. Vol. 33. No. 4. July 1955. pp. 587–604

Bergson, Abram. RUSSIAN DEFENSE EXPENDITURES. Foreign Affairs. Vol. 26. No. 2. January 1948. pp. 373–376

Brodie, Bernard. NUCLEAR WEAPONS: STRATEGIC OR TACTICAL. Foreign Affairs. Vol. 32. No. 2. January 1954. pp. 217–229

Brodie, Bernard. SOME NOTES ON THE EVOLUTION OF AIR

DOCTRINE. World Politics. Vol. 7. No. 3. April 1955. pp. 349–370

Eliot, George Fielding. MILITARY ORGANISATION UNDER THE ATLANTIC PACT. Foreign Affairs. Vol. 27. No. 4. July 1949

Goodpaster, Colonel Andrew T. THE DEVELOPMENT OF SHAPE: 1950–1953. International Organisation. Vol. 9. No. 2. May 1955. pp. 257–262

Head, Brigadier A.H. EUROPEAN DEFENCE. International Affairs. Vol. 27. No. 1. January 1951. pp. 1–10

Kaysen, Carl. THE VULNERABILITY OF THE UNITED STATES TO ENEMY ATTACK. World Politics. Vol. 6. No. 2. January 1954. pp. 190–208

King, Wilfred. FAIR SHARES ON TEETH AND TANKS. Foreign Affairs. Vol. 29. No. 4. July 1951. pp. 608–624

Kruls, General H.J. THE DEFENCE OF EUROPE. Foreign Affairs. Vol. 30. No. 2. January 1952. pp. 265–276

P., M. THE SATELLITE ARMED FORCES. The World Today. Vol. 7. No. 6. January 1951. pp. 231–239

Pick, Otto. ARMIES IN EASTERN EUROPE. The World Today. Vol. 16. No. 12. December 1960. pp. 540–548

S., S. THE ARCTIC FRONTIER AND ITS DEFENCE. The World Today. Vol. 3. No. 7. July 1947. pp. 292–298 (i.e. Canada)

Slessor, Sir John. THE PLACE OF THE BOMBER IN BRITISH POLICY. International Affairs. Vol. 29. No. 3. July 1953. pp. 302–307

Speier, Hans. GERMAN REARMAMENT AND THE OLD MILITARY ELITE. World Politics. Vol. 6. No. 2. January 1954. pp. 147–168

Uhligg, Frank. THE THREAT OF THE SOVIET NAVY. Foreign Affairs. Vol. 30. No. 3. April 1952. pp. 444–454

Wilmot, Chester. IF NATO HAD TO FIGHT. Foreign Affairs. Vol. 31. No. 2. January 1953. pp. 200–214

Wilmot, Chester. BRITAIN'S STRATEGIC RELATIONSHIP TO EUROPE. International Affairs. Vol. 29. No. 4. October 1953. pp. 409–417

Wood, Colonel Robert J. THE FIRST YEAR OF SHAPE. International Organisation. Vol. 6. No. 2. May 1952. pp. 175–191

SECTION II

THE YEARS OF STRAIN AND STRESS: 1955-1962

The adhesion of the Federal Republic of Germany to the Alliance in 1955 entailed the weight of all the Atlantic allies being utilised to obtain the reunification of Germany on terms favourable to the Alliance as a whole. The growing nuclear capability of the Soviet Union enabled this pressure to be resisted and indeed reversed with the re-opening of the Berlin question over the years 1958-1961. Within both Eastern and Western blocs lack of cohesion made itself manifest; on the one hand the Soviet Union had to cope with the runaway de-Stalinisation of Poland and Hungary in 1956, while Britain and France provoked the ire of their super-power patron because of their Suez intervention the same year. While Soviet hegemony was reaffirmed over Eastern Europe, the position of the United States began increasingly to be called into question following the return to office of General de Gaulle in the summer of 1958. Nuclear problems began to bedevil the allies; Britain chose to announce its reliance upon a defence policy based upon the possession of an independent nuclear deterrent and the termination of conscription just as German conscripts began to be provided for the allies by a Federal Republic which had foresworn nuclear weaponry on its entry to the Alliance in 1955.

Meanwhile, credited with a superiority in nuclear delivery systems which its leaders well knew was illusory, the Soviet Union was sustaining a dazzling diplomatic offensive on the West. The advent to the presidency of John F. Kennedy in January 1961 was to herald the dawning realisation that the Alliance had deluded itself; the attempt by Khrushchev to reverse this development and indeed to convert illusion into reality produced the Cuban missile crisis of October 1962. The Cuban issue was essentially a super-power confrontation; within the Western bloc Macmillan had not only restored the harmony which had characterised Anglo-American relations prior to Suez, but had secured American support for the maintenance of a British nuclear deterrent. With the rejection in 1958 of his proposals for a triumvirate to direct the Alliance, President de Gaulle was increasingly to put a distance between France and those whom he began to describe as the 'Anglo-Saxons'; the corollary of this policy was the presentation of France as the most reliable of allies for those members of the Alliance upon the European continent.

The second section of the bibliography treats with these and associated developments. It also reflects the foundation of the Institute for Strategic Studies in London in 1958, and the appearance of new and influential journals in both Western and Soviet zones. Some of the works cited conjure the fervid atmosphere of the late fifties; thus, Albert Wohlstetter's classic article 'On the delicate balance of terror'. Others mark the appearance of luminaries who were to dazzle in the years which followed; thus Henry Kissinger began to establish his reputation on both sides of the Atlantic by his academic publications towards the end of this tormented decade.

Books

Economic Aspects

Hitch, Charles J. and McKean, Roland N. THE ECONOMICS OF DEFENCE IN THE NUCLEAR AGE. Cambridge, Mass.: Harvard University Press. 1960

Ritchie, Ronald S. NATO: THE ECONOMICS OF AN ALLIANCE. Toronto: The Ryerson Press for the Canadian Institute of International Affairs. 1956. (See review article by Malcolm W. Hoag: 'On NATO Pooling' in WORLD POLITICS. Vol. 10. No. 3. April 1958. pp. 475–483)

Legal Aspects

Bathurst, M.E. and Simpson, J.L. GERMANY AND THE NORTH

ATLANTIC COMMUNITY: A LEGAL SURVEY. London: Stevens for the London Institute of World Affairs. 1956
Wiewora, Boleslaw. THE POLISH-GERMAN FRONTIER FROM THE STANDPOINT OF INTERNATIONAL LAW. Pozvan, Warsaw: Wydawnictwo Zachodnie. 1959

National and Regional Aspects

Alexander, Fred. CANADIANS AND FOREIGN POLICY. Toronto: University of Toronto Press. 1960
Ball, M. Margaret. NATO AND THE EUROPEAN UNION MOVEMENT. New York: Praeger for the London Institute of World Affairs. 1959
van Campen, S.I.P. THE QUEST FOR SECURITY; SOME ASPECTS OF NETHERLANDS FOREIGN POLICY 1945–1950. The Hague: Martinus Nijhoff for the Netherlands Institute of International Affairs; London: Batsford. 1958
Chatham House Study Group. BRITAIN IN WESTERN EUROPE: WEU AND THE ATLANTIC ALLIANCE. London: Royal Institute of International Affairs. 1956
Conant, Melvin. THE LONG POLAR WATCH: CANADA AND THE DEFENCE OF THE WEST. New York: Harper for the Council on Foreign Relations. 1961
Davidson, Eugene. THE DEATH AND LIFE OF GERMANY: an account of the American occupation. New York: Knopf. 1959
Deutsch, Karl W. and Edinger, Lewis J. GERMANY REJOINS THE POWERS: mass opinion, interest groups and elites in contemporary German foreign policy. Stanford: Stanford University Press. 1959; London: Oxford University Press. 1960
Feld, Werner. REUNIFICATION AND WEST-GERMAN – SOVIET RELATIONS 1949–1957. The Hague: Nijhoff. 1963
Freund, Gerald. GERMANY BETWEEN TWO WORLDS. New York: Harcourt, Brace and Co. 1961. (See review article by Y. Yemelyanov: 'A Dangerous and Barren Policy' in INTERNATIONAL AFFAIRS (Moscow). 1963. No. 2. pp. 96–97)
Furniss, Edgar S. (ed.). AMERICAN MILITARY POLICY. New York: Rinehart. 1957
Goldman, Eric F. THE CRUCIAL DECADE: AMERICA, 1945–1955.

New York. Knopf. 1956
Grindrod, Muriel. THE REBUILDING OF ITALY. London: Royal
Institute of International Affairs. 1956
Harrison, W.E.C. CANADA IN WORLD AFFAIRS. 1949–1950. New
York: Oxford University Press for the Canadian Institute of International Affairs. 1957
Haviland, H. Field., Jr. (ed.). THE UNITED STATES AND THE
WESTERN COMMUNITY. Haverford, Pa.: Haverford College Press.
1957
Kertesz, Stephen D. (ed.). THE FATE OF EAST-CENTRAL EUROPE.
Notre Dame (Ind.): University of Notre Dame Press. 1956
Khrushchev, Nikita. THE SOVIET STAND ON GERMANY. New York:
Cross-currents Press. 1961
McInnis, Edgar S. (ed.). THE SHAPING OF POST-WAR GERMANY.
London: Dent. 1960
McLin, Jon B. CANADA'S CHANGING DEFENCE POLICY 1957–
1963: THE PROBLEMS OF A MIDDLE POWER IN ALLIANCE.
Baltimore: Johns Hopkins Press; London: Oxford University
Press. 1967
Manderson-Jones, R.B. THE SPECIAL RELATIONSHIP: ANGLO-
AMERICAN RELATIONS AND WESTERN EUROPEAN UNITY
1947–1956. London: Weidenfeld and Nicolson; New York: Crane,
Russak. 1972
Neal, Fred Warner. WAR AND PEACE AND GERMANY. New York:
W.W. Norton and Co. 1962. (a critique of U.S. policy)
Neuchterlein, Donald E. ICELAND, RELUCTANT ALLY. Ithaca:
Cornell University Press. 1961
Prittie, Terence. GERMANY DIVIDED: THE LEGACY OF THE
NAZI ERA. Boston: Atlantic (Little, Brown). 1960 (a critique of
advocates of disengagement)
Ripka, Hubert. EASTERN EUROPE IN THE POST-WAR WORLD.
London: Methuen; New York: Praeger. 1961
Robson, Charles B. BERLIN – PIVOT OF GERMAN DESTINY.
Chapel Hill: The University of North Carolina Press; London:
Oxford University Press. 1960
Siegler, Heinrich von. THE REUNIFICATION AND SECURITY OF
GERMANY: A DOCUMENTARY BASIS FOR DISCUSSION.
Bonn: Seigter and Co., K.G. 1957
Snyder, William P. THE POLITICS OF BRITISH DEFENCE POLICY
1945–1962. Columbus: Ohio State University Press. 1964; London:

Ernest Benn. 1965. (See review by R.N. Rosecrance in INTER-
NATIONAL AFFAIRS. Vol. 41. No. 4. October 1965. p. 704)
Speier, Hans and Davison, W. Phillips. WEST GERMAN LEADERSHIP
AND FOREIGN POLICY. Evanston, Ill.: White Plains: New York:
Row, Peterson. 1957. (See review by B. Ruhm von Oppen in
INTERNATIONAL AFFAIRS. Vol. 34. No. 3. July 1958. pp. 372–
373)
Speier, Hans. DIVIDED BERLIN: the anatomy of Soviet political
blackmail. New York: Frederick A. Praeger. 1961
Spencer, Robert A. CANADA IN WORLD AFFAIRS: FROM U.N. TO
NATO 1946–1949. Toronto: Oxford University Press for the
Canadian Institute of International Affairs. 1959
Stanley, Timothy W. AMERICAN DEFENCE AND NATIONAL
SECURITY. Washington: Public Affairs Press. 1956
Szaz, Zoltan Michael. GERMANY'S EASTERN FRONTIERS: THE
PROBLEM OF THE ODER-NEISSE LINE. Chicago: Regnery.
1960
Tondel, Lyman M., Jr. (ed.). THE ISSUES IN THE BERLIN-
GERMAN CRISIS: the background papers and proceedings of the
first Hammarskjold Forum organised by the Association of the
Bar of the City of New York. Dobbs Ferry, New York: Oceana.
1963
Whitaker, Arthur P. SPAIN AND DEFENCE OF THE WEST. New
York: Harper for the Council on Foreign Relations; London:
Oxford University Press. 1961
Windsor, Philip. CITY ON LEAVE: A HISTORY OF BERLIN 1945–
1962. London: Chatto and Windus. 1963
Wiskemann, Elizabeth. GERMANY'S EASTERN NEIGHBOURS:
PROBLEM RELATING TO THE ODER-NEISSE LINE AND THE
CZECH FRONTIER REGIONS. London: Oxford University Press
for the Royal Institute of International Affairs. 1956
Woodhouse, C.M. BRITISH FOREIGN POLICY SINCE THE 2ND
WORLD WAR. London: Hutchinson. 1961

Politico – Military Aspects

Abel, Elie. THE MISSILES OF OCTOBER: THE STORY OF THE
CUBAN MISSILE CRISIS, 1962. London: MacGibbon and Kee;

(paperback) Mayflower Books. 1966. Originally published as 'The Missile Crisis'. Philadelphia: Lippincott. 1966

Acheson, Dean G. POWER AND DIPLOMACY. Toronto: Saunders. 1958

Aliano, Richard A. AMERICAN DEFENCE POLICY FROM EISENHOWER TO KENNEDY. Columbus: Ohio State University Press. 1975

Beal, John Robinson. JOHN FOSTER DULLES: A BIOGRAPHY. New York: Harper. 1957

Bell, Coral. NEGOTIATION FROM STRENGTH. London: Chatto and Windus. 1962

Brzezinski, Zbigniew K. THE SOVIET BLOC: UNITY AND CONFLICT. Cambridge, Mass.: Harvard University Press. 1960. (See review article by Paul Kecskemeti: 'Diversity and uniformity in Communist bloc politics'. WORLD POLITICS. Vol. 13. No. 2. January 1961. pp. 313–322)

Buchan, Alastair. NATO IN THE 1960'S. London: Weidenfeld and Nicolson. 1960

Campaigne, Jameson C. AMERICAN MIGHT AND SOVIET MYTH. Chicago: Regnery. 1960

Catlin, George. THE ATLANTIC COMMUNITY. London: Coram Publishers Ltd. 1959

Chamberlin, William Henry. APPEASEMENT: ROAD TO WAR. New York: Rolton House. 1962. (Asserts that the Communist powers are unappeasable)

Chayes, Abram. THE CUBAN MISSILE CRISIS. London: Oxford University Press. 1974

Coates, W.P. and Zelda, K. A HISTORY OF ANGLO-SOVIET RELATIONS. Vol. 2.: 1943–50. London: Lawrence. 1958. (consistently pro-Soviet)

Coles, Harry L. (ed.). TOTAL WAR AND COLD WAR: PROBLEMS IN CIVILIAN CONTROL OF THE MILITARY. Columbus: Ohio State University Press. 1962

Collier, David S. and Glaser, Kurt. (ed.). BERLIN AND THE FUTURE OF EASTERN EUROPE. Chicago: Regnery. 1963

Corry, J.A. SOVIET RUSSIA AND THE WESTERN ALLIANCE. Toronto: Canadian Institute of International Affairs. 1958

Dallin, David J. SOVIET FOREIGN POLICY AFTER STALIN. London: Methuen. 1962. (See review by Kurt L. London: 'Krushchev and the new era in Soviet strategy' in ORBIS. Vol. 5.

No. 4. Winter 1962. pp. 512—514)
Davison, W. Phillips. THE BERLIN BLOCKADE: A STUDY IN COLD WAR POLITICS. Princeton: Princeton University Press; London: Oxford University Press. 1958
Deutsch, Karl W. POLITICAL COMMUNITY AND THE NORTH ATLANTIC AREA. Princeton: Princeton University Press. 1957
Dinerstein, H.S. WAR AND THE SOVIET UNION. London: Atlantic Books; New York: Praeger. 1959
Dinerstein, Herbert S. THE MAKING OF A MISSILE CRISIS: OCT. 1962. Baltimore: Johns Hopkins Press. 1976
Donovan, Robert J. EISENHOWER: THE INSIDE STORY. New York: Harper. 1956
Eden, Sir Anthony. FULL CIRCLE. (i.e. The Eden Memoirs. 1951— 1957). London: Cassell. 1960
Eisenhower, Dwight D. THE WHITE HOUSE YEARS. Vol. 1. Mandate for Change 1953—56. Vol. 2. Waging Peace 1956—61. New York: Doubleday. 1965; London: Heinemann. 1966
Eppstein, John. NATO: PAST, PRESENT AND FUTURE. London: British Society for International Understanding. 1959
Farran, Charles d'Olivier. ATLANTIC DEMOCRACY: A COMPARISON OF THE NATO MEMBER STATES. Edinburgh: W. Green; New York: Praeger. 1957
Finletter, Thomas K. FOREIGN POLICY: THE NEXT PHASE. New York: Harper for the Council on Foreign Relations. 1960; London: Oxford University Press. 1961. (i.e. U.S. Foreign policy in the 1960's)
Fleming, D.F. THE COLD WAR AND ITS ORIGINS. 1917—1960. Vol. 1. 1917—1950. Vol. 2. 1950—1960. London: Allen and Unwin. 1961. (See review by M. Nikolayev: 'Why the West has lost the Cold War'. INTERNATIONAL AFFAIRS (Moscow). 1962. No. 3. pp. 96—98)
Gaitskell, Hugh. THE CHALLENGE OF CO-EXISTENCE. Cambridge, Mass.: Harvard University Press; London: Methuen. 1957
Gelber, Lionel. AMERICA IN BRITAIN'S PLACE: the leadership of the West and Anglo-American Unity. London: Allen and Unwin. 1961
George, Alexander L. and Smoke, Richard. DETERRENCE IN AMERICAN FOREIGN POLICY: THEORY AND PRACTICE. New York: Columbia University Press. 1974. (A series of case studies, from the Berlin blockade to the Cuban missile crisis)
Goold-Adams, Richard. JOHN FOSTER DULLES: A REAPPRAISAL. London: Weidenfeld; New York: Appleton-Century Crofts. 1962
Hahn, Walter F. and Neff, John C. AMERICAN STRATEGY FOR THE

NUCLEAR AGE. New York: Doubleday Anchor. 1960
Halle, Louis J. CIVILIZATION AND FOREIGN POLICY. New York: Harper. 1955. (See review article by Wm. G. Carleton: 'Brain trusters of American foreign policy'. WORLD POLITICS. Vol. 7. No. 4. July 1955. pp. 627–639)
Horowitz, David. THE FREE WORLD COLOSSUS: A CRITIQUE OF AMERICAN FOREIGN POLICY IN THE COLD WAR. London: MacGibbon and Kee. 1965. (See review by H.G. Nicholas: INTERNATIONAL AFFAIRS. Vol. 42. No. 4. October 1966. p. 769)
Huntington, S.P. THE COMMON DEFENSE. New York: Columbia University Press. 1961
Kennan, George F. REALITIES OF AMERICAN FOREIGN POLICY. New York: Henry Holt & Co. 1954. (See review article by Wm. G. Carleton: 'Brain-trusters of American foreign policy' in WORLD POLITICS. Vol. 7. No. 4. July 1955. pp. 627–639)
Kennan, George F. MEMOIRS 1950–1963. Boston: Atlantic (Little, Brown). 1972. (See review by Y. Oleshchuk: 'Contained criticism of "containment" ' in INTERNATIONAL AFFAIRS (Moscow). 1973. No. 10. pp. 102–105)
Kennedy, John F. THE STRATEGY OF PEACE. New York: Harper. 1960. (A collection of Kennedy's speeches and statements on foreign policy and national security)
Kennedy, Robert F. THIRTEEN DAYS: THE CUBAN MISSILE CRISIS. New York: Norton. 1969
Kissinger, Henry A. NUCLEAR WEAPONS AND FOREIGN POLICY. New York: Harper for the Council on Foreign Relations; London: Oxford University Press. 1957. (See review by Sir John Slessor: 'Western strategy in the nuclear age' in ORBIS. Vol. 1. No. 3. Fall 1957. pp. 357–364. Also I. Yevgenyev: 'Atomic warmongering continues' in INTERNATIONAL AFFAIRS (Moscow). 1957. No. 12. pp. 151–154. Also W.W. Kaufmann: 'The crisis in military affairs' in WORLD POLITICS. Vol. 10. No. 4. July 1958. pp. 579–603. Also Lt. Col. V. Larionov: 'The doctrine of aggression in doses' in SURVIVAL. Vol. 1. No. 4. September/October 1959. pp. 135–136. (translated from RED STAR. 8 July 1959).)
Kissinger, Henry A. THE NECESSITY FOR CHOICE: PROSPECTS OF AMERICAN FOREIGN POLICY. London: Chatto and Windus. 1960. (See review by J.I. Coffey: 'The Hard Choices of Policy' in ORBIS. Vol. 5. No. 1. Spring 1961. pp. 87–91. Also review by Major-General N. Talensky: 'Search for a safer war' in INTER-

NATIONAL AFFAIRS (Moscow). 1961. No. 10. pp. 101–105)
Knorr, Klaus. (ed.). NATO AND AMERICAN SECURITY. Princeton: Princeton University Press; London: Oxford University Press. 1959. (See also review by Richard G. Stilwell: 'New dimensions of deterence' in ORBIS. Vol. 4. No. 1. Spring 1960. pp. 87–92)
Kraft, Joseph. THE GRAND DESIGN: FROM COMMON MARKET TO ATLANTIC PARTNERSHIP. New York: Harper and Row. 1962. (See review by Robert L. Pfaltzgraff, Jr.: 'Europe and America: partnership or community' in ORBIS. Vol. 6. No. 2. Summer 1962. pp. 331–337)
Kulski, Wladyslaw W. PEACEFUL CO-EXISTENCE: AN ANALYSIS OF SOVIET FOREIGN POLICY. Chicago: Regnery for the Foundation for Foreign Affairs. 1959
Lerner, Daniel and Aron, Raymond (eds.). FRANCE DEFEATS EDC. New York: Praeger for the Massachusetts Institute of Technology; London: Atlantic Press, distributed by Thames and Hudson. 1957
Lippmann, Walter. WESTERN UNITY AND THE COMMON MARKET. Boston: Atlantic (Little, Brown). 1962
Liska, George. NATIONS IN ALLIANCE: THE LIMITS OF INTER-DEPENDENCE. Baltimore: Johns Hopkins Press. 1962. (See review by Max Beloff in SURVIVAL. Vol. 5. No. 2. March/April 1963. pp. 89–90. Also review article by Steven Muller: 'The revival of diplomacy' in WORLD POLITICS. Vol. 15. No. 4. July 1963. pp. 647–655)
Lowenstein, Hubertus Prince zu and von Zuhlsdorff, Volkmar. NATO AND THE DEFENCE OF THE WEST. New York: Praeger. 1962
Lukacs, John. A HISTORY OF THE COLD WAR. New York: Doubleday. 1961
McInnis, Edgar. THE ATLANTIC TRIANGLE AND THE COLD WAR. Toronto: University of Toronto Press for Canadian Institute of International Affairs. 1959. (Anglo-American-relations)
McKitterick, T.E.M. and Younger, Kenneth (eds.). FABIAN INTERNATIONAL ESSAYS. New York: Praeger. 1957. (Essays on contemporary foreign and military affairs)
Mackintosh, J.M. STRATEGY AND TACTICS OF SOVIET FOREIGN POLICY. London: Oxford University Press. 1962. (See review article by L.V.: 'Strategy and Foreign Policy' in SURVEY. No. 46. January 1963. pp. 166–169)
Macmillan, Harold. RIDING THE STORM. (1956–1959). London: Macmillan. 1971. POINTING THE WAY. (1959–1961). London:

Macmillan. 1972. (the Macmillan memoirs)
Marshall, C.B. THE LIMITS OF AMERICAN FOREIGN POLICY. New York: Henry Holt & Co. 1954. (See review article by Wm. G. Carleton: 'Brain-trusters of American foreign policy' in WORLD POLITICS. Vol. 7. No. 4. July 1955. pp. 627–639)
Moore, Ben T. NATO AND THE FUTURE OF EUROPE. New York: Harper for the Council on Foreign Relations. 1958
Noble, G. Bernard. CHRISTIAN A. HERTER. New York: Cooper Square Publishers. 1970
Northedge, F.S. BRITISH FOREIGN POLICY: THE PROCESS OF READJUSTMENT 1945–1961. London: Allen and Unwin. 1962
O'Conor, John F. COLD WAR AND LIBERATION. New York: Vantage Press. 1961. (Urges a program of 'mutual assistance' for the peoples behind the Iron Curtain)
Osgood, Robert Endicott. NATO: THE ENTANGLING ALLIANCE. Chicago: Chicago University Press. 1962. (See also review by Robert L. Pfaltzgraff, Jr.: 'Europe and America: Partnership or Community'. ORBIS. Vol. 6. No. 2. Summer 1962. pp. 331–337)
Osgood, Robert Endicott. ALLIANCES AND AMERICAN FOREIGN POLICY. Baltimore: Johns Hopkins Press. 1968
Patterson, G. and Furniss, E.S. NATO: A CRITICAL REAPPRAISAL. Princeton: Princeton University Press. 1957
Pearson, Lester B. DIPLOMACY IN THE NUCLEAR AGE. Boston, Mass.: Harvard University Press. 1959. (See review by John F. Kennedy: 'On diplomacy in the nuclear age' in INTERNATIONAL JOURNAL. Vol. 29. No. 1. Winter 1973–74. pp. 67–70)
Peeters, Paul. MASSIVE RETALIATION: THE POLICY AND ITS CRITICS. Chicago: Regnery. 1959
Perla, Leo. CAN WE END THE COLD WAR? New York: Macmillan. 1960. (A critique of U.S. foreign policy and a plea for more morality and less militarism)
Pusey, Merlo J. EISENHOWER THE PRESIDENT. New York: Macmillan. 1956
Reitzel, William *et al.* UNITED STATES FOREIGN POLICY 1945–1955. London: Faber; Washington: Brookings Institution. 1956
Roberts, Henry L. RUSSIA AND AMERICA: DANGERS AND PROSPECTS. New York: Harper for the Council on Foreign Relations. 1956
Salvadori, Massino. NATO – A 20TH CENTURY COMMUNITY OF NATIONS. Princeton: Van Nostrand Co. 1957

Schilling, Warner, et al. STRATEGY, POLITICS AND DEFENSE
BUDGETS. 1962. New York: Columbia University Press. (See review
article by Charles Burton Marshall: 'On the uses and limits of defence
planning' in WORLD POLITICS. Vol. 15. No. 4. July 1963. pp.
689–699)
Schlamm, William S. GERMANY AND THE EAST-WEST CRISIS:
THE DECISIVE CHALLENGE TO AMERICAN POLICY. New
York: David McKay. 1959
Schmidt, Helmut. DEFENCE OR RETALIATION: A GERMAN
VIEW. New York: Praeger. 1962
Schuman, Frederick L. THE COLD WAR: RETROSPECT AND
PROSPECT. Baton Rouge: Louisiana State University Press. 1962
Slessor, Marshal of the Royal Air Force Sir John. WHAT PRICE CO-
EXISTENCE? New York: Praeger. 1961. (View on NATO strategy
for the 60's)
Smith, Jean Edward. THE DEFENCE OF BERLIN. Baltimore: John
Hopkins Press; London: Oxford University Press. 1963
Snyder, Glenn. DETERRENCE AND DEFENCE: TOWARDS A
THEORY OF NATIONAL SECURITY. Princeton: Princeton
University Press. 1961
Spaak, Paul-Henri. WHY NATO? Harmondsworth: Penguin Books.
1959
Strachey, John. ON THE PREVENTION OF WAR. London: Macmillan.
1962
Strausz-Hupé, Robert. PROTRACTED CONFLICT. New York: Praeger.
1958. (Effects of Communist strategy upon NATO)
Streit, Clarence K. FREEDOM'S FRONTIER: ATLANTIC UNION
NOW. New York: Harper. 1961
Vagts, Alfred. DEFENCE AND DIPLOMACY: THE SOLDIER AND
THE CONDUCT OF FOREIGN RELATIONS. New York: King's
Crown Press. 1956. (See review by Richard D. Challener: 'The
military and the conduct of foreign policy' in WORLD POLITICS.
Vol. 9. No. 4. July 1957. pp. 610–622)
Various. EUROPEAN SECURITY AND THE MENACE OF WEST
GERMAN MILITARISM. Prague: Orbis for the Institute for
International Politics and Economics. 1962. (Proceedings of a Soviet
bloc conference, May 1961)
Werth, Alexander. THE KHRUSHCHEV PHASE. London: Robert
Hale. 1961
Weymar, Paul. ADENAUER. New York: Dutton. 1957
Wilcox, Francis O. and Haviland, Jr., H. Field (eds.). THE ATLANTIC

COMMUNITY. New York and London: Praeger. 1963
Williams, F. A P.M. REMEMBERS. London: Wm. Heinemann. 1961.
(i.e. Clement Attlee)
Wilson, Thomas W., Jr. COLD WAR AND COMMON SENSE. Greenwich, Conn.: New York Graphic Society. 1962
Wolfers, Arnold (ed.). ALLIANCE POLICY IN THE COLD WAR. Baltimore: Johns Hopkins Press; London: Oxford University Press. 1959
Wolfers, Arnold. DISCORD AND COLLABORATION: ESSAYS ON INTERNATIONAL POLITICS. Baltimore: Johns Hopkins Press. 1962. (See review article by Steven Muller: 'The revival of diplomacy' in WORLD POLITICS. Vol. 15. No. 4. July 1963. pp. 647–655)

Military – Strategic Aspects

Bechhoeffer, Bernhard G. POST-WAR NEGOTIATIONS FOR ARMS CONTROL. Washington: Brookings Institution. 1961
Bennett, John C. (ed.). NUCLEAR WEAPONS AND THE CONFLICT OF CONSCIENCE. New York: Scribner. 1962
Blackett, P.M.S. ATOMIC WEAPONS AND EAST-WEST RELATIONS. Cambridge: Cambridge University Press. 1956. (See review by I. Kirim: 'Western scientists and atomic and hydrogen weapons' in INTERNATIONAL AFFAIRS (Moscow). 1957. No. 5. pp. 147–151)
Blackett, P.M.S. STUDENTS OF WAR. Edinburgh: Oliver and Boyd. 1962
Gallois, General Pierre. THE BALANCE OF TERROR: STRATEGY FOR THE NUCLEAR AGE. Boston: Houghton Mifflin Co. 1961. (See review by S. Filshtinsky: 'The atomic gospel of General Gallois' in INTERNATIONAL AFFAIRS (Moscow). 1961. No. 3. pp. 108–111)
Garthoff, Raymond L. SOVIET STRATEGY IN THE NUCLEAR AGE. London: Stevens (Atlantic Books); New York: Praeger; Toronto: Burns and MacEachern. 1958
Garthoff, Raymond L. THE SOVIET IMAGE OF FUTURE WAR. Washington: Public Affairs Press. 1959
Gollancz, Victor. THE DEVIL'S REPERTOIRE, OR, NUCLEAR BOMBING AND THE LIFE OF MAN. Garden City: Doubleday.

1959. (An appeal for unilateral nuclear disarmament)
Gouré, Leon. CIVIL DEFENCE IN THE SOVIET UNION. Berkeley, Los Angeles: University of California Press; Cambridge: Cambridge University Press. 1962
Hinterhoff, Eugene. DISENGAGEMENT. London: Stevens and Sons Ltd. 1959. (See review article by Glenn H. Snyder: 'Deterrence, Defence and Disengagement' in WORLD POLITICS. Vol. 14. No. 2. January 1962. pp. 393–403)
Howard, Michael. DISENGAGEMENT IN EUROPE. Harmondsworth: Penguin Books. 1958
Kahn, Herman. ON THERMONUCLEAR WAR. Princeton: Princeton University Press. 1960
Kaufmann, William W. et al. MILITARY POLICY AND NATIONAL SECURITY. Princeton: Princeton University Press; London: Oxford University Press. 1956
King-Hall, Stephen. DEFENCE IN THE NUCLEAR AGE. London: Gollancz. 1958. (See review article by P.M.S. Blackett: 'Nuclear weapons and defence: comments on Kissinger, Kennon and King-Hall' in INTERNATIONAL AFFAIRS. Vol. 34. No. 4. pp. 421–434)
Kingston-McCloughry, Air Vice-Marshal E.J. DEFENCE: POLICY AND STRATEGY. New York: Praeger. 1960. (A critique of current strategy)
Knorr, Klaus and Read, Thornton (eds.). LIMITED STRATEGIC WAR. New York: Praeger. 1962
Liddell Hart, B.H. (ed.). THE RED ARMY. New York: Harcourt. 1956
Liddell Hart, B.H. DETERRENT OR DEFENCE. London: Stevens and Sons; New York: Frederick A. Praeger Inc. 1960. (See review article by Glenn H. Snyder: 'Deterrenee, Defence and Disengagement' in WORLD POLITICS. Vol. 14. No. 2. January 1962. pp. 393–403)
Miksche, F.O. THE FAILURE OF ATOMIC STRATEGY. London: Faber; New York: Praeger. 1959. (A vigorous critique of Western military strategy)
Morgenstern, Oskar. THE QUESTION OF NATIONAL DEFENCE. New York: Random House. 1959
Osgood, Robert Endicott. LIMITED WAR: THE CHALLENGE TO AMERICAN STRATEGY. Chicago: University of Chicago Press. 1957
Saunders, Commander M.G. (ed.). THE SOVIET NAVY. New York: Praeger. 1958
Sokol, Anthony. SEA POWER IN THE NUCLEAR AGE. Washington,

D.C.: Public Affairs Press. 1961
Speier, Hans. GERMAN REARMAMENT AND ATOMIC WAR: THE VIEWS OF THE GERMAN MILITARY AND POLITICAL LEADERS. Evanston. Ill.: White Plains: New York: Row, Peterson. 1957
Stern, Frederick Martin. THE CITIZEN ARMY: KEY TO DEFENCE IN THE ATOMIC AGE. New York: St. Martin's Press. 1957. (See also review by Alexander Marwald: 'The case for the citizen soldier' in ORBIS. Vol. 2. No. 2. Summer 1958. pp. 254–256)
Taylor, General Maxwell D. THE UNCERTAIN TRUMPET. New York: Harper. 1960. (A critique of U.S. strategic and defence policies)
Toynbee, Philip, et al. THE FEARFUL CHOICE. Detroit: Wayne State University Press. 1959. (Arguments for and against British participation in a nuclear war)

Reports, Papers and Pamphlets

Economic Aspects

Rowan, Sir Leslie. ARMS AND ECONOMICS: THE CHANGING CHALLENGE (The Lees Knowles Lecture 1960). Cambridge: Cambridge University Press. 1960
Warburton, Anne and Wood, John. PAYING FOR NATO. London: Friends of Atlantic Union. 1956

National and Regional Aspects

Gellner, John. PROBLEMS OF CANADIAN DEFENCE. Toronto: Canadian Institute of International Affairs. 1959. (Behind the Headlines. Vol. 18. No. 6)
Kokot, Jozef. THE LOGIC OF THE ODER-NEISSE FRONTIER. Poznan, Warsaw: Wydawnictwo Zachodnie. 1959. London: Embassy of the Polish People's Republic. 1960

Legien, R. THE FOUR POWER AGREEMENTS ON BERLIN: ALTERNATIVE SOLUTIONS TO THE STATUS QUO? Berlin: Carl Heymanns Verlag. 1960

Rzhevsky, Yuri. WEST BERLIN: A SPECIAL POLITICAL ENTITY. Moscow: Novosti Press Agency. n.d.

Politico – Military Aspects

Buchan, Alastair. NATO TODAY. Toronto: Canadian Institute of International Affairs. 1959. (Behind the Headlines. Vol. 14. No. 1)

DeWeerd, H.A. BRITAIN AND THE DEFENSE OF WESTERN EUROPE. Santa Monica: Rand Corporation. June 1956. (Rand Paper P – 697)

Deutsch, Harold C. NEW CRISIS ON BERLIN. Toronto: Canadian Institute of International Affairs. 1959. (Behind the Headlines. Vol. 14. No. 2)

Healey, Denis. A NEUTRAL BELT IN EUROPE? London: Fabian Society. 1958. (Fabian Tract 311)

H.M.S.O. THE HUNGARIAN UPRISING: an abridgement of the report of the U.N. Special Committee on the Problem of Hungary, published on June 20, 1957. London: H.M.S.O. 1957

Knorr, Klaus. IS THE AMERICAN DEFENSE EFFORT ENOUGH? Princeton: Center of International Studies, Princeton University. 1957 (Memorandum No. 14)

MacLachlan, Donald and de Freitas, Geoffrey. NATO IS NOT ENOUGH – TWO APPROACHES TO AN ATLANTIC ASSEMBLY. London: Friends of Atlantic Union. 1957

U.N.O. REPORT OF THE SPECIAL COMMITTEE ON THE PROBLEM OF HUNGARY. New York: United Nations; London: H.M.S.O. 1957

Articles

Economic Aspects

Blackaby, F.T. and Paige, D.C. DEFENCE EXPENDITURE – BURDEN OR STIMULUS?: an analysis of British defence expenditure. Survival. Vol. 2. No. 6. November/December 1960. pp. 242–247

Blagoradov, G. ECONOMIC CONTRADICTIONS OF THE U.S.A. AND ITS NATO PARTNERS. International Affairs (Moscow). No. 8. pp. 37–45

Day, A.C.L. . . . AND THE COST OF DEFENCE. Survival. Vol. 2. No. 2. March/April 1960. pp. 81–85. (A reprint from THE POLITICAL QUARTERLY. Spring 1960)

Diebold, William, Jr. THE CHANGED ECONOMIC POSITION OF WESTERN EUROPE: some implications for United States policy and international organisation. International Organisation. Vol. 14. No. 1. Winter 1960. pp. 1–19

Duprez, Jean-Jacques. THE STRATEGIC EMBARGO: DOCTRINE AND PRACTICE. The World Today. Vol. 19. No. 9. September 1963. pp. 374–379

Finogenov, V. THE PROBLEM OF SOVIET-AMERICAN TRADE. International Affairs (Moscow). 1959. No. 12. pp. 60–66

Franks, Lord. CO-OPERATION IS NOT ENOUGH. Foreign Affairs. Vol. 41. No. 1. October 1962. pp. 24–35. (The economic problems ahead of the Atlantic nations)

G., M. ECONOMIC IMPLICATIONS OF GERMAN REARMAMENT. The World Today. Vol. 2. No. 3. March 1955. pp. 117–129

G., M. WEST GERMAN PROSPERITY SURVEYED. The World Today. Vol. 14. No. 4. April 1958. pp. 168–180

Gordon, Lincoln. ECONOMIC ASPECTS OF COALITION DIPLOMACY: THE NATO EXPERIENCE. International Organisation. Vol. 10. No. 4. Autumn 1956. pp. 529–543

Harnwell, Gaylord P. SCIENCE, TECHNOLOGY AND THE NORTH ATLANTIC COMMUNITY. Orbis. Vol. 2. No. 2. Summer 1958. pp. 209–220

Hoeffding, Oleg. STRATEGY AND ECONOMICS: A SOVIET VIEW. World Politics. Vol. 2. No. 2. January 1959. pp. 316–324

Kodachenko, A. NATO: ECONOMIC FOUNDATION? International Affairs (Moscow). 1961. No. 2. pp. 85–87

Manrischat, G. ECONOMIC PREPARATION FOR WAR IN WEST GERMANY. International Affairs (Moscow). 1961. No. 7. pp. 59–60

Oakeshott, Robert. THE STRATEGIC EMBARGO: AN OBSTACLE TO EAST-WEST TRADE. The World Today. Vol. 19. No. 6. June 1963. pp. 240–247
S., S.E. THE POLITICAL ASPECT OF EAST-WEST TRADE: THE SOVIET APPROACH. The World Today. Vol. 12. No. 10. October 1956. pp. 409–417
Vernon, Raymond. FOREIGN TRADE AND NATIONAL DEFENCE. Foreign Affairs. Vol. 34. No. 1. October 1955. pp. 77–88
Yudin, Y. 'PAY MORE!' THE U.S.A. TELLS ITS NATO ALLIES. International Affairs (Moscow). 1961. No. 12. pp. 32–36

Legal Aspects

Korovin, Y. AERIAL ESPIONAGE AND INTERNATIONAL LAW. International Affairs (Moscow). 1960. No. 6. pp. 49–51
Tunkin, G. THE BERLIN PROBLEM AND INTERNATIONAL LAW. International Affairs (Moscow). 1959. No. 2. pp. 36–48

National and Regional Aspects

A., E. SOVIET-YUGOSLAV RELATIONS: TEN YEARS AFTER THE COMMUNIST BAN. The World Today. Vol. 14. No. 8. August 1958. pp. 356–367
A., J. CZECHOSLOVAKIA AND THE EAST EUROPEAN FERMENT The World Today. Vol. 13. No. 4. April 1957. pp. 145–152
Abo, Hermann J. GERMANY AND THE LONDON AND PARIS AGREEMENTS. (September and October 1954). International Affairs: Vol. 31. No. 2. April 1955. pp. 167–173
Afanasyeva, O. ATLANTIC PLANS FOR DENMARK. International Affairs (Moscow). 1957. No. 3. pp. 100–102
Alexandrov, V. THE INTERNAL POLITICAL DEVELOPMENT OF FEDERAL GERMANY AND HER FOREIGN POLICY PROBLEMS. International Affairs (Moscow): 1956. No. 12. pp. 49–56; 1957. No. 1. pp. 60–69; 1957. No. 2. pp. 29–38
Allemann, F.R. ADENAUER'S EASTERN POLICY. Survey. No. 44/45.

October 1962. pp. 29−36
Almond, Gabriel A. THE POLITICAL ATTITUDES OF GERMAN
BUSINESS. World Politics. Vol. 8. No. 2. January 1956. pp. 157−
186
Anghelatos, A.G. NEW-FOUND POLITICAL STABILITY IN GREECE.
The World Today. Vol. 18. No. 3. March 1962. pp. 102−112
Anon. WEST GERMANY AND NATO. International Affairs (Moscow).
1956. No. 9. pp. 127−129
Anon. WEST GERMAN FOREIGN POLICY AT THE CROSSROADS.
International Affairs (Moscow). 1958. No. 4. pp. 59−64
Anon. CYPRUS AND THE NATO INTERVENTION. The World Today.
Vol. 14. No. 7. July 1958. pp. 277−279
Anon. THE BERLIN CRISIS. The World Today. Vol. 17. No. 8.
August 1961. pp. 319−322
Barkway, Michael. CANADA'S CHANGING ROLE IN NATO DEFENCE.
International Journal. Vol. 14. No. 2. Spring 1959. pp. 99−110
Bartel, W. PSYCHOLOGICAL WEAPONS OF THE BONN
MILITARISTS. International Affairs (Moscow). 1961. No. 3.
pp. 26−32
Bartel, W. WEST GERMAN REVANCHISM THREATENING THE
PEACE OF EUROPE. International Affairs (Moscow). 1961. No. 7.
pp. 49−51
Beedham, Brian. CUBA AND THE BALANCE OF POWER. The World
Today. Vol. 19. No. 1. January 1963. pp. 36−41
Birnbaum, Immanuel. GERMAN EASTERN POLICY: YESTERDAY
AND TOMORROW. International Affairs. Vol. 31. No. 4. October
1955. pp. 427−434
Brandt, Willy. THE EAST-WEST PROBLEM AS SEEN FROM
BERLIN. International Affairs. Vol. 34. No. 3. July 1958. pp. 297−
304
Brzezinski, Zbigniew K. THE ORGANISATION OF THE COMMUNIST
CAMP. World Politics. Vol. 13. No. 2. January 1961. pp. 175−209
Buchwitz, O. GERMAN UNITY AND THE GERMAN WORKING
CLASS. International Affairs (Moscow). 1959. No. 10. pp. 59−66
Burbank, Lyman B. SCANDINAVIAN INTEGRATION AND WESTERN
DEFENCE. Foreign Affairs. Vol. 36. No. 1. October 1956. pp. 144−
150
C., N. CYPRUS: CONFLICT AND RECONCILIATION. The World
Today. Vol. 15. No. 4. April 1959. pp. 137−147
Chelnakov, I. THE BALTIC MUST BECOME A SEA OF PEACE.

International Affairs (Moscow). 1957. No. 12. pp. 135—136
Chilcote, Robert H. POLITICS IN PORTUGAL AND HER EMPIRE.
The World Today. Vol. 17. No. 9. September 1961. pp. 376—387
Clay, General Lucius D. BERLIN. Foreign Affairs. Vol. 41. No.1.
October 1962. pp. 47—58
Conant, Melvin. CANADA'S ROLE IN WESTERN DEFENCE. Foreign
Affairs. Vol. 40. No. 3. April 1962. pp. 431—442
Courtade, P. FRANCE AND THE UNITED STATES I. International
Affairs (Moscow). 1958. No. 2. pp. 31—38
Courtade, P. FRANCE AND THE UNITED STATES II. International
Affairs (Moscow). 1958. No. 3. pp. 59—65
Courtade, P. THE PARIS-BONN AXIS AND THE FUTURE OF
FRANCE. International Affairs (Moscow). 1959. No. 7. pp. 18—25
Deter, A. WEST GERMAN REMILITARIZATION AND THE WORKING CLASS. International Affairs (Moscow). No. 8. pp. 99—102
Eayrs, James. CANADA, NATO AND NUCLEAR WEAPONS.
Survival. Vol. 3. No. 2. March/April 1961. pp. 76—83
Epstein, Leon D. PARTISAN FOREIGN POLICY: BRITAIN IN THE
SUEZ CRISIS. World Politics. Vol. 12. No. 2. January 1960.
pp. 201—224
Ferguson, George. CANADA AND THE 'ATLANTIC ALLIANCE'.
International Journal. Vol. 12. No. 2. Spring 1957. pp. 83—89
Frankland, Noble. BRITAIN'S CHANGING STRATEGIC POSITION
(reflections provoked by the 1957 Defence White Paper).
International Affairs. Vol. 33. No. 4. October 1957. pp. 416—426
Frei, Otto. THE BARRIER ACROSS BERLIN AND ITS CONSEQUENCES. The World Today. Vol. 17. No. 11. November 1961.
pp. 459—470
Furniss, Edgar S. DE GAULLE'S FRANCE AND NATO: AN
INTERPRETATION. International Organisation. Vol. 15. No. 3.
Summer 1961. pp. 349—365
Gerasev, N. REVIVAL OF GERMAN MONOPOLY CAPITALISM
AND REMILITARIZATION OF WEST GERMANY. International
Affairs (Moscow). 1956. No. 11. pp. 93—101
Gomulka, Wladyslaw. THE POLICY OF THE POLISH PEOPLE'S
REPUBLIC. Foreign Affairs. Vol. 38. No. 3. April 1960. pp. 402—418
Gooch, G.P. FRANCO-GERMAN CO-EXISTENCE AT LAST? Foreign
Affairs. Vol. 37. No. 3. April 1959. pp. 432—442
Grigoryev, K. SOVIET-TURKISH RELATIONS. International Affairs

(Moscow). 1956. No. 4. pp. 52–64

Grigoryev, K. EFFECTS OF TURKEY'S MILITARIZATION. International Affairs (Moscow). 1960. No. 1. pp. 73–79

Guppi, L. ITALY AND NATO. International Affairs (Moscow). 1956. No. 5. pp. 54–60

Hahn, Walter F. THE GERMANS AND THE WEST. Orbis. Vol. 1. No. 2. Summer 1957. pp. 184–198

Harrison, W.E.C. CANADA IN WORLD AFFAIRS 1949–1950. Toronto and London: Oxford University Press for the Canadian Institute of International Affairs. 1957

Hildebrand, George H. THE POST-WAR ITALIAN ECONOMY: ACHIEVEMENTS, PROBLEMS AND PROSPECTS. World Politics. Vol. 8. No. 1. October 1955. pp. 46–70

Hiscocks, Richard. PROGRESS EAST OF THE ODER-NEISSE: RECENT DEVELOPMENTS IN THE POLISH WESTERN TERRITORIES. The World Today. Vol. 16. No. 12. December 1960. pp. 491–500

Holmes, John W. CANADA AND THE UNITED STATES IN WORLD POLITICS. Foreign Affairs. Vol. 40. No. 1. October 1961. pp. 105–117

Jaster, Robert S. THE DEFEAT OF KHRUSHCHEV'S PLAN TO INTEGRATE EASTERN EUROPE. The World Today. Vol. 19. No. 12. December 1963. pp. 514–522

Kent, Tom. THE CHANGING PLACE OF CANADA. Foreign Affairs. Vol. 35. No. 4. July 1957. pp. 581–592. (vis-à-vis U.S.A. and within the Western alliance)

Kobysh, Y. PEACE PLAN FOR NORTHERN EUROPE AND ITS OPPONENTS. International Affairs (Moscow). 1959. No. 8. pp. 63–66

L., G. ICELAND: RELUCTANT ALLY. The World Today. Vol. 12. No. 8. August 1956. pp. 321–330

L., H.G. BERLIN REVISITED (after 3 years). The World Today. Vol. 12. No. 3. March 1956. pp. 93–101

L., H.G. THE PROBLEM OF GERMANY AND EUROPEAN SECURITY: BACKGROUND TO THE FORTHCOMING EAST-WEST CONFERENCES. The World Today. Vol. 15. No. 5. May 1959. pp. 205–220

Lachs, Manfred. POLAND'S QUEST FOR EUROPEAN SECURITY. International Affairs. Vol. 35. No. 3. July 1959. pp. 305–309

Lachs, Manfred. AN ATOM-FREE ZONE IN CENTRAL EUROPE.

International Affairs (Moscow). 1959. No. 8. pp. 19—24
Lapatin, Y. ITALY AND 'ATLANTICISM'. International Affairs (Moscow). 1960. No. 9. pp. 37—47
Leites, Nathan and della Malène, Christian. PARIS FROM EDC TO WEU. World Politics. Vol. 9. No. 2. January 1957. pp. 193—219
Lerner, Daniel and Robinson, Richard D. SWORDS AND PLOUGHSHARES: THE TURKISH ARMY AS A MODERNISING FORCE. World Politics. Vol. 13. No. 1. October 1960. pp. 19—44
Lewis, Flora. THE UNSTABLE STATUS OF GERMANY. Foreign Affairs. Vol. 38. No. 4. July 1960. pp. 588—597
Lloyd, Trevor. OPEN SKIES IN THE ARCTIC. International Journal. Vol. 14. No. 1. Winter 1958/59. pp. 42—49
M — S., H. BELGIUM ON THE EVE OF THE INTERNATIONAL EXHIBITION. The World Today. Vol. 14. No. 4. April 1958. pp. 148—152
Meisner, J. THE CZECHOSLOVAK PEOPLE AND THE GERMAN PROBLEM. International Affairs (Moscow). 1957. No. 8. pp. 105—109
Miller, Margaret. POLAND AND KHRUSHCHEV'S RUSSIA. The World Today. Vol. 19. No. 10. October 1963. pp. 422—430
Molchanov, N. THE SOVIET UNION AND FRANCE. International Affairs (Moscow). 1956. No. 5. pp. 27—36
Moltke, K. A THREAT TO DANISH INDEPENDENCE. International Affairs (Moscow). 1958. No. 6. pp. 43—48
Norlund, I. THE SCANDINAVIAN COUNTRIES AND THE NEW GERMAN THREAT. International Affairs (Moscow). 1958. No. 1. pp. 47—54
Pipinelis, Panayotis. THE GRECO-TURKISH FEUD REVIVED. Foreign Affairs. Vol. 37. No. 2. January 1959. pp. 306—316
Pogodin, A. MAKE NORTHERN EUROPE A PEACE ZONE. International Affairs (Moscow). 1962. No. 7. pp. 27—32
Pogodin, A. BONN'S STRATEGIC PLANS IN THE BALTIC. International Affairs (Moscow). 1961. No. 9. pp. 33—38
Pogodin, A. CONCERNING DANISH AND NORWEGIAN FOREIGN POLICY. International Affairs (Moscow). 1960. No. 10. pp. 48—53
R., A. THE HUNGARIAN REVOLUTION. The World Today. Vol. 13. No. 1. January 1957. pp. 3—16
R., A. THE AFTERMATH OF THE HUNGARIAN REVOLUTION. The World Today. Vol. 13. No. 11. November 1957. pp. 458—472
Ritchie, Ronald S. PROBLEMS OF A DEFENCE POLICY FOR

CANADA. International Journal. Vol. 14. No. 3. Summer 1959.
pp. 202—212
S., K.R. THE HARD ROAD TO AN AUSTRIAN TREATY. The World
Today. Vol. 11. No. 5. May 1955. pp. 190—202
Sethe, P. RELATIONS BETWEEN FEDERAL GERMANY AND THE
SOVIET UNION. International Affairs (Moscow). 1957. No. 4.
pp. 72—75
Shaposhnichenko, P. WEST GERMANY AND NATO. International
Affairs (Moscow). 1958. No. 6. pp. 26—33
Soustelle, Jacques. FRANCE LOOKS AT HER ALLIANCES. Foreign
Affairs. Vol. 35. No. 1. October 1956. pp. 116—130. (In the light
of no allied support in Algeria and the Far East)
Spencer, Robert A. TRIANGLE INTO TREATY: CANADA AND
THE ORIGINS OF NATO. International Journal. Vol. 14. No. 2.
Spring 1959. pp. 87—98
Thompson, R.W. CANADA, A UNITED EUROPE AND NATO.
International Journal. Vol. 12. No. 3. Summer 1957. pp. 220—226
Tomala, M. GERMAN MILITARISM — THE DIRECT ENEMY OF
THE POLISH PEOPLE. International Affairs (Moscow). 1957. No. 8.
pp. 112—116
Wilkinson, Joe R. DENMARK AND NATO: THE PROBLEM OF A
SMALL STATE IN A COLLECTIVE SECURITY SYSTEM. International Organisation. Vol. 10. No. 3. Summer 1956. pp. 390—401
Williams, J. Emlyn. WESTERN GERMANY BEFORE THE SUMMIT.
The World Today. Vol. 16. No. 2. February 1960. pp. 63—70
Winzer, O. SOME FEATURES OF WEST GERMAN FOREIGN
POLICY. International Affairs (Moscow). 1956. No. 8. pp. 60—61

Politico — Military Aspects

Acheson, Dean. THE ILLUSION OF DISENGAGEMENT. Foreign
Affairs. Vol. 36. No. 3. April 1958. pp. 371—382
Acheson, Dean. THE PREMISES OF AMERICAN POLICY. Orbis.
Vol. 3. No. 3. Fall 1959. pp. 269—281
Adenauer, Konrad. THE GERMAN PROBLEM, A WORLD PROBLEM.
Foreign Affairs. Vol. 41. No. 1. October 1962. pp. 59—65
Anon. THE POWERS AND BERLIN. The World Today. Vol. 14.
No. 12. December 1958. pp. 507—510

Anon. ARMS FOR TUNISIA. The World Today. Vol. 14. No. 12. December 1958. pp. 510–512
Anon. A GERMAN PEACE TREATY: – THE DEMAND OF THE HOUR. International Affairs (Moscow). 1959. No. 2. pp. 71–76
Anon. A PEACEFUL SETTLEMENT WITH GERMANY NOW. International Affairs (Moscow). 1959. No. 4. pp. 3–7
Anon. BONN AND A PEACE TREATY. International Affairs (Moscow). 1960. No. 2. pp. 64–69
Anon. U.S. BASES IN BRITAIN. The World Today. Vol. 16. No. 8. August 1960. pp. 319–325
Anon. RUSSIA AND THE WESTERN POWERS: a chronology since the Vienna meeting of 3–4 June 1961. The World Today. Vol. 17. No. 12. December 1961. pp. 503–511
Anon. ON THERMONUCLEAR CO-EXISTENCE. Survey. No. 39. December 1961. pp. 3–16. Survival. Vol. 5. No. 1. January/ February 1962. pp. 34–42
Aron, Raymond. THE FRANCO-AMERICAN DEBATE: THE FRENCH PERSPECTIVE. Survival. Vol. 4. No. 4. July/August 1962. pp. 159–162. (See also Walter Lippman: 'The Franco-American debate: the French perspective'. SURVIVAL as above, pp. 153–158)
Arzumanyan, A. EUROPEAN SECURITY AND THE ATOMIC ARMING OF THE FEDERAL REPUBLIC OF GERMANY. International Affairs (Moscow). 1961. No. 7. pp. 44–45
Aust, H. THE BERLIN QUESTION AND THE INTERESTS OF PEACE. International Affairs (Moscow). 1959. No. 1. pp. 46–53
Barghoorn, Frederick C. THE SOVIET VIEW OF AMERICA. Orbis. Vol. 2. No. 1. Spring 1958. pp. 96–107
Beloff, Max. THE ATLANTIC COMMUNITY: THE DEBATE IN AMERICA. Survival. Vol. 4. No. 2. March/April 1962. pp. 69–70. (Reprint from The Times, 2 February 1962)
Beaufre, General André. NATO IN 1962. Survival. Vol. 4. No. 3. May/ June 1962. pp. 120–124
Belonsov, M. WHO, THEN, IS RESPONSIBLE FOR THE COLD WAR? International Affairs (Moscow). 1958. No. 11. pp. 89–95
Bevan, Aneurin. BRITAIN AND AMERICA AT LOGGERHEADS. Foreign Affairs. Vol. 36. No. 1. October 1957. pp. 60–67. (i.e. in the post-Suez period)
Bieri, Ernst. AN ATLANTIC DIALOGUE IN BRUGES. Orbis. Vol. 1. No. 4. Winter 1958. pp. 397–407
Birrenbach, Kurt. THE REORGANISATION OF NATO. Orbis. Vol. 6.

No. 2. Summer 1962. pp. 244–257
Brandt, Willy. THE MEANS SHORT OF WAR. Foreign Affairs. Vol. 39. No. 2. January 1961. pp. 196–207. (i.e. to solve the Berlin and German problems)
Brentano, Heinrich von. GOALS AND MEANS OF THE WESTERN ALLIANCE. Foreign Affairs. Vol. 39. No. 3. April 1961. pp. 416–429
Brodie, Bernard. THE POSSIBILITY OF TOTAL WAR. Survival. Vol. 4. No. 6. November/December 1962. pp. 242–249
Brown, George W. THE 'ATLANTIC ALLIANCE' IN PERSPECTIVE. International Journal. Vol. 12. No. 2. Spring 1957. pp. 79–82
Brown, Neville. A NEW POLICY FOR NATO? The World Today. Vol. 20. No. 10. October 1964. pp. 423–431
Buchan, Alastair. STRATEGIC FACTORS AND THE SUMMIT. The World Today. Vol. 16. No. 4. April 1960. pp. 141–149
Buchan, Alastair. THE REFORM OF NATO. Foreign Affairs. Vol. 40. No. 2. January 1962. pp. 165–182. (The central machinery, the structure for defence, and nuclear relations)
Buchan, Alastair. EUROPE, AMERICA AND NATO: A BRITISH VIEW. Survival. Vol. 4. No. 1. January/February 1962. pp. 9–12
Bundy, McGeorge. FRIENDS AND ALLIES. Foreign Affairs. Vol. 41. No. 1. October 1962. pp. 14–23. (General review of U.S. relations with her allies as at October 1962)
Carleton, William G. BRAIN-TRUSTERS OF AMERICAN FOREIGN POLICY. World Politics. Vol. 7. No. 4. July 1958. pp. 627–639. (Review article on studies by L.J. Halle, G.F. Kennan and C.B. Marshall)
Challener, Richard D. THE MILITARY AND THE CONDUCT OF FOREIGN POLICY. World Politics. Vol. 9. No. 4. July 1957. pp. 610–622. (Review of Alfred Vagts: 'Defence and diplomacy: the soldier and the conduct of foreign relations'. New York: King's Crown Press. 1956)
Chamberlin, Waldo. THE NORTH ATLANTIC BLOC IN THE U.N. GENERAL ASSEMBLY. Orbis. Vol. 1. No. 1. Winter 1958. pp. 459–473
Collins, General J. Lawton. NATO: STILL VITAL FOR PEACE. Foreign Affairs. Vol. 34. No. 3. April 1956. pp. 367–379
Cottrell, Alvin J. and Dougherty, James E. NUCLEAR WEAPONS, POLICY AND STRATEGY. Orbis. Vol. 1. No. 2. Summer 1957. pp. 138–160

Couve de Murville, Maurice. NATO: A FRENCH VIEW. International Journal. Vol. 14. No. 2. Spring 1959. pp. 85–86

Croan, Melvin. REALITY AND ILLUSTION IN SOVIET-GERMAN RELATIONS. Survey. Nos. 44/45. October 1962. pp. 12–28

Crowther, Geoffrey. RECONSTRUCTION OF AN ALLIANCE. Foreign Affairs. Vol. 35. No. 2. January 1957. pp. 173–183. (i.e. in the aftermath of Suez)

Dadyants, G. COLD WAR, PAST AND PRESENT. International Affairs (Moscow). 1960. No. 6. pp. 5–11

Degras, Jane. THE COMMUNIST CAMP TEN YEARS AFTER STALIN. The World Today. Vol. 19. No. 3. March 1963. pp. 108–115

DeWeerd, H.A. BRITAIN'S CHANGING MILITARY POLICY. Foreign Affairs. Vol. 34. No. 1. October 1955. pp. 102–116

Dinerstein, Herbert S. SOVIET GOALS AND MILITARY FORCE. Orbis. Vol. 5. No. 4. Winter 1962. pp. 425–436

Dodd, Thomas J. IF CO-EXISTENCE FAILS: THE KHRUSHCHEV VISIT (TO U.S.A.) EVALUATED. Orbis. Vol. 3. No. 4. Winter 1960. pp. 393–423

Dougherty, James E. EUROPEAN DETERRENCE AND ATLANTIC UNITY. Orbis. Vol. 6. No. 3. Fall 1962. pp. 371–421

Dulles, John Foster. CHALLENGE AN D RESPONSE IN UNITED STATES POLICY. Foreign Affairs. Vol. 36. No. 1. October 1957. pp. 25–43

Eden, Sir Anthony. THE SLENDER MARGIN OF SAFETY. Foreign Affairs. Vol. 39. No. 1. October 1960. pp. 165–173

Erler, Fritz. THE STRUGGLE FOR GERMAN REUNIFICATION. Foreign Affairs. Vol. 34. No. 3. April 1956. pp. 380–393

Erler, Fritz. THE REUNIFICATION OF GERMANY AND SECURITY FOR EUROPE. World Politics. Vol. 10. No. 3. April 1958. pp. 366–377

Foster, William C. TOWARD A BALANCED DEFENCE. Orbis. Vol. 3. No. 1. Spring 1959. pp. 26–37

Friedmann, Wolfgang. NEW TASKS FOR NATO? International Journal. Vol. 2. No. 3. Summer 1956. pp. 157–164

Friedmann, Wolfgang. MEETING OF EAST AND WEST? (Reflections on the Eisenhower-Khrushchev meetings 1959). International Journal. Vol. 14. No. 4. Autumn 1959. pp. 235–243

Furniss, Edgar S. FRANCE, NATO AND EUROPEAN SECURITY. International Organisation. Vol. 10. No. 4. Autumn 1956. pp. 544–558

Fyodorov, T. A GERMAN PEACE TREATY AND NATO. International Affairs (Moscow). 1962. No. 6. pp. 17–23

Gaitskell, Hugh. DISENGAGEMENT: WHY? HOW? Foreign Affairs. Vol. 36. No. 4. July 1958. pp. 539–556

Galkin, A. THE 'PARADOXES' OF WESTERN FOREIGN POLICY. International Affairs (Moscow). 1960. No. 2. pp. 51–57

Galkin, A. GERMAN MILITARISM AND SOVIET-WEST GERMAN RELATIONS. International Affairs (Moscow). 1961. No. 7. pp. 81–83

de Gaulle, Charles. PRESIDENT DE GAULLE'S FIRST PRESS CONFERENCE 25 MARCH 1959. Excerpts concerning NATO. Survival. Vol. 1. No. 2. May/June 1959. pp. 47–48

Gordon, Lincoln. NATO AND EUROPEAN INTEGRATION. World Politics. Vol. 10. No. 2. January 1958. pp. 219–231

Gordon, Lincoln. NATO IN THE NUCLEAR AGE. Survival. Vol. 1. No. 2. May/June 1959. pp. 35–41

Grosser, Alfred. SUEZ, HUNGARY AND EUROPEAN INTEGRATION. International Organisation. Vol. 11. No. 3. Summer 1957. pp. 470–480

Haas, Ernst B. REGIONALISM, FUNCTIONALISM AND UNIVERSAL INTERNATIONAL ORGANISATION. World Politics. Vol. 8. No. 2. January 1956. pp. 238–263

Haas, Ernst B. PERSISTENT THEMES IN ATLANTIC AND EUROPEAN UNITY. World Politics. Vol. 10. No. 4. July 1958. pp. 614–628

Haas, Ernst B. and Merke, Peter H. PARLIAMENTARIANS AGAINST MINISTERS: THE CASE OF WESTERN EUROPEAN UNION. International Organisation. Vol. 14. No. 1. Winter 1960. pp. 37–39

Haffner, Sebastian. THE BERLIN CRISIS (1958–1962). Survey. Nos. 44/45. October 1962. pp. 37–44

Healey, Denis. 'WHEN SHRIMPS LEARN TO WHISTLE' – THOUGHTS AFTER GENEVA (July 1955). International Affairs. Vol. 32. No. 1. January 1956. pp. 1–10

Healey, Denis. THE CRISIS IN EUROPE. International Affairs. Vol. 38. No. 2. April 1962. pp. 145–155. (Berlin; Britain's approach to the E.E.C.)

Hoag, Malcolm W. NATO: DETERRENT OR SHIELD. Foreign Affairs. Vol. 36. No. 2. January 1958. pp. 278–292

Hoag, Malcolm W. ON NATO POOLING. World Politics. Vol. 10. No. 3. April 1958. pp. 475–583

Hoag, Malcolm W. WHAT INTERDEPENDENCE FOR NATO? Survival.
Vol. 2. No. 3. May/June 1960. pp. 94–106. (Reprint from World
Politics. April 1960)
Home, The Earl of (later Sir Alec Douglas Home). INTERDEPEN-
DENCE: THE BRITISH ROLE. International Affairs. Vol. 37.
No. 2. April 1961. pp. 154–161
Hottelet, Richard C. KHRUSHCHEV'S GERMAN GAMBIT. Orbis.
Vol. 3. No. 1. Spring 1959. pp. 13–25
Hottelet, Richard C. BERLIN AND BEYOND. Orbis. Vol. 5. No. 3.
Fall 1961. pp. 267–291
Howard, Michael. DISENGAGEMENT AND WESTERN SECURITY.
International Affairs. Vol. 34. No. 4. October 1958. pp. 469–476
Illarionov, S. THE U.S.A. AND THE F.R.G. – PARTNERS AND
RIVALS. International Affairs (Moscow). 1960. No. 12. pp. 68–75
Inozemtsev, N. THE WAY TO SETTLE THE GERMAN QUESTION.
International Affairs (Moscow). 1957. No. 8. pp. 122–126
Isayev, N. NATO: MILITARY TRAIN IN AN IMPASSE. International
Affairs (Moscow). 1961. No. 6. pp. 31–39
Jacobi, Claus. GERMAN PARADOXES. Foreign Affairs. Vol. 35.
No. 3. April 1957. pp. 432–440. (The pursuit of German policy
in the light of Suez and Hungary)
Jordan, Amos A. MILITARY ASSISTANCE AND NATIONAL
POLICY. Orbis. Vol. 2. No. 2. Summer 1958. pp. 236–253
Kahn, S. WEST GERMANY'S POLICY OF REARMAMENT AND
REVANCHE. International Affairs (Moscow). 1960. No. 5. pp. 47–
52
Kaplan, Lawrence S. NATO AND ADENAUER'S GERMANY:
UNEASY PARTNERSHIP. International Organisation. Vol. 15.
No. 4 Autumn 1961. pp. 618–629
Kaufmann, William W. THE CRISIS IN MILITARY AFFAIRS. World
Politics. Vol. 10. No. 4. July 1958. pp. 579–603
Kelly, George A. THE POLITICAL BACKGROUND OF THE
FRENCH A-BOMB. Orbis. Vol. 4. Fall 1960. No. 3. pp. 248–306
Kennan, George F. DISENGAGEMENT REVISITED. Foreign Affairs.
Vol. 37. No. 2. January 1959. pp. 187–210
Kennan, George F. and Gibbs, Norman. DISENGAGEMENT AND
DISARMAMENT: a revision of the Reith lectures of 1957 – and
the reply. Survival. Vol. 2. No. 1. January/February 1960. pp. 20–27
Kennan, George F. PEACEFUL CO-EXISTENCE: A WESTERN
VIEW. Foreign Affairs. Vol. 38. No. 2. January 1960. pp. 171–190

Kennedy, John F. SPECIAL MESSAGE TO CONGRESS ON U.S. DEFENCE POLICY 28 MARCH 1961. Survival. Vol. 3. No. 3. May/June 1961. pp. 98–105

Kennedy, John F. A DEMOCRAT LOOKS AT FOREIGN POLICY. Foreign Affairs. Vol. 36. No. 1. October 1957. pp. 44–59

Kennedy, John F. and Khrushchev, Nikita. K. AND K.: ACTION AND REACTION. Survival. Vol. 3. No. 5. September/October 1961. pp. 235–242

Khrushchev, Nikita S. ON PEACEFUL CO-EXISTENCE. Foreign Affairs. Vol. 38. No. 1. October 1959. pp. 1–18

Khvostov, V. THE FOREIGN POLICY OF GERMAN MILITARISM. International Affairs (Moscow). 1957. No. 8. pp. 77–87

Kissinger, Henry A. FORCE AND DIPLOMACY IN THE NUCLEAR AGE. Foreign Affairs. Vol. 34. No. 3. April 1956. pp. 349–366

Kissinger, Henry A. STRATEGY AND ORGANISATION, Foreign Affairs. Vol. 35. No. 3. April 1957. pp. 379–394

Kissinger, Henry A. MISSILES AND THE WESTER ALLIANCE. Foreign Affairs. Vol. 36. No. 3. April 1958. pp. 383–400

Kissinger, Henry A. THE SEARCH FOR STABILITY. Foreign Affairs. Vol. 37. No. 4. July 1959. pp. 525–536

Kissinger, Henry A. TOWARDS WESTERN COHESION: AN AMERICAN VIEW. Survival. Vol. 3. No. 2. March/April 1961. pp. 69–74

Kissinger, Henry A. THE UNSOLVED PROBLEMS OF EUROPEAN DEFENCE. Foreign Affairs. Vol. 40. No. 4. July 1962. pp. 515–541

Kissinger, Henry A. EUROPEAN DEFENCE. Survival. Vol. 4. No. 5. September/October 1962. pp. 217–225

Kohn, Hans. THE ATLANTIC COMMUNITY AND THE WORLD. Orbis. Vol. 1. No. 4. Winter 1958. pp. 418–427

Kohn, Hans. THE DIFFICULT ROAD TO WESTERN UNITY. Orbis. Vol. 3. No. 3. Fall 1959. pp. 297–312

Kohn, Hans. THE U.S. AND WESTERN EUROPE: A NEW ERA OF UNDERSTANDING. Orbis. Vol. 6. No. 1. Spring 1962. pp. 13–24

Komarov, M. CO-EXISTENCE OF THE TWO GERMAN STATES AND THE PEACE TREATY. International Affairs (Moscow). 1962. No. 7. pp. 6–11

Korovin, Y. COLD WAR: THEORY AND PRACTICE. International Affairs (Moscow). 1959. No. 6. pp. 6–13

Kozyakov, V. THE COLD WAR AND CONGRESS. International Affairs (Moscow). 1959. No. 11. pp. 105–106

Kryukov, P. WHO INSPIRED THE INSURGENTS IN HUNGARY? International Affairs (Moscow). 1956. No. 12. pp. 105–110

Kryukov, P. and Mulin, V. A PEACE TREATY – A HISTORICAL NECESSITY. International Affairs (Moscow). 1959. No. 12. pp. 14–19

Kryukov, P. A PEACE TREATY AND EUROPEAN SECURITY. International Affairs (Moscow). 1961. No. 7. pp. 77–80

Kryukov, P. and Mulin, P. BONN: ENEMY OF PEACEFUL CO-EXISTENCE. International Affairs (Moscow). 1962. No. 12. pp. 57–62

Kurganov, E. and Nikolayev, E. WHAT THE U.S. MUTUAL SECURITY PROGRAMME MEANS. International Affairs (Moscow). 1956. No. 4. pp. 72–83

L., H.G. THE GERMAN PROBLEM ON THE EVE OF THE FOUR-POWER TALKS. The World Today. Vol. 2. No. 7. July 1955. pp. 280–290

L., H.G. THE FOUR POWERS AND GERMANY: THE RE-UNIFICATION ISSUE. The World Today. Vol. 2. No. 2. November 1955. pp. 471–482

Labour Party and T.U.C. THE NEXT STEP: DISARMAMENT AND NUCLEAR WAR. Survival. Vol. 1. No. 4. September/October 1959. pp. 119–122

Lachs, Manfred. THE WARSAW TREATY AND THE NORTH ATLANTIC TREATY. International Affairs (Moscow). 1956. No. 2. pp. 113–116

Larionov, Lt. Col. V. THE DOCTRINE OF AGGRESSION IN DOSES – a critique of Henry Kissinger's 'Nuclear Weapons and Foreign Policy'. Survival. Vol. 1. No. 4. September/October 1959. pp. 135–136. (Translated from RED STAR 8 July 1959)

Lavergne, B. DEEP DIFFERENCES BETWEEN PARIS AND BONN. International Affairs (Moscow). 1960. No. 12. pp. 65–68

Lawson, Ruth C. CONCERTING POLICIES IN THE NORTH ATLANTIC COMMUNITY. International Organisation. Vol. 12. No. 2. Spring 1958. pp. 163–179

Lippman, Walter. INTERVIEW WITH KHRUSHCHEV. Survival. Vol. 3. No. 4. July/August 1961. pp. 154–158

Lippman, Walter. THE FRANCO-AMERICAN DEBATE: THE AMERICAN PERSPECTIVE. Survival. Vol. 4. No. 4. July/August 1962. pp. 153–158. (See also Raymond Aron: 'The Franco-American Debate: the French perspective'. SURVIVAL as above,

pp. 159–162)
Lvov, M. and Mishin, A. FRANCE AND WEST GERMANY. International Affairs (Moscow). 1959. No. 4. pp. 21–30
Lvov, M. and Grigoryev, V. SUPER – NATO? International Affairs (Moscow). 1959. No. 6. pp. 36–43
McNamara, Robert S. THE ANN ARBOR SPEECH 16 JUNE 1962: excerpt on the Alliance, and European reactions. Survival. Vol. 4. No. 5. September/October 1962. pp. 194–200
Macdonald, H.I. DISENGAGEMENT RECONSIDERED. International Journal. Vol. 14. No. 1. Winter 1958/59. pp. 21–32
Madzojewski, S. BRITAIN AND GERMAN IMPERIALISM. International Affairs (Moscow). 1958. No. 1. pp. 39–47
Madzojewski, S. THE SECURITY OF BRITAIN AND ANGLO-AMERICAN RELATIONS. International Affairs (Moscow). No. 10. pp. 45–52
Madzojewski, S. BRITAIN AND WESTERN EUROPE. International Affairs (Moscow). 1960. No. 1. pp. 41–48
Mayor, John. PRESIDENT KENNEDY'S 'GRAND DESIGN': THE UNITED STATES AND A UNITED EUROPE. The World Today. Vol. 18. No. 9. September 1962. pp. 383–389
Malinovsky, Marshal R.Y. WARNING TO THE WEST: speech to the 22nd Party Congress, 24 October 1961. Survival. Vol. 4. No. 1. January/February 1962. pp. 32–32. (See also Marshal Savitsky: 'Be on your guard'. Survival as above, pp. 32–33)
Malinovsky, Marshal R.Y. et al. THE 'NEW LOOK' IN MOSCOW: abstracts from speeches to the Supreme Soviet by senior military, January 1960. Survival. Vol. 2. No. 2. March/April 1960. pp. 43–46
Matveyeva, N. PRESENT TRENDS IN U.S. FOREIGN POLICY. International Affairs (Moscow). 1957. No. 4. pp. 37–48
Mayo, H.B. CO-EXISTENCE – IS IT POSSIBLE? International Journal. Vol. 10. No. 3. Summer 1955. pp. 157–170
Meissner, W. FOR A PEACEFUL SETTLEMENT OF THE GERMAN QUESTION. International Affairs (Moscow). 1959. No. 8. pp. 3–9
Melnikov, D. THE TROJAN HORSE IN FONTAINEBLEAU. International Affairs (Moscow). 1957. No. 4. pp. 105–111
Melnikov, D. GERMAN MILITARISM TODAY. International Affairs (Moscow). 1957. No. 8. pp. 66–77
Melnikov, D. NEW WAYS OF ENSURING EUROPEAN SECURITY. International Affairs (Moscow). 1958. No. 9. pp. 10–17
Melnikov, D. THE GERMAN PEACE TREATY AND THE INTERESTS

OF EUROPEAN SECURITY. International Affairs (Moscow). 1959. No. 5. pp. 18–24

Melnikov, D. WEST GERMANY AND NATO. International Affairs (Moscow). 1961. No. 7. pp. 70–72

Melnikov, D. THE WEST AND A GERMAN PEACE TREATY. International Affairs (Moscow). 1959. No. 11. pp. 28–34

Melnikov, D. WEST GERMANY AND EUROPEAN PEACE. International Affairs (Moscow). 1960. No. 3. pp. 50–57

Melnikov, D. WEST GERMANY AND NATO POLICY. International Affairs (Moscow). 1960. No. 11. pp. 29–35

Miksche, F.O. THE CASE FOR NUCLEAR SHARING. Orbis. Vol. 5. No. 3. Fall 1961. pp. 292–305

Mosely, Philip E. SOVIET FOREIGN POLICY: NEW GOALS OR NEW MANNERS? Foreign Affairs. Vol. 34. No. 4. July 1956. pp. 541–554. (Reflections on the 20th Party Congress)

Mosely, Philip E. THE MEANING OF CO-EXISTENCE. Foreign Affairs. Vol. 41. No. 1. October 1962. pp. 36–46

Moulin, Leo. ANTI-AMERICANISM IN EUROPE. Orbis. Vol. 1. No. 5. Winter 1958. pp. 448–458

Muhlen, Norbert. POST-WAR GERMANY: MIRACLE OR MIRAGE? Orbis. Vol. 3. No. 3. Fall 1959. pp. 351–353

Nakropin, O. NEW TROUBLE FOR NATO. International Affairs (Moscow). 1957. No. 12. pp. 136–138

Nakropin, O. and Stroganov, A. THE CARDINAL SOLUTION OF THE GERMAN PROBLEM. International Affairs (Moscow). 1959. No. 3. pp. 24–29

Nalin, Y. NATO – WEAPON OF AGGRESSION. Survival. Vol. 1. No. 2. May/June 1959. pp. 42–43. (Translated from RED STAR. 28 March 1959)

Nalin, Y. THE 'ATLANTIC CONGRESS' IN LONDON. International Affairs (Moscow). 1959. No. 7. pp. 100–101

Nalin, Y. NATO: WATCHDOG OF COLONIALISM. International Affairs (Moscow). 1961. No. 5. pp. 60–65

Nathan, James A. THE MISSILE CRISIS: HIS FINEST HOUR NOW. World Politics. Vol. 27. No. 2. January 1975. pp. 256–281. (i.e. President Kennedy in October 1962)

Nazarenko, I. THE COMMON MARKET IN THE SERVICE OF NATO. International Affairs (Moscow). 1962. No. 12. pp. 28–37

Nelson, Harold I. THE GERMAN PROBLEM, 1955. International Journal. Vol. 10. No. 3. Summer 1955. pp. 183–191

Niemeyer, Gerhard. THE PROBABILITY OF WAR IN OUR TIME. Orbis. Vol. 1. No. 2. Summer 1957. pp. 161–183

Niemeyer, Gerhard. NATO'S STRENGTH AND WEAKNESS. Orbis. Vol. 2. No. 1. Spring 1958. pp. 83–95

Nitze, Paul H. ATOMS, STRATEGY AND POLICY. Foreign Affairs. Vol. 34. No. 2. January 1956. pp. 187–198

Nitze, Paul H. POLITICAL ASPECTS OF A NATIONAL STRATEGY. Survival. Vol. 2. No. 6. November/December 1960. pp. 219–226

Novoseltsev, E. THE WESTERN POWERS ARE AGAINST GERMAN REUNIFICATION. International Affairs (Moscow). 1959. No. 7. pp. 108–113

Novsky, N. THE SMALL COUNTRIES AND NATO. International Affairs (Moscow). 1961. No. 12. pp. 69–73

Nutting, Anthony. DISARMAMENT, EUROPE AND SECURITY. International Affairs. Vol. 36. No. 1. January 1960. pp. 1–6

Oleshchuk, Y. CONTAINED CRITICISM OF 'CONTAINMENT'. (Review of G.F. Kennan: 'Memoirs 1950–1963'. Boston: Little Brown & Co. 1972). International Affairs (Moscow). 1973. No. 10. pp. 102–105

Pearson, Lester B. AFTER GENEVA: A GREATER TASK FOR NATO. Foreign Affairs. Vol. 34. No. 1. October 1955. pp. 14–23

Pearson, Lester B. A MEASURED DEFENCE FOR THE WEST. Orbis. Vol. 1. No. 4. Winter 1958. pp. 428–434

Pearson, Lester B. NATO: RETROSPECT AND PROSPECTS. International Journal. Vol. 14. No. 2. Spring 1959. pp. 79–86

Pleven, René. FRANCE IN THE ATLANTIC COMMUNITY. Foreign Affairs. Vol. 38. No. 1. October 1959. pp. 19–30

Pross, Harry. WEST GERMANY: UNFINISHED DEMOCRACY. Orbis. Vol. 2. No. 3. Fall 1958. pp. 356–370

Razmerov, V. THE WEST GERMAN ATOMIC PROGRAMME AND PREPARATION FOR MILITARY ATOMIC PRODUCTION. International Affairs (Moscow). 1961. No. 7. pp. 61–63

Rockefeller, Nelson A. PURPOSE AND POLICY. Foreign Affairs. Vol. 38. No. 3. April 1960. pp. 370–390

Rogers, Lindsay. OF SUMMITS. Foreign Affairs. Vol. 34. No. 1. October 1955. pp. 141–147

Rothstein, A. THE STRUGGLE TO IMPROVE BRITISH-SOVIET RELATIONS. International Affairs (Moscow). 1957. No. 10. pp. 66–74

Rubinsky, Y. THE NATO COUNCIL'S LAST SESSION. International

Affairs (Moscow). 1957. No. 6. pp. 114–116
Ruhm von Oppen, Beate. THE END OF THE ADENAUER ERA.
The World Today. Vol. 19. No. 8. August 1963. pp. 343–352
Salisbury, Harrison E. CHARACTERISTICS OF SOVIET FORIEGN
POLICY. International Journal. Vol. 11. No. 4. Autumn 1956.
pp. 243–250
Sanakoyev, S. THE STRUGGLE OF THE TWO IDEOLOGIES AND
THE COLD WAR. International Affairs (Moscow). 1960. No. 7.
pp. 60–64
Sanakoyev, S. THE THREAT OF WEST GERMAN MILITARISM: ITS
FORM AND CONTENTS AT THE PRESENT STAGE. International
Affairs (Moscow). 1961. No. 7. pp. 68–70
Schmelz, R. WEST GERMANY'S PLACE IN AMERICAN IMPERIALIST
PLANS. International Affairs (Moscow). 1957. No. 8. pp. 90–94
Schmidt, Helmut. THE DEFENCE DEBATE IN GERMANY: THE
OPPOSITION VIEW. Survival. Vol. 3. No. 4. July/August 1961.
pp. 178–181. (See also Franz Josef Strauss: 'The defence debate
in Germany: the government view'. SURVIVAL. as above, pp. 176–
178)
Schuman, Robert. THE ATLANTIC COMMUNITY AND EUROPE.
Orbis. Vol. 1. No. 4. Winter 1958. pp. 408–410
Schumann, Maurice. FRANCE AND GERMANY IN THE NEW
EUROPE. Foreign Affairs. Vol. 41. No. 1. October 1962. pp. 66–77
Schutz, Wilhelm Wolfgang. NEW INITIATIVES FOR A NEW AGE:
A GERMAN VIEW. Foreign Affairs. Vol. 36. No. 3. April 1958.
pp. 460–471. (i.e. disengagement and German reunification)
Schutz, Wilhelm Wolfgang. GERMAN FOREIGN POLICY:
FOUNDATIONS IN THE WEST, AIMS IN THE EAST. International
Affairs. Vol. 35. No. 3. July 1959. pp. 310–315
von Senger und Etterlin, General F. NATO – DISPUTED DEVELOP-
MENT. Survival. Vol. 1. No. 2. May/June 1959. pp. 44–46
Seton-Watson, Hugh. SOVIET FOREIGN POLICY ON THE EVE OF
THE SUMMIT. (May 1960). International Affairs. Vol. 36. No. 3.
July 1960. pp. 287–298
Smith, Sydney E. NATO AND THE CHALLENGE OF THE MISSILE
AGE. International Journal. Vol. 13. No. 3. Summer 1958. pp. 165–
174
Snyder, Glenn H. DETERRENCE, DEFENCE AND DISENGAGEMENT.
World Politics. Vol. 14. No. 2. January 1962. pp. 393–403
Sojak, V. PEACEFUL CO-EXISTENCE – THE ONLY WAY TO

EUROPEAN SECURITY. International Affairs (Moscow). 1961. No. 7. pp. 56–59

Spaak, Paul-Henri. THE WEST IN DISARRAY. Foreign Affairs. Vol. 35. No. 2. January 1957. pp. 184–190. (Reactions to Suez and Hungary)

Spaak, Paul-Henri. NATO AND THE COMMUNIST CHALLENGE. International Journal. Vol. 13. No. 4. Autumn 1958. pp. 243–250

Spaak, Paul-Henri. THE ATLANTIC COMMUNITY AND NATO. Orbis. Vol. 1. No. 4. Winter 1958. pp. 411–417

Spaak, Paul-Henri. NEW TESTS FOR NATO. Foreign Affairs. Vol. 37. No. 2. April 1959. pp. 357–365

Speier, Hans. SOVIET ATOMIC BLACKMAIL AND THE NORTH ATLANTIC ALLIANCE. World Politics. Vol. 9. No. 3. April 1957. pp. 307–328

Spencer, Robert A. GERMANY AND THE 'LONG HAUL'. International Journal. Vol. 11. No. 1. Winter 1955/56. pp. 1–15. (i.e. reunification)

Spinelli, Altiero. ATLANTIC PACT OR EUROPEAN UNITY. Foreign Affairs. Vol. 40. No. 4. April 1962. pp. 542–552

Strauss, Franz Josef. SOVIET AIMS AND GERMAN UNITY. Foreign Affairs. Vol. 37. No. 3. April 1959. pp. 366–377. (Not only political; also includes a consideration of disengagement)

Strauss, Franz Josef. THE DEFENCE DEBATE IN GERMANY: THE GOVERNMENT VIEW. Survival. Vol. 3. No. 4. July/August 1961. pp. 176–178. (See also Helmut Schmidt: 'The Defence debate in Germany: the opposition view'. SURVIVAL as above, pp. 178–181)

Strauss, Franz Josef. EUROPE, AMERICA AND NATO: A GERMAN VIEW. Survival. Vol. 4. No. 1. January/February 1962. pp. 5–8

Strauss-Hupé, Robert. PROTRACTED CONFLICT: A NEW LOOK AT COMMUNIST STRATEGY. Orbis. Vol. 2. No. 1. Spring 1958. pp. 13–38

Tolmachov, P. FAILURE OF THE COLD WAR POLICY. International Affairs (Moscow). 1959. No. 10. pp. 19–28

Tyulpanov, S. and Chernetsovsky, Y. THE NATO 'INTERNATIONAL' AND ITS PROGRAMME. International Affairs (Moscow). 1962. No. 6. pp. 82–87

Ulam, Adam B. SOVIET IDEOLOGY AND SOVIET FOREIGN POLICY. World Politics. Vol. 11. No. 2. January 1959. pp. 153–172

Verrier, Anthony. KENNEDY AND EUROPE: THE END OF A CHAPTER. The World Today. Vol. 20. No. 1. January 1964. pp. 39–46

Victorov, Y. BEHIND THE SCENES OF NATO. International Affairs (Moscow). 1959. No. 1. pp. 68–76

Vidyasova, L. THE AGGRESSIVE POLICY OF THE U.S.A. AND NATO. International Affairs (Moscow). 1960. No. 10. pp. 28–34

Vladimirov, S. and Yanin, I. U.S. BASES AND EUROPEAN SECURITY. International Affairs (Moscow). 1960. No. 7. pp. 17–23

W., J.F.A. TEN YEARS OF EAST-WEST RELATIONS IN EUROPE: THE STRUGGLE FOR GERMANY. The World Today. Vol. 11. No. 6. June 1955. pp. 246–254

Wiles, P.J.D. THE PURSUIT OF DISENGAGEMENT. Survival. Vol. 2. No. 1. January/February 1960. pp. 28–33. (Reprint from THE WORLD TODAY. April 1959)

Wolfe, Bertram D. COMMUNIST IDEOLOGY AND SOVIET FOREIGN POLICY. Foreign Affairs. Vol. 41. No. 1. October 1962. pp. 152–170

Wolfers, Arnold. EUROPE AND THE NATO SHIELD. International Organisation. Vol. 12. No. 4. Autumn 1958. pp. 425–439

Woodhouse, C.M. ATTITUDES OF THE NATO COUNTRIES TOWARD THE UNITED STATES. World Politics. Vol. 10. No. 2. January 1958. pp. 202–218

Yeremenko, A. THE STRATEGIC AND POLITICAL VALUE OF MILITARY BASES. International Affairs (Moscow). 1960. No. 11. pp. 57–62

Yermolenko, D. THE IDEOLOGICAL ARTIFICES OF THE NATO APOLOGISTS. International Affairs (Moscow). 1957. No. 1. pp. 85–94

Yerusalimsky, A. GERMAN MILITARISM AND COLLECTIVE SECURITY IN EUROPE. International Affairs (Moscow). 1957. No. 8. pp. 86–90

Zhukov, Y. A NEW NATO WEAPON: IDEOLOGICAL SUBVERSION. International Affairs (Moscow). 1962. No. 9. pp. 70–77

Zilliacus, K. BRITAIN AND THE MENACE OF GERMAN MILITARISM. International Affairs (Moscow). 1959. No. 3. pp. 38–46

Military – Strategic Aspects

Anon. THE NEXT FIVE YEARS: SUGGESTIONS FOR THE BRITISH DEFENCE REVIEW 1962. Survival. Vol. 4. No. 1. January/February 1962. pp. 43–44. (Reprint from THE ECONOMIST. 2 December 1961)

Anon. NUCLEAR SUPPORT FOR NATO: commentary on the North Atlantic Council Meeting, Athens. May 1962. Survival. Vol. 4. No. 4. July/August 1962. pp. 184–185

Baudissin, Count Wolf. THE NEW GERMANY ARMY. Foreign Affairs. Vol. 34. No. 1. October 1955. pp. 1–13

Baz, Colonel I. THE CHARACTERISTICS OF MODERN WAR. Survival. Vol. 1. No. 5. November/December 1959. pp. 180–184. (Translated from MILITARY HERALD. Moscow. June 1958)

Bethe, Hans A. DISARMAMENT AND STRATEGY. Survival. Vol. 4. No. 6. November/December 1962. pp. 267–276. (Reprint from THE BULLETIN OF THE ATOMIC SCIENTISTS. September 1962)

Bernard, Stephan. SOME POLITICAL AND TECHNICAL IMPLICATIONS OF DISARMAMENT. World Politics. Vol. 8. No. 1. October 1955. pp. 71–90

Blackett, P.M.S. NUCLEAR WEAPONS AND DEFENCE: comments on Kissinger, Kennan and King-Hall. International Affairs. Vol. 34. No. 4. October 1958. pp. 421–434

Brown, Neville. BRITAIN'S STRATEGIC WEAPONS I: the manned bomber. The World Today. Vol. 20. No. 7. July 1964. pp. 293–298

Brown, Neville. BRITAIN'S STRATEGIC WEAPONS II: the Polaris A-3. The World Today. Vol. 20. No. 8. August 1964. pp. 358–364

Buzzard, Rear Admiral Sir Anthony W. MASSIVE RETALIATION AND GRADUATED DETERRENCE. World Politics. Vol. 8. No. 2. January 1966. pp. 228–237

Buzzard, Anthony; Slessor, John and Lowenthal, Richard. THE H-BOMB: MASSIVE RETALIATION OR GRADUATED DETERRENCE? International Affairs. Vol. 32. No. 2. April 1956. pp. 148–165

Dinerstein, H.S. CURRENT SOVIET STRATEGIC IDEAS. Survey. No. 34. October/December 1960. pp. 74–79

Dougherty, James E. KEY TO SECURITY: DISARMAMENT OR ARMS STABILITY. Orbis. Vol. 4. No. 3. Fall 1960. pp. 261–283

Dupuy, T.N. CAN AMERICA FIGHT A LIMITED NUCLEAR WAR? Orbis. Vol. 5. No. 1. Spring 1961. pp. 31–42

Gallois, General Pierre. NEW TEETH FOR NATO. Foreign Affairs.

Vol. 39. No. 1. October 1960. pp. 67–80

Gallois, General Pierre. COLLECTIVE DEFENCE. Survival. Vol. 1. No. 2. May/June 1959. p. 49

Gareau, Frederick H. NUCLEAR DETERRENCE: A DISCUSSION OF THE DOCTRINE. Orbis. Vol. 5. No. 2. Summer 1961. pp. 182–197

Gellner, John and Jackson, James. MODERN WEAPONS AND THE SMALL POWER. International Journal. Vol. 13. No. 2. Spring 1958. pp. 87–99. (i.e. nuclear weapons and Canada)

Geneste, Lt. Col. M.E. PROFESSIONAL VIEWS ON TACTICAL WEAPONS: A FRENCH VIEW. Survival. Vol. 4. No. 5. September/October 1962. pp. 212–214. (See also Lt. Col. L.M. Jones: 'Professional views on tactical weapons: an American view'. Survival. as above, pp. 214–216)

Glazov, Colonel V. WHAT IS LOCAL WAR? Survival. Vol. 3. No. 5. September/October 1961. pp. 226–228

Goold-Adams, Richard. THE BRITISH ARMY IN THE NUCLEAR AGE. Survival. Vol. 1. No. 5. November/December 1959. pp. 155–163

Healey, Denis. THE SPUTNIK AND WESTERN DEFENCE. International Affairs. Vol. 34. No. 2. April 1958. pp. 145–156

Hirshleifer, Jack. SOME THOUGHTS ON THE SOCIAL STRUCTURE AFTER A BOMBING DISASTER. World Politics. Vol. 8. No. 2. January 1956. pp. 206–227

Hoopes, Townsend. OVERSEAS BASES IN AMERICAN STRATEGY. Foreign Affairs. Vol. 37. No. 1. October 1958. pp. 69–82

Howard, Michael. BRITAIN'S DEFENSES. Foreign Affairs. Vol. 39. No. 1. October 1960. pp. 81–91. Survival. Vol. 3. No. 1. January/February 1961. pp. 35–40

Hughes, E. U.S. BASES IN BRITAIN. International Affairs (Moscow). 1960. No. 9. pp. 44–47

Hunter, Robert E. THE POLITICS OF U.S. DEFENCE 1963: MANNED BOMBERS VERSUS MISSILES. The World Today. Vol. 19. No. 3. March 1963. pp. 98–107

Hunter, Robert E. THE POLITICS OF U.S. DEFENCE 1963. The World Today. Vol. 19. No. 4. April 1963. pp. 155–166

Illarionov, S. NATO'S NUCLEAR MISSILES PROBLEMS. International Affairs (Moscow). 1961. No. 7. pp. 23–28

Iovlev, Colonel A.M. THE VALUE OF NUMBERS IN THE NUCLEAR AGE: A SOVIET VIEW. Survival. Vol. 3. No. 5. September/October 1961. pp. 233–234. (See also General Pickert: 'The value of numbers

in the nuclear age: a German view'. Survival. as above, pp. 229–232)
Jones, Lt. Col. L.M. PROFESSIONAL VIEWS ON TACTICAL WEAPONS: AN AMERICAN VIEW. Survival. Vol. 4. No. 5. September/October 1962. pp. 214–216. (See also Lt. Col. M.E. Geneste: 'Professional views on tactical weapons: a French view'. Survival. as above, pp. 212–214)
K., J. THE SOVIET GENERAL STAFF TAKES STOCK: CHANGES IN MILITARY DOCTRINE. The World Today. Vol. 11. No. 11. November 1955. pp. 492–502
Kahn, Herman; Fromm, Erich and Maccoby, Michael. A DEBATE ON THE QUESTION OF CIVIL DEFENCE. Survival. Vol. 4. No. 2. March/April 1962. pp. 50–67
Kintner, William R. and Possony, Stefan T. NATO'S NUCLEAR CRISIS. Orbis. Vol. 6. No. 2. Summer 1962. pp. 217–244
King, James E., Jr. NUCLEAR PLENTY AND LIMITED WAR. Foreign Affairs. Vol. 35. No. 2. January 1957. pp. 238–256
Kissinger, Henry A. LIMITED WAR: NUCLEAR OR CONVENTIONAL? Survival. Vol. 3. No. 1. January/February 1961. pp. 2–11
Knorr, Klaus. NUCLEAR WEAPONS: 'HAVES' AND 'HAVE-NOTS'. Foreign Affairs. Vol. 36. No. 1. October 1957. pp. 167–178. (The broader issues raised by the British decision to develop thermo-nuclear power as announced in the Defence White Paper 1957)
Knowlton, Lt. Col. William A. EARLY STAGES IN THE ORGANISATION OF SHAPE. International Organisation. Vol. 13. No. 1. Winter 1959. pp. 1–18
Kononenko, A. PRESENT-DAY U.S. MILITARY THINKING AND THE ARMS DRIVE. International Affairs (Moscow). 1958. No. 7. pp. 34–41
Kozlov, Colonel S. MODERN WAR – A RUSSIAN VIEW. Survival. Vol. 3. No. 4. July/August 1961. pp. 159–160. (Translated from ARMED FORCES COMMUNIST. January 1961)
Kurasov, Army General V.V. ON THE QUESTION OF A FORE-STALLING BLOW. Survival. Vol. 1. No. 1. March/April 1959. pp. 3–5. (Translated from RED STAR 27 April 1958)
Kurochkin, Army General P. CONVENTIONAL FORCES IN THE NUCLEAR AGE. Survival. Vol. 3. No. 6. November/December 1961. pp. 282–283. (Translated from MILITARY HISTORICAL JOURNAL. August 1961)
Lemnitzer, General Lyman L. FORWARD STRATEGY RE-

APPRAISED. Survival. Vol. 3. No. 1. January/February 1961.
pp. 22–25
Liddell Hart, B.H. SHIELD FORCES FOR NATO. Survival. Vol. 2.
No. 3. May/June 1960. pp. 108–110
Lilov, Lt. Col. L. et al. THE SOVIET MISSILE PROGRAMME.
Survival. Vol. 4. No. 2. March/April 1962. pp. 86–91. (Reprints
from THE PEOPLES ARMY (Bulgaria) and RED STAR)
Lvov, M. NATO'S MEDITERRANEAN NUCLEAR-ROCKET AXIS.
International Affairs (Moscow). 1959. No. 10. pp. 49–55
M., J.M. CHANGING MILITARY THOUGHT IN THE SOVIET
UNION. The World Today. Vol. 13. No. 12. December 1957.
pp. 517–528
Mackintosh, Malcolm. SOVIET STRATEGY IN WORLD WAR III.
Survival. Vol. 2. No. 4. July/August 1960. pp. 151–158
Mackintosh, Malcolm. SOVIET STRATEGY POSTURES. Survival.
Vol. 4. No. 3. May/June 1962. pp. 116–119
Malinovsky, Marshal S.Y. SOVIET STRATEGY. Survival. Vol. 4.
No. 5. September/October 1962. pp. 229–232. (From
KOMMUNIST May 1962)
Matteson, Robert E. THE DISARMAMENT DILEMMA. Orbis. Vol. 2.
No. 3. Fall 1958. pp. 285–299
Messmer, Pierre. THE FRENCH MILITARY ESTABLISHMENT OF
TOMORROW. Orbis. Vol. 6. No. 2. Summer 1962. pp. 205–216
Messmer, Pierre. FRENCH NUCLEAR FORCES: an interview with
the French Minister of Defence. September 1962. Survival. Vol. 4.
No. 6. November/December 1962. pp. 277–281. (Reprint from
U.S. NEWS AND WORLD REPORT. 24 September 1962)
Muhlen, Norbert. THE NEW ARMY OF A NEW GERMANY. Orbis.
Vol. 1. No. 3. Fall 1957. pp. 278–290
Mulley, Fred. A EUROPEAN NUCLEAR DETERRENT. Survival.
Vol. 2. No. 1. January/February 1960. pp. 34–36
Norstad, General Lauris. NATO AS THE FOURTH ATOMIC
POWER. Survival. Vol. 2. No. 3. May/June 1960. p. 107
Norstad, General Lauris. THE DEFENCE OF EUROPE: speech to
the NATO Parliamentarians. 21 November 1960. Survival. Vol. 3.
No. 1. January/February 1961. pp. 26–30
Norstad, General Lauris. SAUCEUR'S VIEWS – 1961: speech to the
NATO Parliamentarians. 13 November 1961. Survival. Vol. 4. No. 1.
January/February 1962. pp. 13–14
Pickert, General. THE VALUE OF NUMBERS IN THE NUCLEAR

AGE: A GERMAN VIEW. Survival. Vol. 3. No. 5. September/ October 1961. pp. 229–232. (See also Colonel A.M. Iovlev: 'The value of numbers in the nuclear age: a Soviet view'. Survival. as above, pp. 233–234)

Pugh, George E. STRATEGY AND ARMS CONTROL. Survival. Vol. 5. No. 6. November/December 1963. pp. 273–281. (Reprint from ORBIS. Summer 1963)

Rathjens, George W., Jr. NOTES ON THE MILITARY PROBLEMS OF EUROPE. World Politics. Vol. 10. No. 2. January 1958. pp. 182–201

Rudoi, G. THE BUNDESWEHR – INSTRUMENT OF REVANCHE AND AGGRESSION. International Affairs (Moscow). 1959. No. 4. pp. 82–87

Schelling, Thomas C. NUCLEAR STRATEGY IN EUROPE. World Politics. Vol. 14. No. 3. April 1962. pp. 421–432. Survival. Vol. 4. No. 5. September/October 1962. pp. 206–211

Schwarz, Urs. STRENGTHENING EUROPE'S DEFENSIVE POWER. Survival. Vol. 2. No. 5. September/October 1960. pp. 210–214. (See also Frederick M. Stern: 'Citizen armies for multi-dimensional defence'. Survival. as above, pp. 203–209)

Shatrov, V. NATO'S NUCLEAR CRISIS. International Affairs (Moscow). 1962. No. 8. pp. 47–51

Slessor, Marshal of the R.A.F. Sir John. BRITISH DEFENCE POLICY. Foreign Affairs. Vol. 35. No. 4. July 1957. pp. 551–563

Slessor, Sir John. WESTERN STRATEGY IN THE NUCLEAR AGE. Orbis. Vol. 1. No. 3. Fall 1957. pp. 357–364. (A review of Henry A. Kissinger: 'Nuclear Weapons and Foreign Policy'. New York: Harper for the Council on Foriegn Relations; London: Oxford University Press. 1957)

Slessor, Sir John. A NEW LOOK AT STRATEGY FOR THE WEST. Orbis. Vol. 2. No. 3. Fall 1958. pp. 320–336

Slessor, Sir John. SWORD AND SHIELD. Survival. Vol. 3. No. 1. January/February 1961. pp. 12–15

Slessor, Sir John. NUCLEAR POWER AND BRITAIN'S DEFENCE. Survival. Vol. 4. No. 6. November/December 1962. pp. 250–254

Stern, Frederick M. CITIZEN ARMIES FOR MULTI-DIMENSIONAL DEFENCE. Survival. Vol. 2. No. 5. September/October 1960. pp. 203–209. Orbis. Vol. 3. No. 4. Winter 1960. pp. 469–481. (See also Urs Schwarz: 'Strengthening Europe's defensive power'. Survival. as above, pp. 210–214)

Strachey, John. IS OUR DETERRENT VULNERABLE? A DISCUSSION OF WESTERN DEFENCE IN THE 1960'S. International Affairs. Vol. 37. No. 1. January 1961. pp. 1–8
Talensky, Major-General N. THE STRATEGIC CONCEPT OF GERMAN MILITARISM. International Affairs (Moscow). 1957. No. 8. pp. 94–99
Talensky, Major-General N. MILITARY STRATEGY AND FOREIGN POLICY. International Affairs (Moscow). 1958. No. 3. pp. 26–33
Talensky, Major-General N. THE MILITARY ASPECT OF COEXISTENCE. International Affairs (Moscow). 1960. No. 7. pp. 64–67
Talensky, Major-General N. ON THE CHARACTER OF MODERN WARFARE. International Affairs (Moscow). 1960. No. 10. pp. 23–28. Survival. Vol. 3. No. 1. January/February 1961. pp. 16–21
Taylor, General Maxwell D. SECURITY WILL NOT WAIT. Foreign Affairs. Vol. 39. No. 2. January 1961. pp. 174–184. (A critique of U.S. policy in the Cold War)
Teplinsky, B. MILITARY BASES AND AMERICAN STRATEGIC DOCTRINE. International Affairs (Moscow). 1959. No. 9. pp. 79–86
U.S. Democratic National Committee. THE MILITARY FORCES WE NEED. Survival. Vol. 1. No. 4. September/October 1959. pp. 107–116
Verrier, Anthony. TEST-BAN TREATY: AFTERMATH IN NATO. The World Today. Vol. 19. No. 9. September 1963. pp. 369–371
Warner, Geoffrey. THE NASSAU AGREEMENT AND NATO. The World Today. Vol. 19. No. 2. February 1963. pp. 61–69
Waskow, Arthur I. AMERICAN MILITARY DOCTRINE. Survival. Vol. 4. No. 3. May/June 1962. pp. 106–115
Weinstein, Adalbert. HARMONIOUS STRATEGY — THE CASE FOR INCREASED CONVENTIONAL FORCES. Survival. Vol. 1. No. 5. September/October 1959. pp. 117–118
Wohlstetter, Albert. THE DELICATE BALANCE OF TERROR. Foreign Affairs. Vol. 37. No. 2. January 1959. pp. 211–234. Survival. Vol. 1. No. 1. March/April 1959. pp. 8–17. (A condensed version of the article)
Wohlstetter, Albert. NUCLEAR SHARING: NATO AND THE N + 1 COUNTRY. Foreign Affairs. Vol. 39. No. 3. April 1961. pp. 355–388
Yeremenko, Marshal A. ARGUMENTS AGAINST FOREIGN BASES.

Survival. Vol. 3. No. 2. March/April 1961. pp. 62–66
Yermashov, I. THE CRISIS OF AMERICAN 'ATOMIC AGE STRATEGY'. International Affairs (Moscow). 1960. No. 11. pp. 48–57
Z., X.Y. DISARMAMENT: PROPOSALS AND NEGOTIATIONS 1946–1955. The World Today. Vol. 11. No. 8. August 1955. pp. 334–348
Zhukov, G. AN ATOM-FREE ZONE IN EUROPE. International Affairs (Moscow). 1959. No. 5. pp. 50–56
Zilliacus, K. BRITAIN AND THE H-BOMB. International Affairs (Moscow). 1958. No. 4. pp. 40–45

SECTION III

THE SEARCH FOR A *MODUS VIVENDI*: 1962–1970

The conclusions drawn from the experience of the Cuban missile crisis of October 1962 varied. Prime Minister Harold Macmillan saw it as a confirmation of the earlier insistence of his government that Britain needed an independent nuclear deterrent and at the end of the year struck the agreement at Nassau whereby Britain obtained the *Polaris* missile from the United States. While sharing Macmillan's view concerning nuclear weapons, President de Gaulle chose to regard the Cuban crisis more balefully and began to accelerate the withdrawal of France from the integrated military structures of the Alliance. The designations 'Atlanticist' and 'European' began more freely to be applied to those German politicians and commentators who chose to place their trust in the United States or in France, and then, in the summer of 1964, Khrushchev, Macmillan and Adenauer were one way or another moved from the centre of the European political stage.

Their departure, coupled with the steady increase in the number and sophistication of nuclear delivery systems, coincided with the growing realisation that whatever kept the two power blocs in Europe apart they yet shared one common interest — the avoidance of any conflict of interest which might lead to nuclear war. This entailed a re-assessment of those issues which had kept the blocs in confrontation. Far and away the most important of these issues was the insistence of the Atlantic allies that Germany be reunited as the outcome of procedures known to be unacceptable to the Soviet Union. The Federal Republic being the only member of the Alliance which could rescue the Alliance as a whole from a dilemma of its own creation, there followed the process of accommodation to political realities in Central Europe which was widely and accurately described as the *Ostpolitik*.

The process was not an even one, and the Atlantic Alliance was not able to determine its pace; from 1966 the Warsaw Pact powers pressed for a conference on European security. The initial response of the West was to repeat its established conviction that the major problem in respect of European security was the military imbalance between the East and the West, and hence there followed a counter-proposal that discussions should rather be focussed on mutual and balanced force reductions. The acceptance by the North Atlantic Council of the Harmel Report in December 1967, however, committed the Alliance to the active pursuit of detente as well as the maintenance of a credible deterrent posture and a sound defence capability, and the seventies opened with the recognition of the German Democratic Republic, the Four-Power agreements on Berlin and an acceptance of the proposals of the Warsaw Pact to discuss not only security but co-operation in Europe.

The material selected in the following section not only reflects these developments; it also indicates that cohesion was no more to be taken for granted in the Warsaw Pact than in the Atlantic Alliance, as most vividly demonstrated by the events in Czechoslovakia in summer 1968.

Books

Economic Aspects

Alder-Karlsson, Gunnar. WESTERN ECONOMIC WARFARE 1947–1967. Stockholm: Almquist and Wiksell. 1968. (See review by Michael Kaser in SURVIVAL. Vol. 11. No. 7. July 1969)

Cooper, Richard N. THE ECONOMICS OF INTERDEPENDENCE: ECONOMIC POLICY IN THE ATLANTIC COMMUNITY. New York: McGraw-Hill for the Council on Foreign Relations. 1968

Hardt, John P., *et al.* THE COLD WAR ECONOMIC GAP: THE INCREASING THREAT TO AMERICAN SECURITY. New York: Praeger, 1961

Harvey, Mose L. EAST-WEST TRADE AND UNITED STATES POLICY. New York: National Association of Manufacturers. 1966

Hinshaw, Randall. THE EUROPEAN COMMUNITY AND AMERICAN TRADE: a study in Atlantic economics and policy. New York:

Praeger for the Council on Foreign Relations. 1964
Hitch, Charles J. and McKean, Roland N. THE ECONOMICS OF
DEFENCE IN THE NUCLEAR AGE. Cambridge, Mass.: Harvard
University Press; Toronto: S.J. Reginald Saunders. 1960
Krause, Lawrence B. EUROPEAN ECONOMIC INTEGRATION AND
THE UNITED STATES. Washington: Brookings Institution. 1968
Maddison, Angus. ECONOMIC GROWTH IN THE WEST: COM-
PARATIVE EXPERIENCE IN EUROPE AND NORTH AMERICA.
New York: Twentieth Century Fund. 1964
Schwartz, Harry. THE SOVIET ECONOMY SINCE STALIN.
Philadelphia: Lippincott. 1965
Sutton, Anthony C. WESTERN TECHNOLOGY AND SOVIET
ECONOMIC DEVELOPMENT, 1945-1965. Stanford: Hoover
Institution Press. 1973

Legal, Institutional and Organisational Aspects

Eriksen, Bjarne, THE COMMITTEE SYSTEM OF THE NATO
COUNCIL. Oslo: Universitetsforlaget. 1967
Hovey, J. Allan. THE SUPERPARLIAMENTS: INTERPARLIAMEN-
TARY CONSULTATION AND ATLANTIC CO-OPERATION.
New York: Praeger. 1966
Jordan, R.S. THE NATO INTERNATIONAL STAFF/SECRETARIAT
1952-57: a study in international administration. London: Oxford
University Press. 1967
MacCloskey, Brig.-Gen. Monro. NORTH ATLANTIC TREATY
ORGANISATION: GUARDIAN OF PEACE AND SECURITY.
New York: Richards Rosen Press Inc. 1966
Stanger, Roland J. (ed.). WEST BERLIN: THE LEGAL CONTEXT.
Columbus: Ohio State University Press. 1966

National and Regional Aspects

Amme, Carl H. NATO WITHOUT FRANCE: A STRATEGIC RE-
APPRAISAL. Stanford: The Hoover Institution. 1967. (See review
article by Harald von Riekhoff: 'NATO without France' in

INTERNATIONAL JOURNAL. Vol. 23. No. 2. Spring 1968. pp. 281–286. Also review by Christoph Bertram in SURVIVAL. Vol. 11. No. 9. September 1969. pp. 299–300)

Aronson, James. THE PRESS AND THE COLD WAR. (i.e. U.S. press). New York: Bobbs-Merrill; Toronto: Thomas Allen. 1970. (See review by Philip Deane in INTERNATIONAL JOURNAL. Vol. 27. No. 2. Spring 1972. pp. 324–325)

Bader, William B. AUSTRIA BETWEEN EAST AND WEST. Stanford: Stanford University Press. 1966

Barnet, Richard J. and Raskin, Marcus G. AFTER 20 YEARS: ALTERNATIVES TO THE COLD WAR IN EUROPE. New York: Random House. 1965

Beaufre, André. NATO AND EUROPE. London: Faber. 1967. (See review by V. Grigoriev: 'NATO devotee's self-deception' in INTERNATIONAL AFFAIRS (Moscow). 1967. No. 5. p. 104)

Beloff, Max. THE UNITED STATES AND THE UNITY OF EUROPE. Washington: Brookings Institution. 1963

Beloff, Max. THE FUTURE OF BRITISH FOREIGN POLICY. London: Secker and Warburg; New York: Taplinger. 1969

van der Beugel, Ernst H. FROM MARSHALL AID TO ATLANTIC PARTNERSHIP: EUROPEAN INTEGRATION AS A CONCERN OF AMERICAN FOREIGN POLICY. New York: Elsevier. 1966

Birrenbach, Kurt. THE FUTURE OF THE ATLANTIC COMMUNITY: TOWARDS EUROPEAN-AMERICAN PARTNERSHIP. New York: Frederick A. Praeger; Toronto: Burns and MacEachern. 1963

Bloomfield, Lincoln P. WESTERN EUROPE TO THE MID-SEVENTIES. Cambridge, Mass.: M.I.T. Press. 1968

Bolling, Klaus. REPUBLIC IN SUSPENSE: POLITICS, PARTIES AND PERSONALITIES IN POST-WAR GERMANY. New York: Praeger. 1964

Brandon, Donald. AMERICAN FOREIGN POLICY: BEYOND UTOPIANISM AND REALISM. New York: Appleton. 1966

Brandt, Willy. A PEACE POLICY FOR EUROPE. New York: Toronto: Holt, Rinehart and Winston. 1968

von Brentano, H. GERMANY AND EUROPE. London: André Deutsch. 1964

Brewin, Andrew. STAND ON GUARD: THE SEARCH FOR A CANADIAN DEFENCE POLICY. Toronto and Montreal: McClelland and Stewart. 1965

Brown, Neville. ARMS WITHOUT EMPIRE. (A study of British defence

policy since 1945). Harmondsworth: Penguin. 1967
Brinton, Crane. THE AMERICANS AND THE FRENCH. Cambridge: Harvard University Press. 1968
Buchan, Alastair and Windsor, Philip. ARMS AND STABILITY IN EUROPE. London: Chatto and Windus; New York: Frederick A. Praeger; Toronto: Burns and MacEachern. 1963. (See review by J.I. Coffey in INTERNATIONAL JOURNAL. Vol. 19. No. 2. Spring 1964. pp. 243–244)
Burgess, Philip M. ELITE IMAGES AND FOREIGN POLICY OUTCOMES: A STUDY OF NORWAY. Columbus: Ohio State University Press. 1969
Calleo, David C. EUROPE'S FUTURE: THE GRAND ALTERNATIVES. New York: Horizon Press. 1965
Calleo, David P. BRITAIN'S FUTURE. New York: Horizon Press. 1969
Campbell, John C. AMERICAN POLICY TOWARDS COMMUNIST EASTERN EUROPE: THE CHOICES AHEAD. Minneapolis: University of Minnesota Press. 1965
de Carmoy, Guy. THE FOREIGN POLICIES OF FRANCE 1944–1968. Chicago: University of Chicago Press. 1970
Clarkson, Stephen (ed.). AN INDEPENDENT FOREIGN POLICY FOR CANADA? Toronto: McClelland and Stewart for the University League for Social Reform. 1968
Conant, Melvin. THE LONG POLAR WATCH: CANADA AND THE DEFENCE OF NORTH AMERICA. London: Oxford University Press; Hamish Hamilton. New York: Harper for the Council on Foreign Relations; Toronto: Musson Book Co. 1962
Conquest, Robert. RUSSIA AFTER KHRUSHCHEV. New York: Praeger. 1965
Couloumbis, Theodore. GREEK POLITICAL REACTION TO AMERICAN AND NATO INFLUENCES. London: Oxford University Press; New Haven: Yale University Press. 1966
Cromwell, William C. (ed.), et al. POLITICAL PROBLEMS OF ATLANTIC PARTNERSHIP: NATIONAL PERSPECTIVES. Bruges: College of Europe. 1969. (i.e. America, British and German perspectives)
Deutsch, Karl W., et al. FRANCE, GERMANY AND THE WESTERN ALLIANCE: a study of elite attitudes on European integration and world politics. New York: Charles Scribner's Sons. 1967
Donelan, Michael. THE IDEAS OF AMERICAN FOREIGN POLICY. London: Chapman. 1963

Druks, Herbert. HARRY S. TRUMAN AND THE RUSSIANS. New York: Speller. 1967

Dulles, Eleanor Lansing. BERLIN: THE WALL IS NOT FOREVER. Chapel Hill: University of North Carolina Press. 1967

Dulles, Eleanor Lansing. ONE GERMANY OR TWO: THE STRUGGLE AT THE HEART OF EUROPE. Stanford: Hoover Institution Press. 1970

Erler, Fritz. DEMOCRACY IN GERMANY. Cambridge, Mass.: Harvard University Press. 1965

Feld, Werner. REUNIFICATION AND WEST GERMAN-SOVIET RELATIONS. The Hague: Nijhoff. 1963

Fischer-Galati, Stephen. (ed.). EASTERN EUROPE IN THE SIXTIES. New York: Praeger. 1964

Floyd, David. RUMANIA: RUSSIA'S DISSIDENT ALLY. New York: Praeger. 1965

Graebner, Norman A. COLD WAR DIPLOMACY: American Foreign Policy 1945–1960. Princeton: Van Nostrand. 1962

Grosser, Alfred. FRENCH FOREIGN POLICY UNDER DE GAULLE. Boston, Mass., and Toronto: Little, Brown & Co. 1967

Halle, L.G. AMERICAN FOREIGN POLICY: THEORY AND REALITY. London: George Allen and Unwin. 1960. (See review by Y. Melnikov: 'Still in the grip of illusions' in INTERNATIONAL AFFAIRS (Moscow). 1961. No. 11. pp. 105–108)

Hammond, Paul. THE COLD WAR YEARS: American foreign policy since 1945. New York: Harcourt Brace and World Inc. 1969

Hangen, Welles. THE MUTED REVOLUTION: East Germany's challenge to Russia and the West. New York: Knopf. 1966

Hanreider, Wolfram F. WEST GERMAN FOREIGN POLICY 1949–1963. Stanford: Stanford University Press. 1967

Hartmann, Frederick H. GERMANY BETWEEN EAST AND WEST. Englewood Cliffs: Prentice-Hall. 1965

Hayter, Sir William. RUSSIA AND THE WORLD: A STUDY OF SOVIET FOREIGN POLICY. London: Secker and Warburg. 1970

Hertzman, Lewis, et al. ALLIANCES AND ILLUSIONS: CANADA AND THE NATO – NORAD QUESTION. Edmonton: M.G. Hurtig. 1969. (See review by R.F. Swanson in INTERNATIONAL JOURNAL. Vol. 26. No. 1. Winter 1970. pp. 286–288)

Hiscocks, Richard. THE ADENAUER ERA. Philadelphia: Lippincott. 1966

Hoffmann, Stanley. GULLIVER'S TROUBLES, OR THE SETTING OF

AMERICAN FOREIGN POLICY. New York: McGraw-Hill for
Council for Foreign Relations. 1968
Hugo, Grant. BRITAIN IN TOMORROW'S WORLD: PRINCIPLES
OF FOREIGN POLICY. New York: Columbia University Press.
1969
Hunter, Robert. SECURITY IN EUROPE. London: Elek. 1969
James, Robert Rhodes (ed.). THE CZECHOSLOVAK CRISIS 1968.
London: Weidenfeld and Nicolson for the Institute for the Study
of International Organisations, University of Sussex. 1969. (See
review by Geoffrey Jukes in SURVIVAL. Vol. 11. No. 10.
October 1969. pp. 329–331)
Jaspers, Karl. THE FUTURE OF GERMANY. Chicago. University
of Chicago Press. 1967
de Kadt, Emanuel J. BRITISH DEFENCE POLICY AND NUCLEAR
WAR. London: Frank Cass. 1964; New York: Humanities Press.
1966
Kaiser, Karl. GERMAN FOREIGN POLICY IN TRANSITION: BONN
BETWEEN EAST AND WEST. New York: Oxford University
Press for the Royal Institute of International Affairs. 1968
Kaplan, Lawrence S. RECENT AMERICAN FOREIGN POLICY:
CONFLICTING INTERPRETATIONS. Homewood, Ill.: Dorsey
Press. 1969
Kogan, Norman. A POLITICAL HISTORY OF POST-WAR ITALY.
New York: Praeger. 1966
Kolkowicz, Roman. THE SOVIET MILITARY AND THE
COMMUNIST PARTY. Princeton, N.J.: Princeton University
Press. 1967
Kulski, W.W. DE GAULLE AND THE WORLD: THE FOREIGN
POLICY OF THE FIFTH FRENCH REPUBLIC. Syracuse: Syracuse
University Press. 1966
Landauer, Carl. GERMANY: ILLUSIONS AND DILEMMAS. New
York: Harcourt, Brace and World. 1969. (A plea for greater realism
in Western initiatives towards the East)
Lerner, Daniel and Gorden, Morton. EURATLANTICA: CHANGING
PERSPECTIVES OF THE EUROPEAN ELITES. Cambridge: M.I.T.
Press. 1969
Linden, Carl A. KHRUSHCHEV AND THE SOVIET LEADERSHIP
1957–1964. Baltimore: Johns Hopkins Press in co-operation with
the Institute for Sino-Soviet Studies, George Washington University.
1966

Liska, George. EUROPE ASCENDANT: THE INTERNATIONAL POLITICS OF UNIFICATION. Baltimore: Johns Hopkins Press. 1964
Littell, Robert (ed.). THE CZECH. BLACK BOOK. London: Pall Mall. 1969. (See review by Geoffrey Jukes in SURVIVAL. Vol. 11. No. 10. October 1969. pp. 329–331)
Lochen, Einar. NORWAY IN EUROPEAN AND ATLANTIC CO-OPERATION. Oslo: Universitetsforlaget. 1964
Lyon, Peyton V. THE POLICY QUESTION: a critical appraisal of Canada's role in world affairs. Toronto: McClelland. 1963
MacDonald, R. St. J. (ed.). THE ARCTIC FRONTIER. London and Toronto: University of Toronto Press. 1966
McLin, John B. CANADA'S CHANGING DEFENCE POLICY 1957–1963: the problems of a middle power in alliance. Baltimore: Johns Hopkins; London: Oxford University Press; Toronto: Capp Clark. 1967
Majonica, Ernst. EAST-WEST RELATIONS: A GERMAN VIEW. New York: Praeger. 1969
Mander, John. BERLIN: HOSTAGE FOR THE WEST. Harmondsworth: Penguin. 1962
Martin, Paul. CANADA AND THE QUEST FOR PEACE. New York: Columbia University Press. 1967. (3 lectures delivered in 1967 by the Canadian Minister for External Affairs)
Mayhew, Christopher. BRITAIN'S ROLE TOMORROW. London. Hutchinson. 1967. (See review by O. Orestov: 'Legitimate Alarm' in INTERNATIONAL AFFAIRS (Moscow). No. 6. 1967. pp. 103–104)
Mendl, Wolf. DETERRENCE AND PERSUASION: FRENCH NUCLEAR ARMAMENTS IN THE CONTEXT OF NATIONAL POLICY 1945–1964. New York: Praeger; London: Faber and Faber. 1970. (See review by John Newhouse in SURVIVAL. Vol. 12. No. 12. December 1970. pp. 427–429)
Middleton, Drew. THE SUPREME CHOICE: BRITAIN AND EUROPE. New York: Knopf. 1963
Newhouse, John. DE GAULLE AND THE ANGLO-SAXONS. London: André Deutsch; New York: Viking Press. 1970
Nicholas, Herbert. BRITAIN AND THE U.S.A. Baltimore: Johns Hopkins Press. 1963. (British relations with U.S.A. since 1939)
Northedge, F.S. BRITISH FOREIGN POLICY: THE PROCESS OF READJUSTMENT 1945–1961. London: Allen and Unwin. 1962

Osgood, Robert E. ALLIANCES AND AMERICAN FOREIGN POLICY. Baltimore: Johns Hopkins Press. 1968

Pethybridge, R.W. A HISTORY OF POST-WAR RUSSIA. New York: New American Library. 1966

Pickles, Dorothy. THE UNEASY ENTENTE: FRENCH FOREIGN POLICY AND FRANCO-BRITISH MISUNDERSTANDINGS. London: Oxford University Press for the Royal Institute of International Relations. 1966

Pierre, Andrew J. NUCLEAR POLITICS: THE BRITISH EXPERIENCE WITH AN INDEPENDENT STRATEGIC FORCE 1939-1970. London: Oxford University Press. 1972. (See review by V. Repnitsky: 'Recipes for nuclear "Europeanisation" of NATO' in INTERNATIONAL AFFAIRS (Moscow). 1974. No. 4. pp. 92-94)

Planck, Charles R. THE CHANGING STATUS OF GERMAN REUNIFICATION IN WESTERN DIPLOMACY. 1955-1966. Baltimore: Johns Hopkins Press. 1967. (A review of NATO policy re. Bonn's preferences)

Pounds, Norman J.G. DIVIDED GERMANY AND BERLIN. Princeton: Van Nostrand. 1962

Pritt, D.N. UNREPENTANT AGGRESSORS: AN EXAMINATION OF WEST GERMAN POLICIES. London: Lawrence and Wishart. 1969 (The view of a celebrated British communist)

Richardson, James L. GERMANY AND THE ATLANTIC ALLIANCE: THE INTERACTION OF STRATEGY AND POLITICS. Cambridge, Mass.: Harvard University Press. 1966. (See review by V. Polyakov: 'A British apologist of the Bonn militarists'. INTERNATIONAL AFFAIRS (Moscow). 1967. No. 8. pp. 90-92)

Rosecrance, R.N. DEFENCE OF THE REALM: BRITISH STRATEGY IN THE NUCLEAR EPOCH. New York: Columbia University Press. 1968

Sapin, Burton M. THE MAKING OF UNITED STATES FOREIGN POLICY. Washington: Brookings Institution. 1966

Scheinman, Lawrence. ATOMIC ENERGY POLICY IN FRANCE UNDER THE FOURTH REPUBLIC. Princeton: Princeton University Press. 1965

Schutz, Wilhelm Wolfgang. RETHINKING GERMAN POLICY: NEW APPROACHES TO REUNIFICATION. New York: Frederick A. Praeger; Toronto: Burns and MacEachern. 1967. London: Pall Mall. 1968

Seaburg, Paul and Wildavsky, Aaron. U.S. FOREIGN POLICY: PER-

SPECTIVES AND PROPOSALS FOR THE 1970'S. New York: McGraw-Hill. 1969

Serfaty, Simon. FRANCE, DE GAULLE AND EUROPE. Baltimore: Johns Hopkins Press. 1968

Smith, Jean Edward. THE DEFENCE OF BERLIN. Baltimore: Johns Hopkins Press. 1963

Smith, Mark E. and Johns, Claude J. (eds.). AMERICAN DEFENCE POLICY. Baltimore: Johns Hopkins Press. 1968

Staar, Richard F. THE COMMUNIST REGIMES IN EASTERN EUROPE: AN INTRODUCTION. Stanford: Hoover Institution. 1967

Stahl, Walter. THE POLITICS OF POST-WAR GERMANY. New York: Praeger for Atlantik-Brucke. 1963

Strauss, Franz Josef. THE GRAND DESIGN: A EUROPEAN SOLUTION TO GERMAN REUNIFICATION. London: Weidenfeld and Nicolson. 1965; New York: Praeger. 1966

Strauss, Franz Josef. CHALLENGE AND RESPONSE: A PROGRAMME FOR EUROPE. London: Weidenfeld and Nicolson. 1969; New York: Atheneum. 1970

Vali, Ferenc A. THE QUEST FOR A UNITED GERMANY. Baltimore: Johns Hopkins Press. 1967

Vali, Ferenc A. THE TURKISH STRAITS AND NATO. Stanford: Hoover Institution. 1972

Various (Soviet). ON EVENTS IN CZECHOSLOVAKIA: FACTS, DOCUMENTS, PRESS REPORTS AND EYE WITNESS ACCOUNTS. Moscow: Press Group of Soviet Journalists. 1968

Watt, D.C. BRITAIN LOOKS TO GERMANY. London: Wolff. 1965. (British policy towards Germany since the 2nd. World War)

Whitney, Thomas P. (ed.). KHRUSHCHEV SPEAKS. Ann Arbor: University of Michigan Press. 1963. (An anthology, with commentary, 1949–61)

Wighton, Charles. ADENAUER: A CRITICAL BIOGRAPHY. New York: Coward-McCann. 1964

Willis, F.R. FRANCE, GERMANY AND THE NEW EUROPE. Stanford: Stanford University Press; London: Oxford University Press. 1965. (See review by V. Polyakov: 'Professor Willis's Delusions' in INTERNATIONAL AFFAIRS (Moscow). 1966. No. 7. pp. 93–94)

Windsor, Philip. CITY ON LEAVE: A HISTORY OF BERLIN 1945–1962. New York: Praeger. 1963

Windsor, Philip. GERMAN REUNIFICATION. London: Elek. 1969

Windsor, Philip and Roberts, Adam. CZECHOSLOVAKIA 1968. London:

Chatto and Windus for the Institute of Strategic Studies. 1969
Wolfe, James H. INVISIBLE GERMANY: ILLUSION OR REALITY. The Hague: Martinus Nijhoff. 1963
Younger, Kenneth. CHANGING PERSPECTIVES IN BRITISH FOREIGN POLICY. London: Oxford University Press for the Royal Institute of International Affairs. 1964. (i.e. after de Gaulle's 1963 veto)

Politico – Military Aspects

Acheson, Dean. PRESENT AT THE CREATION: MY YEARS IN THE STATE DEPARTMENT. New York: W.W. Norton. Toronto: George J. McLeod. 1969
Adenauer, Konrad. MEMOIRS 1945–1953. Chicago: Regnery; London: Weidenfeld and Nicolson. 1966
Allison, Graham T. ESSENCE OF DECISION: EXPLAINING THE CUBAN MISSILE CRISIS. Boston: Little, Brown. 1971
Alperovitz, Gar. COLD WAR ESSAYS. New York: Doubleday, Anchor Books. 1970
Aptheker, Herbert. AMERICAN FOREIGN POLICY AND THE COLD WAR: A MARXIST-LENINIST VIEW. New York: New Century. 1962
Ball, George W. THE DISCIPLINE OF POWER: ESSENTIALS OF A MODERN WORLD STRUCTURE. Boston: Atlantic (Little, Brown). 1968
Beaufre, André. NATO AND EUROPE. London: Faber and Faber. 1967. (See review by V. Grigoriev: 'NATO devotee's self-deception' in INTERNATIONAL AFFAIRS (Moscow). 1967. No. 5. p. 104)
Beer, Francis.A. INTEGRATION AND DISINTEGRATION IN NATO. Columbus: Ohio State University Press. 1969. (See review by V. Repnitsky: 'Atlantic integration strife' in INTERNATIONAL AFFAIRS (Moscow). 1971. No. 1. pp. 83–85. Also review by Robert L. Rothstein: 'New perspectives on NATO' in INTERNATIONAL ORGANISATION. Vol. 24. No. 3. Summer 1970. pp. 566–577)
Bell, Coral. THE DEBATEABLE ALLIANCE. London: Oxford University Press for the Royal Institute of International Affairs. 1964

Bieri, Ernst, *et al.* BASIC VALUES OF THE ATLANTIC COMMUNITY.
London: Pall Mall Press for the Conference on Atlantic Community.
1962
Birnbaum, Karl E. PEACE IN EUROPE: EAST-WEST RELATIONS
1966–1968. London: Oxford University Press. 1970. (See review by
N. Yurin: 'Europe: Strength of realities' in INTERNATIONAL
AFFAIRS (Moscow). 1971. No. 5. pp. 94–96)
Bloomfield, Lincoln P. *et al.* KHRUSHCHEV AND THE ARMS RACE.
Cambridge, Mass.: M.I.T. Press; Toronto: General Publishing Co.
1969
Bohlen, Charles E. THE TRANSFORMATION OF AMERICAN
FOREIGN POLICY. New York: W.W. Norton; Toronto: George J.
McLeod. 1969
Bohlen, Charles E. WITNESS TO HISTORY. 1929–1969. New York:
W.W. Norton; Toronto: George J. McLeod. 1973. (Notable for an
account of U.S. policy towards the Soviet Union 1933–1969 by a
distinguished actor in the process)
Bowie, Robert R. SHAPING THE FUTURE: FOREIGN POLICY IN
AN AGE OF TRANSITION. New York: Columbia University Press.
1964
Brandt, Willy. THE ORDEAL OF CO-EXISTENCE. Cambridge, Mass.:
Harvard University Press; London: Oxford University Press. 1963
Brzezinski, Zbigniew and Huntington, Samuel P. POLITICAL POWER:
U.S.A./U.S.S.R. New York: Viking. 1964
Brzezinski, Zbigniew. ALTERNATIVE TO PARTITION: FOR A
BROADER CONCEPTION OF AMERICA'S ROLE IN EUROPE.
New York: McGraw-Hill for the Council on Foreign Relations. 1965
Brockmeijer, M.W.J.M. DEVELOPING COUNTRIES AND NATO.
Leyden: Sijthoff. 1963
Bromke, Adam and Uren, Philip (eds.). THE COMMUNIST STATES
AND THE WEST. London: Pall Mall. 1967
Brown, Seyom. THE FACES OF POWER: CONSTANCY AND
CHANGE IN UNITED STATES FOREIGN POLICY FROM
TRUMAN TO JOHNSON. New York: Columbia University Press.
1968
Buchan, Alastair and Windsor, Philip. ARMS AND STABILITY IN
EUROPE. New York: Praeger for the I.S.S. London. 1963
Buchan, Alastair, *et al.* THE SOVIET THREAT TO EUROPE: AN
ANALYSIS OF SOVIET INTENTIONS AND POTENTIALS.
London: Foreign Affairs Publishing Co. 1969

Calleo, David. THE ATLANTIC FANTASY. Baltimore: Johns Hopkins
Press. 1970
Catlin, George. THE ATLANTIC COMMONWEALTH. Harmondsworth:
Penguin. 1969
Cerami, Charles A. ALLIANCE BORN OF DANGER: AMERICA, THE
COMMON MARKET AND THE ATLANTIC PARTNERSHIP. New
York: Harcourt, Brace and World. 1963
Cerny, K.H. and Briefs, H.W. NATO IN QUEST OF COHESION. London:
Pall Mall; New York: Praeger for the Hoover Institution. 1965
Cleveland, Harlan. NATO – THE TRANSATLANTIC BARGAIN.
New York: Harper and Row. 1970
Cleveland, H. van B. THE ATLANTIC IDEA AND ITS EUROPEAN
RIVALS. New York: McGraw for the Council for Foreign Relations.
1966
Collier, David S. and Glaser, Kurt (eds.). THE CONDITIONS FOR
PEACE IN EUROPE: PROBLEMS OF DETENTE AND SECURITY.
Washington, D.C.: Public Affairs Press. 1969
Connery, Robert H. (ed.). THE 'ATLANTIC COMMUNITY' RE-
APPRAISED. New York: Academy of Political Science. 1968
Cottrell, Alvin J. and Dougherty, James E. THE POLITICS OF THE
ATLANTIC ALLIANCE. New York: Frederick A. Praeger. 1964.
(See review by V. Polyakov: 'NATO's insoluble problems'. INTER-
NATIONAL AFFAIRS (Moscow). 1965. No. 6. p. 80)
Dallin, David J. SOVIET FOREIGN POLICY AFTER STALIN. New
York: Lippincott; Toronto: McClelland and Stewart. 1961
Dallin, Alexander and Larson, Thomas B. (eds.). SOVIET POLITICS
SINCE KHRUSHCHEV. Englewood Cliffs: Prentice-Hall. 1968
Deutsch, Karl W. ARMS CONTROL AND THE ATLANTIC
ALLIANCE. London and New York: John Wiley. 1967
Deutscher, Isaac. IRONIES OF HISTORY: ESSAYS ON CONTEM-
PORARY COMMUNISM. New York: Oxford University Press. 1966
Dulles, Eleanor Lansing and Crane, Robert Dickson (eds.). DETENTE: COLD
WAR STRATEGIES IN TRANSITION. New York: Praeger for the
Center for Strategic Studies, Georgetown University. 1965
Etzioni, Amitai. WINNING WITHOUT WAR. Garden City: Doubleday.
1964
Fedder, E.H. and Robinson, J.A. BEYOND HEGEMONY: THE U.S.
AND THE FUTURE OF NATO. Columbus: Ohio State University
Press for the Mershan Center for Education in National Security. 1967
Finer, Herman. DULLES OVER SUEZ: THE THEORY AND PRACTICE

OF HIS DIPLOMACY. Chicago: Quadrangle Books. 1964
Fontaine, André. HISTORY OF THE COLD WAR: FROM THE KOREAN WAR TO THE PRESENT. New York: Pantheon Books. 1969
Fox, W.T.R. and Fox, Annette Baker. NATO AND THE RANGE OF AMERICAN CHOICE. New York: Columbia University Press. 1967. (See review by Robert L. Rothstein: 'New perspectives on NATO' in INTERNATIONAL ORGANISATION. Vol. 24. No. 3. Summer 1970. pp. 566–577)
Freymond, Jacques. WESTERN EUROPE SINCE THE WAR. London: Pall Mall; New York: Praeger. 1964
Fulbright, J. William. PROSPECTS FOR THE WEST. Cambridge, Mass.: Harvard University Press. 1963
Fulbright, J. William. OLD MYTHS AND NEW REALITIES. New York: Random House. 1964. (See critique by Morton A. Kaplon: 'Old realities and new myths' in WORLD POLITICS. Vol. 17. No. 2. January 1965. pp. 334–367)
Furniss, Edgar S., Jr. (ed.). THE WESTERN ALLIANCE: ITS STATUS AND PROSPECTS. Columbus: Ohio State University Press. 1965. (See review by Harald von Riekhoff in INTERNATIONAL JOURNAL. Vol. 3. Summer 1966. pp. 373–374)
Gardner, Lloyd C. ARCHITECTS OF ILLUSION: MEN AND IDEAS IN AMERICAN FOREIGN POLICY. Chicago: Quadrangle Books. 1970
Gehlen, Michael P. THE POLITICS OF CO-EXISTENCE: SOVIET METHODS AND MOTIVES. Bloomington: Indiana University Press. 1967
Gelber, Lionel. THE ALLIANCE OF NECESSITY: BRITAIN'S CRISIS, THE NEW EUROPE AND AMERICAN INTERESTS. New York: Stein and Day; Toronto: Saunders. 1966. London: Robert Hale. 1967
Goldwin, Robert A. (ed.). BEYOND THE COLD WAR. Chicago: Rand McNally. 1966
Halle, Louis J. THE COLD WAR AS HISTORY. New York: Harper and Row. 1967
Hartley, Livingston. ATLANTIC CHALLENGE. New York: Oceana Publications Inc. 1965
Hastings, Paul. THE COLD WAR 1945–1969. London: Ernest Benn. 1969
Heath, Edward. OLD WORLD, NEW HORIZONS: BRITAIN, THE COMMON MARKET AND THE ATLANTIC ALLIANCE. (The Godkin lectures at Harvard). London: Oxford University Press. 1970

Herter, Christian A. TOWARDS AN ATLANTIC FUTURE. New York: Harper and Row for the Council on Foreign Relations. 1963
Herz, Martin F. BEGINNINGS OF THE COLD WAR. Bloomington: Indiana University Press. 1966
Hodson, H.V. (ed.). THE ATLANTIC FUTURE. London: Longmans. 1964
Horelick, Arnold L. and Rush, Myron. STRATEGIC POWER AND SOVIET FOREIGN POLICY. Chicago: University of Chicago Press; Toronto: University of Toronto Press. 1966
Horowitz, David. FROM YALTA TO VIETNAM: AMERICAN FOREIGN POLICY IN THE COLD WAR. Harmondsworth: Penguin Books. 1969
Hudson, G.F. THE HARD AND BITTER PEACE: WORLD POLITICS SINCE 1945. New York: Frederick A. Praeger; Toronto: Burns and MacEachern. 1967
Hughes, Emmet John. THE ORDEAL OF POWER: A POLITICAL MEMOIR OF THE EISENHOWER YEARS. New York: Atheneum. 1963. (A critique, notably of Dulles)
Huntley, James R. THE NATO STORY. New York: Manhattan Publishing Co. 1969
Jackson, Henry M. (ed.). THE ATLANTIC ALLIANCE: SENATE SUBCOMMITTEE HEARINGS AND FINDINGS. New York: Frederick A. Praeger; Toronto: Burns and MacEachern. 1967
Jaquet, L.G.M. (ed.). EUROPEAN AND ATLANTIC CO-OPERATION. The Hague: Martinus Nijhoff. 1965
Joyce, J.A. END OF AN ILLUSION. London: Allen and Unwin. 1969. (A highly critical appraisal of NATO)
Kaplan, Lawrence S. NATO AND THE POLICY OF CONTAINMENT. Boston: D.C. Heath and Co. 1968
Kaufmann, William W. THE MCNAMARA STRATEGY. New York: Harper and Row. 1964. (See also Bernard Brodie: 'The McNamara phenomenan'. WORLD POLITICS. Vol. 17. No. 4. July 1965. pp. 672–686)
Kennan, George F. ON DEALING WITH THE COMMUNIST WORLD. New York: Harper and Row for the Council on Foreign Relations. 1964
Kennedy, Robert F. THIRTEEN DAYS: A MEMOIR OF THE CUBAN MISSILE CRISIS. London: Macmillan; New York: Norton. 1969
Kim, Young Hum. (ed.). TWENTY YEARS OF CRISES: THE COLD WAR ERA. Englewood Cliffs: Prentice-Hall. 1968
Kissinger, Henry A. THE TROUBLED PARTNERSHIP: A REAPPRAISAL OF THE ATLANTIC ALLIANCE. New York: McGraw-

Hill for the Council on Foreign Relations. 1965. (See review by T.C. Achilles: 'Whither the Atlantic Alliance?'. ORBIS. Vol. 9. No. 2. Summer 1965. pp. 494–496. Also review by L. Moskvin: 'Deplorable results' in INTERNATIONAL AFFAIRS (Moscow). 1966. No. 6. pp. 99–100)

Kissinger, Henry A. (ed.). PROBLEMS OF NATIONAL STRATEGY. New York and London: Praeger and Pall Mall. 1966

Kissinger, Henry A. AMERICAN FOREIGN POLICY: THREE ESSAYS. London: Weidenfeld and Nicolson; New York: W.W. Norton and Co. 1969

Kleiman, R. ATLANTIC CRISIS: AMERICAN DIPLOMACY CONFRONTS A RESURGENT EUROPE. New York: William Norton. 1964. (See review by Y. Rubinsky: 'Futile attempt' in INTERNATIONAL AFFAIRS (Moscow). 1965. No. 8. pp. 96–97)

Knapp, Wilfrid. A HISTORY OF WAR AND PEACE 1939–1965. London: Oxford University Press for the Royal Institute of International Affairs. 1967

Kohler, Foy D. UNDERSTANDING THE RUSSIANS: A CITIZEN'S PRIMER. New York: Harper and Row. 1970

LaFeber, Walter. AMERICA, RUSSIA AND THE COLD WAR 1945–1966. New York: Wiley. 1968

LaFeber, Walter (ed.). AMERICA IN THE COLD WAR 1947–1967. London: John Wiley. 1969

Larson, David L. (ed.). THE 'CUBAN CRISIS' OF 1962. Boston: Houghton. 1963. (A compilation of public statements together with a chronology)

Larson, Thomas B. DISARMAMENT AND SOVIET POLICY. 1964–1968. Englewood Cliffs: Prentice-Hall. 1969

Legault, Albert. DETERRENCE AND THE ATLANTIC ALLIANCE. Toronto: Canadian Institute for International Affairs. 1966

Lerche, Charles O., Jr. THE COLD WAR AND AFTER. Englewood Cliffs: Prentice-Hall. 1965

Lerche, Charles O., Jr. LAST CHANCE IN EUROPE. Chicago: Quadrangle Books. 1967

Lichtheim, G.A. EUROPE AND AMERICA. London: Thames and Hudson. 1963

Luard, Evan. (ed.). THE COLD WAR. London: Thames and Hudson. 1964

McCloy, John J. THE ATLANTIC ALLIANCE: ITS ORIGIN AND ITS FUTURE. New York: Columbia University Press for Carnegie-Mellon University. 1969

McInnis, Edgar. THE ATLANTIC TRIANGLE AND THE COLD WAR. Toronto: University of Toronto Press for the Canadian Institute of International Affairs. 1959

McNamara, Robert S. THE ESSENCE OF SECURITY: REFLECTIONS IN OFFICE. London: Hodder and Stoughton; New York: McGraw-Hill. 1968. (See review by I. Mikhailov: 'Noteworthy admissions' in INTERNATIONAL AFFAIRS (Moscow). 1970. No. 1. pp. 103–105. Also commentary by E. Pasternak: 'U.S. concepts of crisis diplomacy' in INTERNATIONAL AFFAIRS (Moscow). 1972. No. 6. pp. 96–98)

Macmillan, Harold. AT THE END OF THE DAY. (The Macmillan Memoirs. Vol. 5.). London: Macmillan. 1973

Middleton, Drew. CRISIS IN THE WEST. London: Secker and Warburg. 1965

Middleton, Drew. THE ATLANTIC COMMUNITY: A STUDY IN UNITY AND DISUNITY. New York: McKay. 1965. (See review by V. Polyakov: 'American journalist's illusions' in INTERNATIONAL AFFAIRS (Moscow). 1967. No. 2. p. 106)

Morgenthau, Hans J. A NEW FOREIGN POLICY FOR THE UNITED STATES. New York: Praeger for the Council on Foreign Relations. 1969

Moulton, J.L. DEFENCE IN A CHANGING WORLD. London: Eyre and Spottiswoode. 1964

Mulley, F.W. THE POLITICS OF WESTERN DEFENCE. London: Thames and Hudson. 1962.

Munk, Frank. ATLANTIC DILEMMA: PARTNERSHIP OR COMMUNITY. New York: Oceana Publications. 1964

Northedge, F.S. (ed.). THE FOREIGN POLICIES OF THE POWERS. London: Faber. 1968

Osgood, Robert E. ALLIANCES AND AMERICAN FOREIGN POLICY. Baltimore: Johns Hopkins Press. 1968

Pachter, Henry M. COLLISION COURSE: THE CUBAN MISSILE CRISIS. New York: Frederick A. Praeger; Toronto: Burns and MacEachern. 1963

Pfaltzgraff, Robert L., Jr. THE ATLANTIC COMMUNITY: A COMPLEX IMBALANCE. New York: Van Nostrand Reinhold. 1969. (A study of U.S.-European relations since the creation of the Alliance)

Posvar, Wesley W., et al. AMERICAN DEFENCE POLICY. Baltimore: Johns Hopkins Press. 1965

Radmann, Martin. POTSDAM: AGREEMENT AND 20 YEARS LATER. Dresden: Verlag Zeit im Bild for the Peace Council of the German Democratic Republic. 1965

Rees, David. THE AGE OF CONTAINMENT. London: Macmillan. 1967

von Riekhof, Harald. NATO: ISSUES AND PROSPECTS. Toronto: Canadian Institute of International Affairs. 1967

Roach, J.R. (ed.). THE UNITED STATES AND THE ATLANTIC COMMUNITY: ISSUES AND PROSPECTS. (Public lectures by, *inter al.*, Henry Kissinger, Fritz Erler, John McCloy.) Austin: University of Texas Press. 1969

Rock, Vincent P. A STRATEGY OF INTERDEPENDENCE: A PROGRAM FOR THE CONTROL OF CONFLICT BETWEEN THE UNITED STATES AND THE SOVIET UNION. New York: Charles Scribner's Sons. 1964

Rosecrance, R.N. (ed.). THE DISPERSION OF NUCLEAR WEAPONS: STRATEGY AND POLITICS. New York: Columbia University Press. 1964

Schick, Jack M. THE BERLIN CRISIS 1958–1962. Philadelphia: University of Pennsylvania Press. 1971

Schuman, Frederick L. THE COLD WAR: RETROSPECT AND PROSPECT. Baton Rouge: Louisiana State University Press; Toronto: Burns and MacEachern. 1962

Seabury, Paul. THE RISE AND DECLINE OF THE COLD WAR. New York and London: Basic Books Inc., under the auspices of the Center for International Affairs, Harvard University. 1967

Shulman, Marshall D. STALIN'S FOREIGN POLICY REAPPRAISED. Cambridge, Mass.: Harvard University Press. 1963

Slambuk, George. AMERICAN MILITARY FORCES ABROAD. Columbus: Ohio State University Press. 1963

Slusser, Robert M. THE BERLIN CRISIS OF 1961: SOVIET-AMERICAN RELATIONS AND THE STRUGGLE FOR POWER IN THE KREMLIN, JUNE – NOVEMBER 1961. Baltimore: Johns Hopkins Press. 1973

Stanley, Timothy W. NATO IN TRANSITION: THE FUTURE OF THE ATLANTIC ALLIANCE. London: Pall Mall; New York: Praeger for the Council on Foreign Relations; Toronto: Burns and MacEachern. 1965. (See review by L. Moskvin: 'Confessions of a NATO booster'. INTERNATIONAL AFFAIRS (Moscow). 1966. No. 9. pp. 118–120)

Steel, Ronald. THE END OF ALLIANCE: AMERICA AND THE FUTURE OF EUROPE. New York: Viking. 1964. (A critique of

NATO)
Stikker, Dirk U. MEN OF RESPONSIBILITY. New York: Harper and Row. 1966. (Evaluation of Acheson, Adenauer, de Gaulle, Norstad and Schuman)
Strausz-Hupé, Robert, et al. BUILDING THE ATLANTIC WORLD. New York: Haper and Row; Toronto: Musson. 1963. (See review article by Edgar McInnis in INTERNATIONAL JOURNAL. Vol. 19. No. 1. Winter 1963. pp. 109–110)
Szent-Miklosy, Istvan. THE ATLANTIC UNION MOVEMENT: ITS SIGNIFICANCE IN WORLD POLITICS. New York: Fountainhead Publishers. 1965
Talbott, Strobe (trans. and ed.). KHRUSHCHEV REMEMBERS: THE LAST TESTAMENT. Boston: Little, Brown. 1974.
Terchek, Ronald J. THE MAKING OF THE TEST-BAN TREATY. The Hague: Nijhoff. 1970
Triska, Jan F. and Finley, David D. SOVIET FOREIGN POLICY. New York: Macmillan; London: Collier Macmillan. 1968
Ulam, Adam B. EXPANSION AND CO-EXISTENCE: THE HISTORY OF SOVIET FOREIGN POLICY. 1917–1967. London: Secker and Warburg; New York: Praeger. 1968. (See review by Max Beloff in Survival. Vol. 11. No. 11. November 1969. pp. 362–363)
Uri, Pierre. PARTNERSHIP FOR PROGRESS: A PROGRAM FOR TRANSATLANTIC ACTION. New York: Harper and Row for the Atlantic Institute. 1963
Urwin, D.W. WESTERN EUROPE SINCE 1945: A SHORT POLITICAL HISTORY. London: Longmans. 1968
Warburg, James. THE UNITED STATES IN THE POSTWAR WORLD: A CRITICAL APPRAISAL. London: Gollancz. 1966
Watson, Hugh Seton. NATIONALISM AND COMMUNISM: Essays 1946–1963. New York: Praeger. 1964
Werth, Alexander. RUSSIA: HOPES AND FEARS. New York: Simon and Schuster. 1969. (Soviet progress since 1945)
Wesson, Robert G. SOVIET FOREIGN POLICY IN PERSPECTIVE. Homewood, Illinois: The Dorsey Press. 1969
Wilcox, Francis O. and Haviland, H. Field (eds.). THE ATLANTIC COMMUNITY: PROGRESS AND PROSPECTS. New York: Frederick A. Praeger. 1964
Wilson, Thomas W., Jr. COLD WAR AND COMMON SENSE. Greenwich: New York Graphic Society. 1962
Wolfe, Thomas W. SOVIET STRATEGY AT THE CROSSROADS.

Cambridge, Mass.: Harvard University Press. 1964. (Mainly post-Cuba 1962)
Wolfe, Thomas. SOVIET POWER AND EUROPE. 1945–1970. Baltimore: Johns Hopkins Press. 1970
Wolfers, Arnold (ed.). ALLIANCE POLICY IN THE COLD WAR. Baltimore: Johns Hopkins Press. 1959
Wolfers, Arnold (ed.) CHANGING EAST-WEST RELATIONS AND THE UNITY OF THE WEST. Baltimore: Johns Hopkins Press. 1964
Zimmerman, William. SOVIET PERSPECTIVES ON INTERNATIONAL RELATIONS 1956–1967. Princeton: Princeton University Press. 1969. (See review article by G. Arbatov: 'Sovietology or Kremlinology': in SURVIVAL. Vol. 12. No. 6. June 1970. pp. 208–209)

Military-- Strategic Aspects

Aron, Raymond. THE GREAT DEBATE: THEORIES OF NUCLEAR STRATEGY. Garden City: Doubleday. 1965
Beaufre, General André. AN INTRODUCTION TO STRATEGY. New York: Praeger. 1965.
Beaufre, General André. DETERRENCE AND STRATEGY. New York: Frederick A. Praeger. 1966. (See review by Edward A. Kolodziej: 'French strategy emergent' in WORLD POLITICS. Vol. 19. No. 3. April 1967. pp. 417–422)
Beaufre, General André. THE STRATEGY OF ACTION. London: Faber. 1967
Beaufre, General André. STRATEGY FOR TOMORROW. New York: Crane, Russak. 1975
Brodie, Bernard. ESCALATION AND THE NUCLEAR OPTION. Princeton: Princeton University Press. 1966
Brown, Neville. NUCLEAR WAR: THE IMPENDING STRATEGIC DEADLOCK. London: Pall Mall Press; Toronto: Burns and MacEachern. 1965
Clark, Admiral Joseph J. and Barnes, Captain Dwight H. SEA POWER AND ITS MEANING. New York: Watts. 1966
Dallin, Alexander, *et al.* THE SOVIET UNION AND DISARMAMENT. New York: Praeger for the School of International Affairs, Columbia University. 1964
Englebart, Stanley L. STRATEGIC DEFENCES. New York: Crowell. 1966
Forster, Thomas M. THE EAST GERMAN ARMY: A PATTERN OF

COMMUNIST MILITARY ESTABLISHMENT. London: Allen and Unwin. 1967
Garthoff, Raymond L. SOVIET MILITARY POLICY. London: Faber and Faber; New York: Praeger. 1966
Ginsburgh, Colonel Robert N. U.S. MILITARY STRATEGY IN THE SIXTIES. New York: Norton. 1965
Green, Philip. DEADLY LOGIC: THE THEORY OF NUCLEAR DETERRENCE. Columbus: Ohio State University Press. 1966
Gretton, Vice-Admiral Sir Peter. MARITIME STRATEGY: A STUDY OF DEFENCE PROBLEMS. New York: Praeger. 1965
Heilbrunn, Otto. CONVENTIONAL WARFARE IN THE NUCLEAR AGE. London: Allen and Unwin; New York: Praeger. 1965
Herrick, Commander Robert Waring. SOVIET NAVAL STRATEGY: FIFTY YEARS OF THEORY AND PRACTICE. Annapolis: U.S. Naval Institute. 1968. (See review by Geoffrey Jukes in SURVIVAL. Vol. 11. No. 9. September 1969. pp. 298–299)
Kingston-McCloughry, Air Vice-Marshal E.J. DEFENCE POLICY AND STRATEGY. New York: Frederick A. Praeger; Toronto: Burns and MacEachern. 1960
Kintner, William R. and Scott, Harriet Fast (eds.). THE NUCLEAR REVOLUTION IN SOVIET MILITARY AFFAIRS. Norman: University of Oklahoma Press. 1968 (See review by Geoffrey Jukes in SURVIVAL. Vol. 11. No. 1. January 1969. pp. 31–32
Knorr, Klaus. ON THE USES OF MILITARY POWER IN THE NUCLEAR AGE. Princeton: Princeton University Press; London: Oxford University Press. 1966
Mackintosh, Malcolm. JUGGERNAUT: A HISTORY OF SOVIET ARMED FORCES. London: Secker and Warburg; New York: Macmillan. 1967
Martin, L.W. THE SEA IN MODERN STRATEGY. Chatto and Windus for the I.I.S.S. 1967
Martin, Thomas L. and Latham, Donald C. STRATEGY FOR SURVIVAL. Tuscon: University of Arizona Press. 1964. (A plea for Civil Defence)
Palit, Major-General D.K. WAR IN THE DETERRENT AGE. London: Macdonald. 1966
Rapoport, Anatol. STRATEGY AND CONSCIENCE. New York: Harper and Row. 1964
Schelling, Thomas C. ARMS AND INFLUENCE. New Haven: Yale University Press. 1966
Schwarz, Urs. AMERICAN STRATEGY: A NEW PERSPECTIVE.

Garden City: Doubleday. 1966
Sokolovsky, Marshal V.D. (ed.). MILITARY STRATEGY: SOVIET DOCTRINE AND CONCEPTS. Englewood Cliffs: Prentice-Hall for Rand; London: Pall Mall; New York: Praeger. 1963
Tompkins, John S. THE WEAPONS OF WORLD WAR III: THE LONG ROAD BACK FROM THE BOMB. Garden City: Doubleday. 1966
Twining, General Nathan F. NEITHER LIBERTY NOR SAFETY: a hard look at U.S. military policy and strategy. New York: Holt, Rinehart and Winston. 1966
U.S. Department of the Army. NUCLEAR WEAPONS AND THE ATLANTIC ALLIANCE. Washington, D.C.: H.Q. Department of the Army. 1965
Verrier, Anthony. AN ARMY FOR THE SIXTIES: A STUDY IN NATIONAL POLICY, CONTRACT AND OBLIGATION. London: Secker and Warburg. 1966. (i.e. the British Army)

Reports, Papers and Pamphlets

Economic Aspects

Ashcroft, Geoffrey. MILITARY LOGISTIC SYSTEMS IN NATO: THE GOAL OF INTEGRATION. PART I: ECONOMIC ASPECTS. Adelphi Paper No. 62. November 1969. London: I.S.S.
Kramish, A. ATLANTIC TECHNICAL IMBALANCE. (In 'Defence, Technology and the Western Alliance' a report of an I.S.S. Study Group). London: I.S.S. 1965

National and Regional Aspects

Cox, David. CANADIAN DEFENCE POLICY: THE DILEMMAS OF A MIDDLE POWER. ('Behind the Headlines'. Vol. 27. No. 5. 1968). Toronto: Canadian Institute of International Affairs.
Eayrs, James. FUTURE ROLES FOR THE ARMED FORCES OF CANADA. ('Behind the Headlines'. Vol. 28. No. 1–2. 1969). Toronto: Canadian Institute of International Affairs.
Greve, Tim. NORWAY AND NATO. Oslo: Press Department, Royal Ministry of Foreign Affairs. 1968

Klenberg, Jan. THE CAPE AND THE STRAITS: PROBLEMS OF NORDIC SECURITY. (Papers in International Affairs. No. 18. February 1968). Cambridge, Mass.: Center for International Affairs, Harvard University

Martin, L.W. BRITISH DEFENCE POLICY: THE LONG RECESSIONAL. Adelphi Paper No. 61. November 1969. London: I.S.S.

Ministry of Foreign Affairs of the German Democratic Republic. THE PROBLEM OF WEST BERLIN AND SOLUTIONS PROPOSED BY THE GOVERMENT OF THE GERMAN DEMOCRATIC REPUBLIC. Berlin: Ministry of Foreign Affairs of the German Democratic Republic. 1961

Orvik, Nils and Haagerup, Nils J. THE SCANDINAVIAN MEMBERS OF NATO. Adelphi Paper No. 23. December 1965. London: I.S.S.

Paice, Anthony. A DEFENCE FOR BRITAIN. (Unservile State Paper No. 15). London: Liberal Party Research and Information Dept. 1969

Press Group of Soviet Journalists. ON EVENTS IN CZECHOSLOVAKIA: FACTS, DOCUMENTS, PRESS REPORTS AND EYE-WITNESS ACCOUNTS. Moscow: Press Group of Soviet Journalists. 1968

Sherman, Michael E. A SINGLE SERVICE FOR CANADA? (i.e. the fusion of the armed services). Adelphi Paper No. 39. July 1967. London: I.S.S.

Various. WESTERN AND EASTERN EUROPE: THE CHANGING RELATIONSHIP. Adelphi Paper No. 33. March 1967. London: I.S.S.

Windsor, Philip. NATO AND THE CYPRUS CRISIS. Adelphi Paper No. 14. London: I.S.S. 1964

Windsor, Philip. WESTERN EUROPE IN SOVIET STRATEGY. Adelphi Paper No. 8. January 1964. London: I.S.S.

Young, Judith H. THE FRENCH STRATEGIC MISSILE PROGRAMME. Adelphi Paper No. 38. July 1967. London: I.S.S.

Politico-Military Aspects

Acheson, Dean, *et al.* THE EVOLUTION OF NATO: proceedings of the 5th annual conference of the I.S.S. Cambridge, 1963. Adelphi Paper No. 5. October 1963. London: I.S.S.

Anon (Soviet). THE WAY TO EUROPEAN SECURITY. Report of the Karlovy Vary Conference, Czechoslovakia. April 1967. (Soviet Booklets. Vol. 2. No. 5). London: I.S.S. n.d.

Beaufre, General André. MAJOR NATO PROBLEMS. (Adance study

paper No. 14. Conference on 'NATO: Problems and Prospects'. February 1964). Washington, D.C.: Center for Strategic Studies, Georgetown University.

Beglov, Spartak. INTERNATIONAL RELATIONS IN THE NUCLEAR AGE. Moscow: Novosti Press Agency Publishing House. 1968

Bloomfield, Lincoln P. WESTERN EUROPE 1965–1975; FIVE SCENARIOS. (BSR 1127. Bendix Systems Division. April 1965). Ann Arbor: Bendix Systems Division.

Bluhm, Georg R. DETENTE AND MILITARY RELAXATION IN EUROPE: A GERMAN VIEW. Adelphi Paper No. 40. September 1967. London: I.S.S.

Beaton, Leonard. THE WESTERN ALLIANCE AND THE McNAMARA DOCTRINE. Adelphi Paper No. 11. August 1964. London: I.S.S.

Borcier, Paul. EIGHT YEARS WORK FOR EUROPEAN DEFENCE: A POLITICAL SURVEY. Paris: Western European Union. 1964

Brezhnev, Leonid I. THE SOVIET VIEW OF NATO. Washington D.C.: U.S.G.P.O. 1967

British Peace Committee. ARGUMENT ABOUT NATO. London: The British Peace Committee. 1968

Bull, Hedley, et al. SOVIET-AMERICAN RELATIONS AND WORLD ORDER: ARMS LIMITATIONS AND POLICY. Adelphi Paper No. 65. February 1970. London: I.S.S.

Burns, Arthur Lee. ETHICS AND DETERRENCE: A NUCLEAR BALANCE WITHOUT HOSTAGE CITIES? Adelphi Paper No. 69. July 1970. London: I.S.S.

Calman, John. EUROPEAN CO-OPERATION IN DEFENCE TECHNOLOGY: THE POLITICAL ASPECT. (In 'Defence, Technology and the Western Alliance' a report of an I.S.S. Study Group). London: I.S.S. 1965

Catlin, George E.G. CREATING THE ATLANTIC COMMUNITY. (Fabian Tract 360). London: Fabian Society. 1965

Cleveland, Harold Van B. and Joan B. THE ATLANTIC ALLIANCE: PROBLEMS AND PROSPECTS. (Headline Series No. 177. June 1966). New York: Foreign Policy Association.

Coffey, Joseph I. A NATO NUCLEAR DETERENT? (Internal Note 33. Office of National Security Studies, Bendix Systems Division. April 1963). Ann Arbor: Bendix Systems Division.

Coffey, Joseph I. OLD WINE AND NEW BOTTLES: THE U.S. AND THE DEFENSE OF WESTERN EUROPE. (Study Paper No. 3. Office of National Security Studies, Bendix Systems Division.

February 1964). Ann Arbor: Bendix Systems Division.
Coffey, Joseph I. STRATEGY, ALLIANCE POLICY AND NUCLEAR PROLIFERATION. (Study Paper No. 11. Office of National Security Studies, Bendix Systems Division. 1965). Ann Arbor: Bendix Systems Division.
Combaux, General Edmond. THE ATLANTIC ALLIANCE AND DEFENCE PROBLEMS. (Report to the annual conference of the Atlantic Treaty Association; The Hague. September 1970). Paris: Atlantic Treaty Association.
Conservative Political Centre. THE FUTURE OF NATO. London: Conservative Political Centre. October 1968
Crane, Peggy, et al. ARGUMENT ABOUT NATO: THE CASE FOR AND AGAINST THE RENEWAL OF THE TREATY IN 1969. London: British Peace Committee. 1968
Critchley, Julian, et al. THE FUTURE OF NATO. London: Conservative Political Centre. 1968
Duchêne, François. BEYOND ALLIANCE. (The Atlantic Papers. NATO Series 1). Paris: The Atlantic Institute. 1965
Gasteyger, Curt. THE AMERICAN DILEMMA: BIPOLARITY OR ALLIANCE COHESION. Adelphi Paper No. 24. January 1966. London: I.S.S.
Gasteyger, Curt. EUROPE IN THE SEVENTIES. Adelphi Paper No. 37. June 1967. London: I.S.S.
Griffith, William E. and Rostow, Walt. W. EAST-WEST RELATIONS: IS DETENTE POSSIBLE? (3rd Series. Rational Debate Seminars No. 3.). Washington, D.C.: American Enterprise Institute for Public Policy Research. 1969
Gromyko, Andrei A. THE INTERNATIONAL SITUATION AND SOVIET FOREIGN POLICY. (Report to the Supreme Soviet. 10 July 1969). Moscow: Novosti Press Agency. 1969
Hackel, Erwin. MILITARY MANPOWER AND POLITICAL PURPOSE. Adelphi Paper No. 72. December 1970. London: I.S.S.
Hassner, Pierre. CHANGE AND SECURITY IN EUROPE, PART I: THE BACKGROUND. Adelphi Paper No. 45. February 1968. London: I.S.S.
Hassner, Pierre. CHANGE AND SECURITY IN EUROPE, PART II: IN SEARCH OF A SYSTEM. Adelphi Paper No. 49. July 1968. London: I.S.S.
Hassner, Pierre and Newhouse, John. DIPLOMACY IN THE WEST. New York: 20th Century Fund. May 1966

Howard, Michael. THE CENTRAL ORGANIZATION OF DEFENCE.
(i.e. British defence). London: R.U.S.I. 1970

I.S.S. Study Group. THE CONTROL OF WESTERN STRATEGY.
Adelphi Paper No. 3. April 1963. London: I.S.S.

I.S.S. Study Group. THE DEFENCE OF WESTERN EUROPE. Adelphi
Paper No. 4. May 1963. London: I.S.S.

Jackson, Senator Henry M. THE ATLANTIC ALLIANCE: BASIC
ISSUES. (Study pursuant to Senate Resolution 181, 18 February
1966). Washington: U.S.G.P.O. 1966

Knorr, Klaus. NATO AND THE NUCLEAR POLICY. (Advance study
paper No. 5, Conference on 'NATO: Problems and Prospects'.
February 1964). Washington, D.C.: Center for Strategic Studies,
Georgetown University.

Knorr, Klaus. NATO: PAST, PRESENT AND FUTURE. New York:
Foreign Policy Association. 1969

Knorr, Klaus, et al. EUROPE AND AMERICA IN THE 1970'S: II:
SOCIETY AND POWER. Adelphi Paper No. 71. November 1970.
London: I.S.S.

Kohn, Hans. NATIONALISM IN THE ATLANTIC COMMUNITY.
Philadelphia: University of Pennsylvania. 1965

Korbonski, Andrzey. THE WARSAW PACT. (International Conciliation
No. 573). New York: Carnegie Endowment for International Peace.
May 1969

Laloy, Jean, et al. WESTERN AND EASTERN EUROPE: THE
CHANGING RELATIONSHIP. (Proceedings of the 8th annual I.S.S.
Conference, Vienna 1966). Adelphi Paper No. 33. March 1967.
London: I.S.S.

Levin, V. COLLECTIVE SECURITY IN EUROPE. Moscow: Novosti
Press Agency. 1967

Lyon, Peyton, V. NATO AS A DIPLOMATIC INSTRUMENT. Toronto:
The Atlantic Council of Canada. December 1970

Mackintosh, Malcolm. THE EVOLUTION OF THE WARSAW PACT.
Adelphi Paper No. 58. June 1969. London: I.S.S.

Martin, L.W. BALLISTIC MISSILE DEFENCE AND THE ALLIANCE.
Paris: Atlantic Institute. 1969

Mathias, Senator Charles McC., Jr., et al. EUROPE AND AMERICA
IN THE 1970'S: PART I: BETWEEN DETENTE AND CONFRON-
TATION. Adelphi Paper No. 70. November 1970. London: I.S.S.

Maxwell, Stephen. RATIONALITY IN DETERRENCE. Adelphi Paper
No. 50. August 1968. London: I.S.S.

Meissner, Boris. THE BREZHNEV DOCTRINE. (East European Monograph No. 2. December 1970: (Government Research Bureau)). Kansas City: Park College.

Nixon, President Richard. U.S. FOREIGN POLICY FOR THE 1907'S: A NEW STRATEGY FOR PEACE. (Report to Congress, 18 February 1970). Washington: U.S.G.P.O. 1970

Russett, Bruce M. and Cooper, Caroline C. ARMS CONTROL IN EUROPE: PROPOSALS AND POLITICAL CONSTRAINTS. (Monograph Series in World Affairs 4, No. 2. Social Science Foundation and Graduate School of International Studies at the University of Denver). Denver: University of Denver. 1966

Schuckburgh, Sir Evelyn. THE ATLANTIC ALLIANCE AND POLITICAL PROBLEMS. (Report to the annual conference of the Atlantic Treaty Association. The Hague. September 1970). Paris: Atlantic Treaty Association.

Shulman, Marshall D., et al. SOVIET-AMERICAN RELATIONS AND WORLD ORDER: THE TWO AND THE MANY. Adelphi Paper No. 66. March 1970. London: I.S.S.

Spaak, Paul-Henri. THE CRISIS OF THE ATLANTIC ALLIANCE. (Mershon National Security Program No. 5. March 1967). Columbus: Ohio State University Press.

Steibel, Gerald L. DETENTE: DILEMMA OR DISASTER? New York: National Strategy Information Center, Inc. July 1969

Tatu, Michel. THE GREAT POWER TRIANGLE: WASHINGTON – MOSCOW – PEKING. The Atlantic Papers 1970. No. 3. December 1970. Paris: The Atlantic Institute.

Tucker, Robert C., et al. PROPOSAL FOR NO FIRST USE OF NUCLEAR WEAPONS: PROS AND CONS. (Policy Memo No. 28). Princeton: Center of International Studies, Woodrow Wilson School of Public and International Affairs, Princeton University. 1963

U.S. Department of State. NATO AND THE DEFENCE OF EUROPE. (Issues in U.S. Foreign Policy Series). Washington, D.C.: U.S.G.P.O. 1969

Various. THE SHARING OF NUCLEAR RESPONSIBILITIES. (Seminar for *ANCIENS* of the NATO Defence College. June 1965). Paris: NATO Defence College.

Various. THE ATLANTIC COMMUNITY. (Intercom. Vol. 7. No. 2. March/April 1965). New York: Foreign Policy Association.

Various. THE ATLANTIC NATIONS: CONVERGING OR DIVERGING? Prospects for 1975. (Report of the Transatlantic Colloquium.

Royaumont, France. July 1966). Boulogne-sur-Seine: The Atlantic Institute. 1967

Various. THE FUTURE OF THE ATLANTIC ALLIANCE. Tilburg, Netherlands: Center for Atlantic Studies, John F. Kennedy Institute. 1968

Various. EAST-WEST DETENTE: THE EUROPEAN DEBATE. (Journal of International Affairs. Vol. 11. No. 1. 1968). New York: School of International Affairs, Columbia University.

Various. NATO AFTER CZECHOSLOVAKIA 1968. (Special Report Series No. 9. April 1969). Washington, D.C.: Center for Strategic and International Studies.

Various. NATO AND EUROPEAN SECURITY. (Orbis. Vol. 13. Spring 1969. No. 1. Special 20th anniversary issue, with 28 contributors). Philadelphia: Foreign Policy Research Institute, University of Pennsylvania.

von Weizsacker, Carl-Fredrich, *et al.* PROBLEMS OF MODERN STRATEGY, PART II. Adelphi Paper No. 55. March 1969. London: I.S.S.

Young, Judith H. THE FRENCH STRATEGIC MISSILE PROGRAMME. Adelphi Paper No. 38. July 1967. I.S.S.

Military — Strategic Aspects

Ashcroft, Geoffrey. MILITARY LOGISTIC SYSTEMS IN NATO: THE GOAL OF INTEGRATION, PART 1: ECONOMIC ASPECTS. Adelphi Paper No. 62. November 1969. London: I.S.S.

Ashcroft, Geoffrey. MILITARY LOGISTIC SYSTEMS IN NATO: PART II: MILITARY ASPECTS. Adelphi Paper No. 68. June 1970. London: I.S.S.

Brown, Neville. BRITISH ARMS AND STRATEGY 1970—1980. London: R.U.S.I. 1969

Buchan, Alastair. THE MULTILATERAL FORCE: AN HISTORICAL PERSPECTIVE. Adelphi Paper No. 13. October 1964. London: I.S.S.

Buzzard, Rear-Admiral Sir Anthony. THE POSSIBILITIES OF CONVENTIONAL DEFENCE. Adelphi Paper No. 6. December 1965. London: I.S.S.

Eayrs, James. FUTURE ROLES FOR THE ARMED FORCES OF CANADA ('Behind the Headlines'. Vol. 28. No. 1—2. 1969). Toronto: Canadian Institute for International Affairs.

Harlow, C.J.E. THE EUROPEAN ARMS BASE. (in 'Defence, Technology and the Western Alliance': a report of an I.S.S. Study Group). London: I.S.S. 1965

Hunt, Brigadier Kenneth. THE REQUIREMENTS OF MILITARY TECHNOLOGY IN THE 1970'S. (in 'Defence, Technology and the Western Alliance': a report of an I.S.S. Study Group). London: I.S.S. 1965

Hunt, Kenneth. NATO WITHOUT FRANCE: THE MILITARY IMPLICATIONS. Adelphi Paper No. 32. December 1966. London: I.S.S.

James, R.R. STANDARDISATION AND COMMON PROCUREMENT OF WEAPONS IN NATO. (in 'Defence, Technology and the Western Alliance': a report of an I.S.S. Study Group). London: I.S.S. 1965

Osgood, R.E. THE CASE OF THE MLF. Washington: The Washington Center of Foreign Policy Research. 1964

Sherman, Michael E. A SINGLE SERVICE FOR CANADA. (i.e. the fusion of the armed services). Adelphi Paper No. 39. July 1967. London: I.S.S.

Slessor, Sir John. NATO NUCLEAR STRATEGY – SOME LESSONS FROM HISTORY. (Advance Study Paper No. 1. Conference on 'NATO – Problems and Prospects'. February 1964. Georgetown University). Washington, D.C.: Center for Strategic Studies, Georgetown University.

Slessor, Sir John. COMMAND AND CONTROL OF ALLIED NUCLEAR FORCES: A BRITISH VIEW. Adelphi Paper No. 22. August 1965. London: I.S.S.

Smart, Ian. ADVANCED STRATEGIC MISSILES: A SHORT GUIDE. Adelphi Paper No. 63. January 1970. London: I.S.S.

Sokolovsky, Marshal V.D. (ed.). MILITARY STRATEGY. New York: Frederick A. Praeger; London: Pall Mall Press. 1965. (See also review by Philip Windsor: SURVIVAL. Vol. 5. No. 5. September/October 1963).

Various. SOVIET SEA-POWER. (Special Report Series No. 10. Center for Strategic and International Studies). Washington, D.C.: Georgetown University. 1969

Young, Judith H. THE FRENCH STRATEGIC MISSILE PROGRAMME. Adelphi Paper No. 38. July 1967. London: I.S.S.

Articles

Economic Aspects

Bergquist, Mats. TRADE AND SECURITY IN THE NORDIC AREA. Co-operation and Conflict. Vol. 4. 1969. pp. 237–246

Diebold, William Jr. ECONOMIC ASPECTS OF AN ATLANTIC COMMUNITY. International Organisation. Vol. 17. No. 3. Summer 1963. pp. 663–682

Goldman, Marshall I. ECONOMIC REVOLUTION IN THE SOVIET UNION. (i.e. in the late 1960's). Foreign Affairs. Vol. 45. No. 2. January 1967. pp. 319–331

Gruzdev, L. and Sidorov, V. MILITARY-ECONOMIC INTEGRATION IN WESTERN EUROPE. International Affairs (Moscow). No. 2. 1967. pp. 66–72

Kindleberger, Charles P. THE MARSHALL PLAN AND THE COLD WAR. International Journal. Vol. 23. No. 3. Summer 1968. pp. 369–382

Neal, Alfred C. ECONOMIC NECESSITIES AND ATLANTIC COMMUNITIES. Foreign Affairs. Vol. 45. No. 4. July 1967. pp. 694–705. Atlantic Community Quarterly. Vol. 5. No. 3. Fall 1967. pp. 347–358

Pfaltzgraff, Robert L., Jr. THE FUTURE OF ATLANTIC ECONOMIC RELATIONSHIPS. Orbis. Vol. 10. No. 2. Summer 1968. pp. 408–437

Sorensen, Theodore C. WHY WE SHOULD TRADE WITH THE SOVIETS. Foreign Affairs. Vol. 46. No. 3. April 1968. pp. 575–583

Legal Aspects

Stanger, Roland J. (ed.). WEST BERLIN: THE LEGAL CONTEXT. Columbus: Ohio State University Press. 1966

National and Regional Aspects

Alleman, F.R. BERLIN IN SEARCH OF A PURPOSE. Survey. No. 61. October 1969. pp. 129–138

Alphand, Hervé. FRANCE AND HER ALLIES. Orbis. Vol. 7. No. 1. Spring 1963. pp. 17–31

Anatolyev, G. BRITAIN AND EUROPEAN SECURITY. International Affairs (Moscow). 1966. No. 2. pp. 42–45

Anderson, Evelyn. GERMANY IN THE COLD WAR. Survey. No. 58. January 1966. pp. 177–186
Andren, Nils. NORDIC INTEGRATION. Co-operation and Conflict. Vol. 2. 1967. pp. 1–25
Andren, Nils. IN SEARCH OF SECURITY. Co-operation and Conflict. Vol. 3. 1968. pp. 217–239. (Scandinavian links with NATO and West European security)
Andreyev, N. WEST GERMANY: NATO SPEARHEAD IN EUROPE. International Affairs (Moscow). 1965. No. 2. pp. 23–28
Anon. GOOD ALLY: (a post-Nassau analysis of British defence policy). Survival. Vol. 5. No. 2. March/April 1963. pp. 50–51. (Reprint from THE TIMES 23 January 1963)
Anon. GERMANY'S FEARS. Survival. Vol. 5. No. 6. November/December. pp. 246–248. (Reprint from The Economist. 24 August 1963)
Anon. TURNING POINT IN CZECHOSLOVAKIA. (written before 21 August 1968). The World Today. Vol. 24. No. 9. September 1968. pp. 359–366
Anon. CHRONOLOGY OF CZECHOSLOVAK-SOVIET CONFRONTATION. July/August 1968. The World Today. Vol. 24. No. 9. September 1968. pp. 357–359
Aron, Raymond. ALONE AT LAST. Atlantic Community Quarterly. Vol. 4. No. 2. Summer 1966. pp. 208–211. (Domestic opposition to France quitting NATO's military structures)
Aron, Raymond. GAULLIST WORD AND REALITY. Atlantic Community Quarterly. Vol. 4. No. 4. Winter 1966/67. pp. 529–532
Aron, Raymond. FROM INDEPENDENCE TO NEUTRALITY. Atlantic Community Quarterly. Vol. 6. No. 2. Summer 1968. pp. 267–270. (Implications of the 'tous azimuts' French strategy)
Ascherson, Neal. POLAND'S PLACE IN EUROPE. The World Today. Vol. 25. No. 12. December 1969. pp. 520–529
Augstein, Rudolf. THE SPUR OF BERLIN (i.e. to reunification). Survival. Vol. 7. No. 8. November 1965. pp. 296–297
Bailey, George. GERMANY BETWEEN TWO ALLIANCES. Survival. Vol. 8. No. 12. December 1966. pp. 386–391
Barker, Elisabeth. THE BERLIN CRISIS. 1958–1962. International Affairs. Vol. 39. No. 1. January 1963. pp. 59–73
Beaton, Leonard. THE (1964) CANADIAN WHITE PAPER ON DEFENCE. International Journal. Vol. 19. No. 3. Summer 1964. pp. 364–370
Beaton, Leonard. TRANSATLANTIC ALIENATION (reactions to the

Canadian force reductions in Europe). (Reprint from THE TIMES 5 June 1969). Survival. Vol. 11. No. 8. August 1969. pp. 246–247

Beglov, S. BONN-LONDON: NEW AXIS. International Affairs (Moscow). 1969. No. 6. pp. 65–70

Bender, Peter. IN SEARCH OF A NEW POLICY. (i.e. West Germany's pursuit of reunification). Survey. No. 61. October 1966. pp. 80–92

Bender, Peter. INSIDE THE WARSAW PACT. Survey. No. 74/75. Winter/Spring 1970. pp. 253–268

Benediktsson, Bjarni. ICELAND: ATLANTIC LINK. Atlantic Community Quarterly. Vol. 4. No. 3. Fall 1966. pp. 416–421

Birnbaum, Karl E. THE NORDIC COUNTRIES AND EUROPEAN SECURITY. Co-operation and Conflict. Vol. 3. 1968. pp. 1–17

Bjol, Erling. FOREIGN POLICY MAKING IN DENMARK. Co-operation and Conflict. Vol. 1. No. 2. 1966. pp. 1–17

Bjol, Erling. A SOVIET VIEW OF NORTHERN EUROPE. Co-operation and Conflict. Vol. 2. 1967. pp. 112–115

Bjol, Erling. NATO AND DENMARK. Co-operation and Conflict. Vol. 3. 1968. pp. 93–107

Bloemer, Klaus. EAST EUROPEAN POLITICS AND REUNIFICATION. Atlantic Community Quarterly. Vol. 5. No. 2. Summer 1967. pp. 219–223

Brandt, Willy. GERMAN POLICY TOWARDS THE EAST. Foreign Affairs. Vol. 46. No. 3. April 1968. pp. 476–486

Brandt, Willy. GERMAN FOREIGN POLICY. Survival. Vol. 11. No. 12. December 1969. pp. 370–372

Bregman, Alexander. THE COLD WAR IN RETROSPECT: THE POLISH QUESTION. Survey. No. 58. January 1966. pp. 159–167

British Labour Party. BRITISH DEFENCE POLICY: THE LABOUR PARTY'S MANIFESTO 1964. Survival. Vol. 6. No. 6. November/December 1964. pp. 256–257

Bromke, Adam. IDEOLOGY AND NATIONAL INTEREST IN SOVIET FOREIGN POLICY. International Journal. Vol. 22. No. 4. Autumn 1967. pp. 547–562

Bronska-Pampuch, Wanda. RUSSIA IN GERMAN EYES: 1964. Survey. No. 51. April 1964. pp. 93–101

Brown, George. VOICES IN OPPOSITION (to the current British defence policy) Survival. Vol. 6. No. 1. January/February 1964. pp. 23–24

Brown, Neville. SOME FEATURES OF THE (1966) BRITISH DEFENCE REVIEW. The World Today. Vol. 22. April 1966. pp. 171–176

Bruntland, Arne Olav. THE NORDIC BALANCE: PAST AND PRESENT.
Co-operation and Conflict. Vol. 1. No. 2. 1966. pp. 30–63
Bruntland, Arne Olav. NORWEGIAN FOREIGN POLICY. Co-operation
and Conflict. Vol. 3. 1968. pp. 169–183
Buchan, Alastair. THE CHOICES FOR BRITISH DEFENCE POLICY.
International Journal. Vol. 18. No. 3. Summer 1963. pp. 281–290
Burchill, C.S., *et al.* CANADA'S LONG-TERM STRATEGIC
SITUATION: A CRITICAL VIEW. International Journal. Vol. 18.
No. 1. Winter 1962. pp. 75–81. (See also R.J. Sutherland: 'Canada's
long-term strategic situation' in INTERNATIONAL JOURNAL.
Vol. 18. No. 3. Summer 1962. pp. 199–223)
Canadian Department of National Defence. CANADIAN DEFENCE
WHITE PAPER. MARCH 1964. Survival. Vol. 6. No. 3. May/June
1964. pp. 105–111
Conant, Melvin. CANADA AND CONTINENTAL DEFENCE: AN
AMERICAN VIEW. International Journal. Vol. 15. No. 3. Summer
1960. pp. 219–228
Conant, Melvin. CANADA AND NUCLEAR WEAPONS: AN
AMERICAN VIEW. International Journal. Vol. 18. No. 2. Spring
1963. pp. 207–210
Cornides, Wilhelm. GERMAN UNIFICATION AND THE POWER
BALANCE. Survey. No. 58. January 1966. pp. 140–149. Survival.
Vol. 8. No. 5. May 1966. pp. 156–161
Couve de Murville, Maurice. THE ROLE OF FRANCE: (Speech to the
National Assembly. 28 April 1964). Atlantic Community Quarterly.
Vol. 2. No. 2. Summer 1964. pp. 255–261
Couve de Murville, Maurice. FRENCH POLICY TODAY. (as described
by the French foreign minister). Atlantic Community Quarterly.
Vol. 2. No. 4. Winter 1964/65. pp. 614–626
Couve de Murville, Maurice. FRANCE AND HER DESTINY. Atlantic
Community Quarterly. Vol. 4. No. 2. Summer 1966. pp. 197–205.
(The French foreign minister explains why the French quit NATO's
military structures)
Crabb, Cecil V., Jr. THE GAULLIST REVOLT AGAINST THE
ANGLO-SAXONS. Atlantic Community Quarterly. Vol. 2. No. 1.
Spring 1964. pp. 35–44
Croan, Melvin. BONN AND PANKOW. Survey. No. 67. April 1965.
pp. 77–89
Dahrendorf, Ralf. BONN AFTER 20 YEARS: ARE GERMANY'S
PROBLEMS ANY NEARER SOLUTION? The World Today. Vol. 25.

No. 4. April 1969. pp. 158–171

Dimoyannis, D. GREECE – NATO OUTPOST. International Affairs (Moscow). 1969. No. 4. pp. 42–45

Doernberg. S. BONN'S ATOMIC AMBITIONS. International Affairs (Moscow). 1965. No. 3. pp. 9–13

Douglas-Home, Charles, *et al.* BRITISH DEFENCE CUTS (1968). Survival. Vol. 10. No. 3. pp. 70–78. March 1968

Dubrovin, V. MILITARY AND ECONOMIC COLLABORATION BETWEEN FRANCE AND WEST GERMANY. International Affairs (Moscow). 1963. No. 1. pp. 80–85

Edmonds, Martin. INTERNATIONAL COLLABORATION IN WEAPONS PROCUREMENT: THE IMPLICATIONS OF THE ANGLO-FRENCH CASE. International Affairs. Vol. 43. No. 2. April 1967. pp. 252–264

Erhard, Ludwig. GERMANY POLICY TODAY. (Statement on being elected Chancellor. 18 October 1963). Atlantic Community Quarterly. Vol. 1. No. 4. Winter 1963–64. pp. 501–511

Erler, Fritz. GERMANY AND NASSAU. Survival. Vol. 5. No. 3. May/June 1963. pp. 102–106

Erler, Fritz. THE ALLIANCE AND THE FUTURE OF GERMANY. Foreign Affairs. Vol. 43. No. 3. April 1965. pp. 436–446

Fontaine, André. WHAT IS FRENCH POLICY? Foreign Affairs. Vol. 45. No. 1. October 1966. pp. 58–76

Fontaine, François. THE IMPOSSIBLE SCHISM. (a critique of Gaullism). Atlantic Community Quarterly. Vol. 2. No. 3. Fall 1964. pp. 367–376

François-Poncet, André. L'ENFANT TERRIBLE. (Domestic opposition to President de Gaulle). Atlantic Community Quarterly. Vol. 4. No. 2. Summer 1966. pp. 205–208

Frankel, Joseph. COMPARING FOREIGN POLICIES: THE CASE OF NORWAY. International Affairs. Vol. 44. No. 3. July 1968. pp. 482–491

Franklin, William M. ZONAL BOUNDARIES AND ACCESS TO BERLIN. World Politics. Vol. 16. No. 1. October 1963. pp. 1–31

Freund, Gerald. ADENAUER AND THE FUTURE OF GERMANY. International Journal. Vol. 18. No. 4. Autumn 1963. pp. 458–467

Fromm, Ernst Ulrich. PRESIDENT DE GAULLE'S VISION OF EUROPE. (a German view). Atlantic Community Quarterly. Vol. 4. No. 2. Summer 1966. pp. 224–5

Gasteyger, Curt. MOSCOW AND THE MEDITERRANEAN. Foreign Affairs. Vol. 46. No. 4. July 1968. pp. 676–687

Glazunov, N. MILITARISTIC FEVER IN FEDERAL GERMANY. International Affairs (Moscow). 1969. No. 2. pp. 20–27

Goloshubov, V. SCANDINAVIAN WORRIES. International Affairs (Moscow). 1968. No. 8. pp. 65–70

Griffith, William. THE GERMAN PROBLEM AND AMERICAN POLICY. Survey. No. 61. October 1966. pp. 105–117

Grosser, Alfred. GENERAL DE GAULLE AND THE FOREIGN POLICY OF THE FIFTH REPUBLIC. International Affairs. Vol. 39. No. 2. April 1963. pp. 198–213

Hackkerup, Per. WHY DENMARK SHOULD STAY IN NATO. Atlantic Community Quarterly. Vol. 6. No. 3. Fall 1968. pp. 347–352

Hakovirta, Harto. WESTERN EUROPEAN INTEGRATION AND FINNISH NEUTRALITY. Co-operation and Conflict. Vol. 5. 1970. pp. 129–136

Hakovirta, Harto. THE FINNISH SECURITY PROBLEM. Co-operation and Conflict. Vol. 4. 1969. pp. 247–266

Hansen, Guttorm. NORWAY AND NATO. Atlantic Community Quarterly. Vol. 7. No. 2. Summer 1969. pp. 235–241

Hansen, Peter. DENMARK AND EUROPEAN INTEGRATION. Co-operation and Conflict. Vol. 4. 1969. pp. 13–46

Hartley, Anthony. JFK'S FOREIGN POLICY. Foreign Policy. No. 4. Fall 1971. pp. 77–100

Hassner, Pierre. GERMAN AND EUROPEAN REUNIFICATION. Survey. No. 61. October 1966. pp. 14–37

von Herwarth, Hans. ANGLO-GERMAN RELATIONS: A GERMAN VIEW. International Affairs. Vol. 39. No. 4. October 1963. pp. 511–520. (See also Sir Christopher Steel: 'Anglo-German relations: a British view'. International Affairs as above, pp. 521–532)

Holmes, John W. CANADA IN SEARCH OF ITS ROLE. Foreign Affairs. Vol. 41. No. 4. July 1963. pp. 359–672

Holmes, John W. THE NEW PERSPECTIVES OF CANADIAN FOREIGN POLICY. The World Today. Vol. 25. No. 10. October 1969. pp. 450–460. Survival. Vol. 11. No. 11. November 1969. pp. 334–341

Holmes, John W. CANADA AND THE UNITED STATES: POLITICAL AND SECURITY ISSUES. Atlantic Community Quarterly. Vol. 8. No. 3. Fall 1970. pp. 398–418

Holst, Johan J. NORWEGIAN SECURITY POLICY. Co-operation and Conflict. Vol. 1. No. 2. 1966. pp. 64–79

Holst, Johan J. A NORWEGIAN LOOKS INTO THE EARLY SEVENTIES. International Journal. Vol. 24. No. 2. Spring 1969.

pp. 356-366
Holst, Johan J. Review of 'DANMARK OG NATO': a study of Danish security policy. Survival. Vol. 11. No. 5. May 1969. pp. 170-171
Ilyin, V. BONN'S NUCLEAR AMBITIONS. International Affairs (Moscow). 1968. No. 5. pp. 24-29
Janosik, Edward G. THE NUCLEAR DETERRENT AS AN ISSUE IN BRITISH POLITICS. Orbis. Vol. 10. No. 2. Summer 1966. pp. 588-604
Kafman, A. THE SITUATION IN THE MEDITERRANEAN SHOULD BE NORMALISED. International Affairs (Moscow). 1964. No. 7. pp. 49-53
Kerry, Richard J. NORWAY AND COLLECTIVE DEFENCE ORGANISATION. International Organisation. Vol. 17. No. 4. Autumn 1963. pp. 860-871
Knorr, Klaus. CANADA AND WESTERN DEFENCE. International Journal. Vol. 18. No. 1. Winter 1962. pp. 1-16
Komissarov, Y. NORWAY, A NATO BASE: SEARCH FOR AN ALTERNATIVE. International Affairs (Moscow). 1968. No. 2. pp. 96-98
Kondratyev, V. NATO FLAG OVER THE ACROPOLIS. International Affairs (Moscow). 1963. No. 1. pp. 63-67
Konovalov, Y. THE TENTACLES OF 'BASES STRATEGY'. International Affairs (Moscow). 1963. No. 7. pp. 52-57
Korbel, Josef. GERMAN-SOVIET RELATIONS: THE PAST AND PROSPECTS. Orbis. Vol. 10. No. 4. Winter 1967. pp. 1046-1060
Kotov, Y. WEST BERLIN AND ITS PROBLEMS. International Affairs (Moscow). 1966. No. 4. pp. 47-49
Kotov, V. G.D.R., AN IMPORTANT FACTOR OF PEACE IN EUROPE. International Affairs (Moscow). 1967. No. 3. pp. 50-55
Krolikowski, H. NATO'S NORTHERN FLANK. International Affairs (Moscow). 1968. No. 11. pp. 16-21
Krosby, H. Peter. NORWAY IN NATO: A PARTIAL COMMITMENT? International Journal. Vol. 20. No. 1. Winter 1964. pp. 68-78
Kryukov, P. and Mulin, V. BONN: POLICY OF BLACKMAIL AND AGGRESSION. International Affairs (Moscow). 1963. No. 5. pp. 11-16
Kryukov, P. and Novoseltsev, Y. BONN: ILLUSIONS AND REALITY. International Affairs (Moscow). 1964. No. 12. pp. 17-23
Kryukov, P. BONN'S AGGRESSIVE FOREIGN POLICY. International Affairs (Moscow). 1966. No. 6. pp. 13-19

Kryukov, P. THE GERMAN QUESTION AND THE PRESENT SITUATION. International Affairs (Moscow). 1967. No. 2. pp. 11–16

Kryukov, P. FAILURE OF BONN'S 'NEW EASTERN POLICY'. International Affairs (Moscow). 1969. No. 7. pp. 41–46

Kurchatov, A. AGGRESSIVE POLICY OF WEST GERMAN IMPERIALISM. International Affairs (Moscow). 1966. No. 12. pp. 45–50

Lambilliotte, Maurice. WESTERN EUROPE FACES NEW PROBLEMS. International Affairs (Moscow). 1965. No. 12. pp. 34–38

Lambilliotte, Maurice. GERMAN MILITARISM AND WEST GERMANY'S NEIGHBOURS. International Affairs (Moscow). 1966. No. 9. pp. 14–17

Lange, Christian and Goldmann, Kjell. A NORDIC DEFENCE ALLIANCE 1949–1965. Co-operation and Conflict. Vol. 1. No. 1. 1966. pp. 46–63

Lowenthal, Richard. GERMANY'S ROLE IN EAST-WEST RELATIONS. The World Today. Vol. 23. No. 6. June 1967. pp. 240–249

Luthy, Herbert. DE GAULLE: POSE AND POLICY. Foreign Affairs. Vol. 43. No. 4. July 1965. pp. 561–573

Lyon, Peyton V. A CASE FOR THE RECOGNITION OF EAST GERMANY. International Journal. Vol. 15. No. 4. Autumn 1960. pp. 337–346

Magathan, Wallace C., Jr. WEST GERMAN DEFENCE POLICY. Orbis. Vol. 8. No. 2. Summer 1964. pp. 292–315

Malin, A. A BEATEN TRACK LEADING NOWHERE: DENMARK AND NATO. International Affairs (Moscow). 1968. No. 12. pp. 112–113

Martin, Paul. CANADA AND THE ATLANTIC ALLIANCE. (official Canadian sympathy for European demands for greater participation in NATO nuclear arrangements). Atlantic Community Quarterly. Vol. 3. No. 2. Summer 1965. pp. 251–253

Martin, Paul. NATO'S VALUE TO CANADA. (as expressed by the Canadian Secretary of State for External Affairs). Atlantic Community Quarterly. Vol. 5. No. 2. Summer 1967. pp. 177–186

Matthews, Roy A. A NEW ATLANTIC ROLE FOR CANADA. Foreign Affairs. Vol. 47. No. 2. January 1969. pp. 334–347

Matveyev, V. WESTERN EUROPE: ASSET OR LIABILITY IN THE STRUGGLE FOR PEACE. International Affairs (Moscow). 1964. No. 1. pp. 53–56

Nikolayez, G. SOVIET-TURKISH RELATIONS. International Affairs (Moscow). 1968. No. 11. pp. 37–40.

Novoseltsev, Y. BONN'S EXCESSIVE AMBITIONS. International Affairs (Moscow). 1966. No. 2. pp. 29—36

Novoseltsev, Y. BONN'S 'EASTERN POLICY' AND EUROPEAN SECURITY. International Affairs (Moscow). 1968. No. 7. pp. 27—33

Orvik, Nils. SOVIET APPROACHES ON NATO'S NORTHERN FLANK. International Journal. Vol. 20. No. 1. Winter 1964. pp. 54—67

Orvik, Nils. NATO: THE ROLE OF THE SMALL MEMBER. International Journal. Vol. 21. No. 2. Spring 1966. pp. 173—185. Atlantic Community Quarterly. Vol. 4. No. 1. Spring 1966. pp. 92—103

Orvik, Nils. SCANDINAVIA, NATO AND NORTHERN SECURITY. International Organisation. Vol. 20. No. 3. Summer 1966. pp. 380—396

Orvik, Nils. NATO, NAFTA AND THE SMALLER ALLIES. Orbis. Vol. 12. No. 2. Summer 1968. p. 455

Panfilov, Y. WEST GERMANY'S FOREIGN POLICY IMPASSE AND THE BIG COALITION. International Affairs (Moscow). 1967. No. 5. pp. 9—14

Pasternak, E. U.S. CONCEPTS OF CRISIS DIPLOMACY. (a commentary on Robert S. McNamara: 'The Essence of Security'. London: Hodder & Stoughton; New York: McGraw-Hill. 1968). International Affairs (Moscow). 1972. No. 6. pp. 96—98

Pavlov, A. BONN'S FOREIGN POLICY: 'PHILOSOPHY' AND REALITY. International Affairs (Moscow). 1964. No. 5. pp. 79—83

Polyanov, N. BONN'S CHALLENGE TO EUROPE. International Affairs (Moscow). 1969. No. 1. pp. 21—28

Polyanov, N. EUROPE: PEACE ZONE OR HOTBED OF WAR. International Affairs (Moscow). 1969. No. 5. pp. 3—9

Ponomarev, G. BONN OPPOSES A RELAXATION OF TENSION. International Affairs (Moscow). 1963. No. 1. pp. 52—55

Powell, Enoch. THE TORIES AND DEFENCE: speech to the Conservative Conference, Brighton, 14 October 1965. Survival. Vol. 7. No. 9. December 1965. pp. 319—320

Pompidou, Georges. FRANCE: THE REAL EUROPE. Atlantic Community Quarterly. Vol. 3. No. 3. Fall 1965. pp. 326—331. (French premier's defence of French policy and a plea for Europe as a '3rd Force')

Rakhmaninov, Y. ALTERNATIVE TO A DIVIDED EUROPE. International Affairs (Moscow). 1967. No. 4. pp. 41—47

Rakhmaninov, Y. FOR EUROPEAN SECURITY. International Affairs (Moscow). 1967. No. 11. pp. 81—87

Rakhmaninov, Y. EUROPEAN SECURITY: TASKS AND PROSPECTS. International Affairs (Moscow). 1969. No. 6. pp. 10–15
Rakhmaninov, Y. SOVIET-FRENCH RELATIONS AND EUROPEAN SECURITY. International Affairs (Moscow). 1970. No. 11. pp. 33–39
Razmerov, V. WESTERN MODELS FOR THE EUROPE OF THE 1970'S. (i.e. a Soviet review of the Atlantic Alliance on its 20th Anniversary). International Affairs (Moscow). 1969. No. 6. pp. 40–46
Reynolds, P.A. RECENT TRENDS IN BRITISH FOREIGN POLICY. International Journal. Vol. 15. No. 3. Summer 1960. pp. 200–209
Richardson, James. GERMANY'S EASTERN POLICY: PROBLEMS AND PROSPECTS. The World Today. Vol. 24. No. 9. September 1968. pp. 375–386
Rockefeller, Nelson A. VOICES IN OPPOSITION: the Republican party's critique of current U.S. defence policy. (Address to the American Newspaper Publishers Association. April 1963). Survival. Vol. 6. No. 1. January/February 1964. pp. 9–15
Roshchin, K. PENTAGON STEPS UP TENSION IN MEDITERRANEAN. International Affairs (Moscow). 1969. No. 2. pp. 34–37
Rzhevsky, Y. F.R.G. IN THE SYSTEM OF WESTERN ALLIANCES. International Affairs (Moscow). 1968. No. 12. pp. 24–29
Saeter, Martin. CHANGE OF COURSE IN GERMAN FOREIGN POLICY. Co-operation and Conflict. Vol. 2. 1967. pp. 82–101
Salazar, Dr. Antonio de Oliveira. REALITIES AND TRENDS OF PORTUGAL'S POLICIES. International Affairs. Vol. 39. No. 2. April 1963. pp. 169–183
Sanakoyev, Sh., et al. PARIS-BONN AXIS: CONSPIRACY AGAINST PEACE. International Affairs (Moscow). 1963. No. 3. pp. 46–56
Scheinman, Lawrence. THE POLITICS OF NATIONALISM IN CONTEMPORARY FRANCE. International Organisation. Vol. 23. No. 1. Winter 1969. pp. 834–858
Schick, Jack M. THE BERLIN CRISIS OF 1961 AND U.S. MILITARY STRATEGY. Orbis. Vol. 8. No. 4. Winter 1965. pp. 816–831
Schopflin, George. NATO AND THE NORDIC BALANCE. The World Today. Vol. 22. March 1966. pp. 114–122
Schroder, Gerhard. GERMANY LOOKS AT EASTERN EUROPE. Foreign Affairs. Vol. 44. No. 1. October 1965. pp. 15–25
Sedykh, V. INSECURE FOUNDATION FOR 'GRANDEUR': THE FRANCO-GERMAN TREATY.OF 1963. International Affairs (Moscow). 1963. No. 4. pp. 9–14
Shell, Kurt L. BERLIN AND THE GERMAN PROBLEM. World Politics.

Vol. 16. No. 1. October 1963. pp. 137–146
Speier, Hans. THE HALLSTEIN DOCTRINE. Survey. No. 61. October 1966. pp. 93–104
Spencer, Robert. BERLIN, THE BLOCKADE AND THE COLD WAR. International Journal. Vol. 23. No. 3. Summer 1968. pp. 383–407
Steel, Sir Christopher. ANGLO-GERMAN RELATIONS: A BRITISH VIEW. International Affairs. Vol. 39. No. 4. October 1963. pp. 521–532. (See also Hans von Herwath: 'Anglo-German relations: a German view'. International Affairs as above, pp. 511–520)
Stehle, Hansjakob. THE FEDERAL REPUBLIC AND EASTERN EUROPE. Survey. No. 61. October 1966. pp. 70–79
Stenzl, Otto. GERMANY'S EASTERN FRONTIER. Survey. No. 51. April 1964. pp. 118–130
Stikker, Dirk U. FRANCE AND ITS DIMINISHING WILL TO CO-OPERATE. Atlantic Community Quarterly. Vol. 3. No. 2. Summer 1965. pp. 197–205. (French attitudes to NATO during the writer's period of office as Secretary-General)
Strausz-Hupe, Robert. DE GAULLE: PROPHET FOR EUROPE OR DISTURBER OF THE PEACE. Atlantic Community Quarterly. Vol. 2. No. 1. Spring 1964. pp. 45–52
Sutherland, R.J. CANADA'S LONG-TERM STRATEGIC SITUATION. International Journal. Vol. 18. No. 3. Summer 1962. pp. 199–223. (See also C.S. Burchill *et al.* 'Canada's long-term strategic situation: a critical view' in International Journal. Vol. 18. No. 1. Winter 1962. pp. 75–81)
Tornudd, Klaus. 'THE FINNISH MODEL', NEUTRAL STATES AND EUROPEAN SECURITY. International Journal. Vol. 24. No. 2. Spring 1969. pp. 349–355
Vernant, Jacques. FRANCE AND NASSAU. Survival. Vol. 5. No. 3. May/June 1963. pp. 106–109
Verrier, Anthony. BRITISH DEFENCE POLICY UNDER LABOR. Foreign Affairs. Vol. 42. No. 2. January 1964. pp. 282–292
Vershinin, Chief Air Marshal K. AVIATION IN MODERN WAR. Survival. Vol. 5. No. 2. March/April 1963. pp. 83–85. (trans. from Military Review, 24 December 1962)
Vidyasova, L. DISPUTE SIMMERS BETWEEN THE U.S.A. AND FRANCE. International Affairs (Moscow). 1963. No. 12. pp. 23–29
Warner, Geoffrey. GAULLIST FOREIGN POLICY. The World Today. Vol. 21. No. 3. March 1965. pp. 112–119
Watt, Donald. BRITISH OPINION AND THE ODER-NEISSE LINE.

Survey. No. 61. October 1966. pp. 118–128
Watt. D.C. BRITAIN AND GERMANY: THE LAST THREE YEARS.
International Journal. Vol. 23. No. 4. Autumn 1968. pp. 560–569
Whetten, Lawrence J. THE MEDITERRANEAN THREAT: HAS
STRATEGIC PARITY BEEN ACHIEVED? Survey. No. 74/75.
Winter/Spring 1970. pp. 270–281
Whitaker, Arthur P. SPAIN AND THE ATLANTIC ALLIANCE. Orbis.
Vol. 10. No. 1. Spring 1966. pp. 42–78
Yalcin, Aydin. TURKEY: EMERGING DEMOCRACY. Foreign Affairs.
Vol. 45. No. 4. July 1967. pp. 706–714
Yurinov, B. BONN, THE WEST AND THE GERMAN QUESTION.
International Affairs (Moscow). 1964. No. 9. pp. 16–21
Yuryev, N. THE ATOMIC MISSILE RUSH IN WEST GERMANY.
International Affairs (Moscow). 1964. No. 4. pp. 42–48
Yuryev, N. BONN-PARIS AXIS: MURKY PROSPECTS. International
Affairs (Moscow). 1964. No. 11. pp. 16–22
Yuryev, N. FRANCO-AMERICAN DISCORD. International Affairs
(Moscow). 1965. No. 3. pp. 51–55
Yuryev, N. EUROPEAN SECURITY AND THE GERMAN QUESTION.
International Affairs (Moscow). 1965. No. 10. pp. 56–60
Yuryev, N. SOVIET-FRENCH CO-OPERATION AND EUROPEAN
SECURITY. International Affairs (Moscow). 1966. No. 6. pp. 7–12
Zalyotny, A. F.R.G. AND DEVELOPMENTS IN CZECHOSLOVAKIA.
International Affairs (Moscow). 1968. No. 11. pp. 22–27
Zhukov, Y. PARIS-BONN ALLIANCE: WHO STANDS TO GAIN?
International Affairs (Moscow). 1963. No. 8. pp. 60–70
Zilliacus, K. NATO AND THE NATIONAL INDEPENDENCE OF
BRITAIN. International Affairs (Moscow). 1963. No. 10. pp. 32–36
Zilliacus, K. ANGLO-AMERICAN ALLIANCE AT THE CROSSROADS.
International Affairs (Moscow). 1964. No. 10. pp. 31–33

Politico – Military Aspects

Acheson, Dean. THE PRACTICE OF PARTNERSHIP. Foreign Affairs.
Vol. 41. No. 2. January 1963. pp. 247–260
Acheson, Dean. THE DILEMMAS OF OUR TIMES. Atlantic Community
Quarterly. Vol. 1. No. 4. Winter 1963–64. pp. 570–585
Acheson, Dean. EUROPE – DECISION OR DRIFT. Foreign Affairs.
Vol. 44. January 1966. pp. 198–205. Atlantic Community Quarterly.

Vol. 4. No. 1. Spring 1966. pp. 17–24

Acheson, Dean. ONE OF OUR 'FIREMEN' IS RESIGNING. Atlantic Community Quarterly. Vol. 4. No. 2. Summer 1966. pp. 160–166. (The background to NATO's success and de Gaulle's assault on the alliance structure).

Allais, Maurice. PREFACE TO A POLICY OF ATLANTIC UNITY, PART I. Atlantic Community Quarterly. Vol. 2. No. 3. Fall 1964. pp. 350–366. PREFACE TO A POLICY OF ATLANTIC UNITY, PART II. Atlantic Community Quarterly. Vol. 2. No. 4. Winter 1964–65. pp. 537–556

Allen, H.C. THE ANGLO-AMERICAN RELATIONSHIP IN THE SIXTIES. International Affairs. Vol. 39. No. 1. January 1963. pp. 37–48

Andreyev, N. NATO AND THE WAR DANGER IN EUROPE. International Affairs (Moscow). 1965. No. 12. pp. 39–43

Andreyev, N. NATO'S ROLE IN EUROPE. Survival. Vol. 8. No. 5. May 1966. pp. 150–155. (Abridgment of article in INTERNATIONAL AFFAIRS (Moscow). 1965. No. 12)

Anon. NATO AND THE DEFENCE OF EUROPE. Survival. Vol. 7. No. 7. October 1965. pp. 266–267. (Editorial from IL GIORNALE D'ITALIA. 9 June 1965). (See also Francesco Calogero: Letter to the Editor. SURVIVAL. Vol. 7. No. 9. December 1965. p. 344).

Anon. THE AIMS OF SOVIET FOREIGN POLICY. Survival. Vol. 7. No. 7. October 1965. pp. 252–256. (Editorial from PRAVDA. 8 August 1965)

Anon. MUST WE REFORM NATO? Survival. Vol. 8. No. 1. January 1966. pp. 2–8. (Trans. from POLITIQUE ETRANGERE. No. 3. 1965)

Anon. PICKING UP NATO'S PIECES. Atlantic Community Quarterly. Vol. 4. No. 3. Fall 1966. pp. 361–366. (From THE ECONOMIST. 8 May 1966: advances the view that President de Gaulle's attitude towards the Alliance puts at risk policies which contain Germany).

Anon. EUROPEAN SECURITY: AN EAST GERMAN VIEW. Survival. Vol. 11. No. 11. November 1969. pp. 357–358

Aron, Raymond. THE AMERICAN ATOMIC MONOPOLY AND EUROPE. (A reply to Walter Lippmann: 'How many drivers at the nuclear wheel?'. Atlantic Community Quarterly. Vol. 1. No. 1. March 1963. pp. 37–41). Atlantic Community Quarterly. Vol. 1. No. 1. March 1963. pp. 42–44

Aron, Raymond. END OF THE COLD WAR? THE GREAT SCHISM:
A RECONSIDERATION. Survey. No. 50. January 1964. pp. 3–9
Aspaturian, Vernon V. MOSCOW'S FOREIGN POLICY. Survey. No. 65.
October 1967. pp. 35–60
Aspaturian, Vernon V. SOVIET FOREIGN POLICY AT THE CROSS-
ROADS. (i.e. after Czechoslovakia 1968). International Organisation.
Vol. 23. No. 4. Autumn 1969. pp. 589–620)
Atlantic Council of the United States. POLICY STATEMENT. Atlantic
Community Quarterly. Vol. 3. No. 4. Winter 1965–66. pp. 419–424
Atlantic Council of the United States. NON-MILITARY FUNCTIONS
OF NATO. Atlantic Community Quarterly. Vol. 3. No. 4. Winter
1965–66. pp. 425–441
Bader, W.B. NUCLEAR WEAPONS SHARING AND 'THE GERMAN
PROBLEM'. Foreign Affairs. Vol. 44. No. 4. July 1966. pp. 683–692
Ball, George W. THE NUCLEAR DETERRENT AND THE ATLANTIC
ALLIANCE. Atlantic Community Quarterly. Vol. 1. No. 2. Summer
1963. pp. 199–204. (The view of the Under-Secretary of State)
Ball, George W. NATO AND WORLD RESPONSIBILITY. Atlantic
Community Quarterly. Vol. 2. No. 2. Summer 1964. pp. 208–217
Ball, George W. THE DANGERS OF NOSTALGIA. Atlantic Community
Quarterly. Vol. 3. No. 2. Summer 1965. pp. 167–176. (Pre-war
'normalcy' in U.S. and European relations cannot be restored —
interdependence is now the norm)
Barnet, Richard J. INITIATIVE AND RESPONSE IN SOVIET FOREIGN
POLICY. World Politics. Vol. 16. No. 1. October 1963. pp. 173–187
Beaton, Leonard. NATO AFTER THE SOVIET INVASION OF
CZECHOSLOVAKIA. Atlantic Community Quarterly. Vol. 7. No. 1.
Spring 1969. pp. 76–8
Beglov, S. NEW EUROPEAN HORIZONS. International Affairs
(Moscow). 1966. No. 7. pp. 6–12
Beglov, S. EUROPEAN SECURITY DIALOGUE GOES AHEAD. Inter-
national Affairs (Moscow). 1967. No. 3. pp. 44–49
Beloff, Max. BRITAIN, EUROPE AND THE ATLANTIC COM-
MUNITY. International Organisation. Vol. 17. No. 3. Summer 1963.
pp. 574–591
van der Beugel, Ernst H. THE CLASH IN EUROPE. Atlantic Community
Quarterly. Vol. 3. No. 1. Spring 1965. pp. 27–33. (An analysis as to
whether European political community contributes towards Atlantic
co-operation)
van der Beugel, Ernst H. FROM MARSHALL AID TO ATLANTIC

PARTNERSHIP. Atlantic Community Quarterly. Vol. 4. No. 1. Spring 1966. pp. 5–16

van der Beugel, Ernst H. RELATIONS BETWEEN EUROPE AND THE UNITED STATES. Atlantic Community Quarterly. Vol. 5. No. 2. Summer 1967. pp. 173–177

van der Beugel, Ernst H. THE NEED FOR ATLANTIC SOLIDARITY. Atlantic Community Quarterly. Vol. 5. No. 4. Winter 1967–68. pp. 507–512

Billington, James H. FORCE AND COUNTERFORCE IN EASTERN EUROPE. Foreign Affairs. Vol. 47. No. 1. October 1968. pp. 26–35. (Notably Czechoslovakia 1968)

Birgi, Uuri. THE UNFOLDING ALLIANCE. Atlantic Community Quarterly. Vol. 2. No. 3. Fall 1964. pp. 408–412. (A Turkish view)

Birnbaum, Karl E. WAYS TOWARDS EUROPEAN SECURITY. Survival. Vol. 10. No. 6. June 1968. pp. 193–200

Birrenbach, Kurt. EUROPE AND AMERICA: PARTNERS IN AN ATLANTIC COMMUNITY. Atlantic Community Quarterly. Vol. 1. No. 2. Summer 1963. pp. 213–218. (A German contribution to the discussion on U.S.-European relations)

Birrenbach, Kurt. PARTNERSHIP AND CONSULTATION IN NATO. (A German view). Atlantic Community Quarterly. Vol. 2. No. 1. Spring 1964. pp. 62–71

Boel, Baron René. EUROPEAN COMMUNITY – ATLANTIC COMMUNITY. (A Belgian view). Atlantic Community Quarterly. Vol. Vol. 1. No. 1. March 1963. pp. 72–78

de Borchgrave, Arnaud. EUROPE LOOKS AGAIN TO U.S. LEADERSHIP. Atlantic Community Quarterly. Vol. 5. No. 4. Winter 1967–68. pp. 564–569. (The swing from Gaullism to neo-Atlanticism)

Bowie, Robert R. STRATEGY AND THE ATLANTIC ALLIANCE. International Organisation. Vol. 17. No. 3. Summer 1963. pp. 709–732

Bowie, Robert R. TENSIONS WITHIN THE ALLIANCE. Foreign Affairs. Vol. 42. No. 1. October 1963. pp. 49–69. Survival. Vol. 6. No. 1. January/February 1964. pp. 26–36

Bowie, Robert R. SHAPING THE FUTURE. Atlantic Community Quarterly. Vol. 2. No. 3. Fall 1964. pp. 325–349. (The Alliance, European Community, Britain and de Gaulle)

Brandt, Willy. DETENTE OVER THE LONG HAUL. Survival. Vol. 9. No. 10. October 1967. pp. 310–312. (Reprint from AUSSENPOLITIK. August 1967)

Brezhnev, Leonid. EUROPEAN SECURITY: SOVIET VIEW. Survival. Vol. 9. No. 6. June 1967. pp. 174–176

Brosio, Manlio. THE FUTURE OF NATO. (Address to NATO Parliamentarians' Conference. New York. October 1965). Atlantic Community Quarterly. Vol. 3. No. 4. Winter 1965–66. pp. 442–450)

Brosio, Manlio. PAST AND FUTURE TASKS OF THE ALLIANCE: AN ANALYSIS OF THE HARMEL REPORT. Atlantic Community Quarterly. Vol. 6. No. 2. Summer 1968. pp. 231–238

Brosio, Manlio. TWENTY NATO YEARS. Atlantic Community Quarterly. Vol. 7. No. 2. Summer 1969. pp. 209–212

Brosio, Manlio. JUSTIFIED GESTURE. Atlantic Community Quarterly. Vol. 7. No. 4. Winter 1969–70. pp. 480–494. (The initial response – post-Harmel – to Soviet proposals for detente)

Brosio, Manlio. SOVIET POLICY: WEAKNESS, YES, BUT DANGER TOO. Atlantic Community Quarterly. Vol. 6. No. 4. Winter 1968–9. pp. 493–501

Brown, Neville. BRITISH ARMS AND THE SWITCH TOWARDS EUROPE. International Affairs. Vol. 43. No. 3. July 1967. pp. 468–482

Brown, Neville. ANGLO-FRENCH NUCLEAR COLLABORATION? The World Today. Vol. 25. No. 8. August 1969. pp. 351–357

Brown, Seyom. AN ALTERNATIVE TO THE GRAND DESIGN. (i.e. the Kennedy 'Grand Design'). World Politics. Vol. 17. No. 2. January 1965. pp. 232–242

Brzezinski, Zbigniev. THREAT AND OPPORTUNITY IN THE COMMUNIST SCHISM. (i.e. the Sino-Soviet split). Foreign Affairs. Vol. 41. No. 3. April 1963. pp. 513–525. (i.e. for the West in the Sino-Soviet schism or communist ideology)

Brzezinski, Zbigniev. RUSSIA AND EUROPE. Foreign Affairs. Vol. 42. No. 3. April 1964. pp. 428–444

Brzezinksi, Zbigniev. AMERICA AND A LARGER EUROPE. The World Today. Vol. 21. No. 10. October 1965. pp. 419–428

Brzezinskì, Zbigniev. THE FRAMEWORK OF EAST-WEST RECONCILIATION. Foreign Affairs. Vol. 46. No. 2. January 1968. pp. 256–275

Buchan, Alastair. PARTNERS AND ALLIES. Foreign Affairs. Vol. 41. No. 4. July 1963. pp. 621–637. Survival. Vol. 5. No. 5. September/October 1963. pp. 224–231. (U.S.-European relations in the aftermath of de Gaulle's rejection of British membership of E.E.C.)

Buchan, Alastair. THE CHANGED SETTING OF THE ATLANTIC

DEBATE. (i.e. NATO in the late 1960's). Foreign Affairs. Vol. 43. No. 4. July 1965. pp. 574–586

Buchan, Alastair. THE PURPOSE OF NATO AND ITS FUTURE DEVELOPMENT. Atlantic Community Quarterly. Vol. 8. No. 1. Spring 1970. pp. 49–57

Bundy, McGeorge. ATLANTIC ALLIANCE IS NOT AMERICA'S ALONE. Atlantic Community Quarterly. Vol. 4. No. 3. Fall 1966. pp. 330–340

Bundy, McGeorge. AMERICA'S ENDURING LINKS WITH EUROPE. Atlantic Community Quarterly. Vol. 8. No. 1. Spring 1970. pp. 17–31

Bykov, O. ATLANTIC POLICY OF THE U.S.A. AND EUROPEAN SECURITY. International Affairs (Moscow). 1967. No. 9. pp. 39–45

Calvocoressi, Peter. THE EVOLUTION OF EUROPE: THE GAULLIST DESIGN, RUSSIA AND EUROPE, EUROPE AND THE BRITISH QUESTION. (3 broadcast talks). Survival. Vol. 5. No. 5. September/October 1963. pp. 196–205

Camps, Miriam. IS EUROPE OBSOLETE? International Affairs. Vol. 44. No. 3. July 1968. pp. 434–445

de Carmoy, Guy. THE LAST YEAR OF DE GAULLE'S FOREIGN POLICY. International Affairs. Vol. 49. No. 3. July 1969. pp. 424–435

Church, Senator Frank C. NATO – REAPPRAISING AMERICAN POLICY. Survival. Vol. 5. No. 5. September/October 1963. pp. 232–237

Church, Senator Frank C. TOWARDS A MORE PERFECT UNION. Atlantic Community Quarterly. Vol. 3. No. 3. Fall 1965. pp. 285–292. (A plea for a U.S. initiative to create an Atlantic Community)

Church, Senator Frank C. U.S. POLICY AND THE 'NEW EUROPE'. Foreign Affairs. Vol. 45. No. 1. October 1966. pp. 49–57. Survival. Vol. 8. No. 12. December 1966. pp. 300–385

Clemens, Walter C., Jr. THE FUTURE OF THE WARSAW PACT. Orbis. Vol. 11. No. 4. Winter 1968. pp. 996–1033

Cleveland, Harlan. THE REAL DETERRENT. Survival. Vol. 9. No. 12. December 1967. pp. 378–383

Cleveland, Harlan. THE REJUVENATION OF NATO. Atlantic Community Quarterly. Vol. 5. No. 4. Winter 1967–68. pp. 512–520

Cleveland, Harlan. NATO AFTER THE INVASION. (i.e. after the invasion of Czechoslovakia, August 1968). Foreign Affairs. Vol. 47. No. 2. January 1969. pp. 251–265

Cleveland, Harlan. THE IRRELEVANCE OF ANTI-COMMITMENT. Atlantic Community Quarterly. Vol. 6. No. 4. Winter 1968–9.

pp. 520—531

Cleveland, Harlan. THE UNITED STATES AND THE FUTURE OF NATO. Atlantic Community Quarterly. Vol. 7. No. 2. Summer 1969. pp. 216—221

Cleveland, Harlan. THE GOLDEN RULE OF CONSULTATION. Atlantic Community Quarterly. Vol. 8. No. 3. Fall 1970. pp. 334—351

Cleveland, Harold van B. THE ATLANTIC IDEA. (i.e. towards an economic and military but not political community). Atlantic Community Quarterly. Vol. 4. No. 4. Winter 1966—67. pp. 494—509

Coffey, J.I. STRATEGY, ALLIANCE POLICY AND NUCLEAR PROLIFERATION. Orbis. Vol. 11. No. 4. Winter 1968. pp. 975—995

Colonna, Guido. THE STATE OF THE ALLIANCE: AN ITALIAN VIEW. Atlantic Community Quarterly. Vol. 2. No. 3. Fall 1964. pp. 397—407

Combeaux, Edmond. DEBATE ON THE ATLANTIC ALLIANCE. Orbis. Vol. 10. No. 2. Summer 1966. pp. 360—389

Committee of the Atlantic Council of the United States. ARE CHANGES IN THE NORTH ATLANTIC TREATY NECESSARY OR DESIRABLE? Atlantic Community Quarterly. Vol. 3. No. 3. Fall 1965. pp. 314—317

Conquest, Robert. THE LIMITS OF DETENTE. Foreign Affairs. Vol. 46. No. 4. July 1968. pp. 733—742

Coulmas, Peter. THE ATLANTIC DEBATE: PARTNERSHIP AND INTERDEPENDENCE. Survival. Vol. 5. No. 4. July/August 1963. pp. 162—165. (Reprint from AUSSENPOLITIK. April 1963)

Crane, Robert Dickson. THE CUBAN CRISIS: A STRATEGIC ANALYSIS OF AMERICAN AND SOVIET POLICY. Orbis. Vol. 6. No. 4. Winter 1963. pp. 528—563

Crane, Robert Dickson. A NEW (NON-MILITARY) COLD WAR. Survival. Vol. 7. No. 2. March/April 1965. pp. 79—82

Daniels, Robert V. DOCTRINE AND FOREIGN POLICY. (i.e. Soviet policy under Khrushchev). Survey. No. 57. October 1965. pp. 3—11

Dawson, Raymond and Rosecrance, Richard. THEORY AND REALITY IN THE AMERICAN ALLIANCE. World Politics. Vol. 19. No. 1. October 1966. pp. 21—51

Douglas-Home, Charles. RUSSIANS ON THE MOVE. Survival. Vol. 11.

No. 2. February 1969. pp. 63–65. (Reprint from THE TIMES. 10 December 1968)

Duroselle, J.B. THE FUTURE OF THE ATLANTIC COMMUNITY. International Journal. Vol. 21. No. 4. Autumn 1966. pp. 421–446

Eisenhower, Dwight D. 'PROMISE IS NOW A FACT' (NATO: PAST AND FUTURE). Atlantic Community Quarterly. Vol. 7. No. 2. Summer 1969. pp. 221–224

Ellsworth, Robert. THE FUTURE OF THE ATLANTIC ALLIANCE. Atlantic Community Quarterly. Vol. 7. No. 3. Fall 1969. pp. 315–321

Emerson, Rupert. THE ATLANTIC COMMUNITY AND THE EMERGING COUNTRIES. International Organisation. Vol. 17. No. 3. Summer. 1963. pp. 628–648

Erler, Fritz. THE BASIS OF PARTNERSHIP. Foreign Affairs. Vol. 42. No. 1. October 1963. pp. 84–95. Survival. Vol. 6. No. 1. January/February 1964. pp. 16–22

Faddeyev, I. THE NATO SPIDER-WEB IN AFRICA. International Affairs (Moscow). 1963. No. 12. pp. 65–68

Florin, P. EUROPEAN SECURITY AND THE GERMAN DEMOCRATIC REPUBLIC. International Affairs (Moscow). 1965. No. 8. pp. 25–31

Fraser, Blair. CAN WE SUCCEED IN NATO WITHOUT REALLY TRYING. (A Canadian view on the nuclear issue). Atlantic Community Quarterly. Vol. 3. No. 1. Spring 1965. pp. 50–55

Freymond, Jacques. THE EUROPEAN NEUTRALS AND THE ATLANTIC COMMUNITY. International Organisation. Vol. 17. No. 3. Summer 1963. pp. 592–609

Freymond, Jacques. ALTERNATIVES TO PARTITION. Survey. No. 58. January 1966. pp. 128–133

Fulbright, Senator J.W. A COMMUNITY OF FREE NATIONS. Atlantic Community Quarterly. Vol. 1. No. 2. Summer 1963. pp. 113–130

Fulbright, J.W. A CONCERT OF FREE NATIONS. International Organisation. Vol. 17. No. 3. Summer 1963. pp. 787–803

Fulbright, J.W. FOREIGN POLICY – MYTH AND REALITY. (A call for a reappraisal of American attitudes and policies to Communist countries). Survival. Vol. 6. No. 3. May/June 1964. pp. 136–141

Fyodorov, F. NATO AND THE DEMAND OF THE TIMES. International Affairs (Moscow). 1964. No. 2. pp. 38–41

Fyodorov, T. WASHINGTON AND BONN – AN ALLIANCE AGAINST PEACE. International Affairs (Moscow). 1965. No. 4. pp. 14–19

Gabelic, Andro. NEW ACCENT IN SOVIET STRATEGY. (a

Yugoslav viw. Survival. Vol. 10. No. 2. February 1968.
pp. 45–47

Garnett, John. THE UNITED STATES AND EUROPE: DEFENCE, TECHNOLOGY AND THE WESTERN ALLIANCE. International Affairs. Vol. 44. No. 2. April 1968. pp. 282–288

Gasteyger, Curt. END OR REFORM OF THE (post-war military) ALLIANCES? Survival. Vol. 8. No. 8. August 1966. pp. 251–255

Gasteyger, Curt. EUROPE IN THE SEVENTIES. Atlantic Community Quarterly. Vol. 5. No. 3. Fall 1967. pp. 316–317

de Gaulle, Charles. VIEWS ON THE NASSAU AGREEMENT, THE ATLANTIC ALLIANCE AND A NATIONAL NUCLEAR FORCES. (Press Conference. 14 January 1963). Survival. Vol. 5. No. 2. March/April 1963. pp. 58–59

de Gaulle, Charles. THE ATLANTIC ALLIANCE: (Press Conference. 29 July 1963). Survival. Vol. 5. No. 5. September/October 1963. pp. 238–239

de Gaulle, Charles. LONG LIVE FRANCE. Atlantic Community Quarterly. Vol. 3. No. 2. Summer 1965. pp. 155–158

Geiger, Theodore. THE ENDING OF AN ERA IN ATLANTIC POLICY. Atlantic Community Quarterly. Vol. 5. No. 1. Spring 1967. pp. 87–99. (The possible emergence of an American-European rift, and a call for a re-examination of U.S. policy)

Gelber, Lionel. A MARRIAGE OF INCONVENIENCE. (A Canadian perspective on the European-American relationship). Foreign Affairs. Vol. 41. No. 2. January 1963. pp. 310–322. Survival. Vol. 5. No. 2. March/April 1963. pp. 70–77. January 1963

Gelber, Lionel. ANGLO-AMERICAN IMPERATIVES. Orbis. Vol. 7. No. 2. Summer 1963. pp. 250–264

Gelber, Lionel. PEACEFUL CO-EXISTENCE OR A DURABLE PEACE? Orbis. Vol. 8. No. 2. Summer 1964. pp. 316–331

Gelber, Lionel. AMERICA, THE GLOBAL BALANCE AND BRITAIN. Atlantic Community Quarterly. Vol. 6. No. 3. Fall 1968

Giffin, S.F. UNTANGLING AN ALLIANCE. Orbis. Vol. 7. No. 3. Fall 1963. pp. 465–477

Gladwyn, Lord. ATLANTIC DREAMS AND REALITIES. Atlantic Community Quarterly. Vol. 2. No. 1. Spring 1964. pp. 81–93

Gladwyn, Lord. NATO TODAY. (A British view on President de Gaulle's policy towards NATO). Atlantic Community Quarterly. Vol. 4. No. 2. Summer 1966. pp. 215–224

Glagolev, I. and Larionov, V. SOVIET DEFENCE MIGHT AND PEACE-

FUL CO-EXISTENCE. International Affairs (Moscow). 1963. No. 11. pp. 27–33

Goodman, Elliot R. DE GAULLE'S NATO POLICY IN PERSPECTIVE. Orbis. Vol. 10. No. 3. Fall 1966. pp. 690–723. Atlantic Community Quarterly. Vol. 4. No. 3. Fall 1966. pp. 349–361

Goodman, Elliot R. DETENTE: THE SOVIET VIEW. Survey. No. 70/71. Winter/Spring 1969. pp. 121–148

Goodman, Elliot R. NATO AND GERMAN REUNIFICATION. Survey. No. 76. Summer 1970. pp. 30–40

Gordenker, Leon. INTERNATIONAL ORGANISATION AND THE COLD WAR. International Journal. Vol. 23. No. 3. Summer 1968. pp. 357–368

Gordon Walker, P.C. THE LABOR PARTY'S DEFENSE AND FOREIGN POLICY. Foreign Affairs. Vol. 42. No. 3. April 1964. pp. 391–398

Gorokhov, A. WESTERN EUROPE 1966. International Affairs (Moscow). 1966. No. 10. pp. 6–12

Gorokhov, A. NATO: 20 YEAR BALANCE SHEET. International Affairs (Moscow). 1969. No. 3. pp. 20–26

Graebner, Norman A. THE COLD WAR: AN AMERICAN VIEW. International Journal. Vol. 15. No. 2. Spring 1960. pp. 95–112

Graebner, Norman A. WHITHER CONTAINMENT? International Journal. Vol. 24. No. 2. Spring 1969. pp. 246–263

Grosser, Alfred. FRANCE AND GERMANY IN THE ATLANTIC COMMUNITY. International Organisation. Vol. 17. No. 3. Summer 1963. pp. 550–573

Grosser, Alfred. FRANCE AND GERMANY: DIVERGENT OUTLOOKS. Foreign Affairs. Vol. 44. No. 1. October 1965. pp. 26–36

Gutteridge, William. DEFENCE OR DISARMAMENT. International Affairs. Vol. 41. No. 4. October 1965. pp. 676–681

Hackkerup, Per. EUROPE: BASIC PROBLEMS AND PERSPECTIVES – A DANISH VIEW. International Affairs. Vol. 41. No. 1. January 1965. pp. 1–10

Hadik, Laszlo. THE PROCESS OF DETENTE IN EUROPE. Atlantic Community Quarterly. Vol. 8. No. 3. Fall 1970. pp. 325–334

Haigh, Patricia. REFLECTIONS ON THE WARSAW PACT. The World Today. Vol. 24. No. 4. April 1968. pp. 166–172

Halle, Louis J. THE COLD WAR IN RETROSPECT: THE TURNING POINT (I.E. THE MARSHALL PLAN 1947). Survey. No. 58. January 1966. pp. 168–176

Halle, Louis J. A MULTITUDE OF COLD WARS. International Journal.

Vol. 23. No. 3. Summer 1968. pp. 335–343
Hallstein, Walter. THE EUROPEAN COMMUNITY AND ATLANTIC PARTNERSHIP. International Organisation. Vol. 17. No. 3. Summer 1963. pp. 771–786
Hallstein, Walter. NATO AND THE EUROPEAN ECONOMIC COMMUNITY. Orbis. Vol. 6. No. 4. Winter 1963. pp. 564–574
Harned, Joseph. ATLANTIC ASSEMBLY – A GENESIS. (Suggestions for a parliamentary assembly to supervise Atlantic co-operation). Atlantic Community Quarterly. Vol. 3. No. 1. Spring 1965. pp. 43–49
Harrison, S.L.R. AMERICA'S 1969 OPTION. Atlantic Community Quarterly. Vol. 7. No. 3. Fall 1969. pp. 334–342
Hartley, Livingston. AN ATLANTIC COMMISSION. (i.e. proposals for a Commission similar to the European Commission). Orbis. Vol. 7. No. 2. Summer 1963. pp. 300–307
Hartley, Livingston. AN ATLANTIC COMMISSION OF 'WISE MEN'. (Proposal for an 'Atlantic Commission' similar to European Commission). Atlantic Community Quarterly. Vol. 2. No. 4. Winter 1964–65. pp. 557–563
Hartley, Livingston. ON THE POLITICAL INTEGRATION OF THE ATLANTIC COMMUNITY. Orbis. Vol. 6. No. 4. Winter 1963. pp. 645–655. Atlantic Community Quarterly. Vol. 1. No. 2. Summer 1963. pp. 231–242
Hartley, Livingston. ATLANTIC PARTNERSHIP – HOW? Orbis. Vol. 8. No. 1. Spring 1964. pp. 141–152. Atlantic Community Quarterly. Vol. 2. No. 2. Summer 1964. pp. 174–185
Hartley, Livingston. TOWARDS AN ATLANTIC ASSEMBLY. Atlantic Community Quarterly. Vol. 4. No. 1. Spring 1966. pp. 104–113
Hartley, Livingston. THE ATLANTIC ALLIANCE: INSTITUTIONAL DEVELOPMENTS OF THE 1970'S. Atlantic Community Quarterly. Vol. 7. No. 3. Fall 1969. pp. 321–334
von Hassel, Kai-Uwe. DETENTE THROUGH FIRMNESS. Foreign Affairs. Vol. 42. No. 2. January 1964. pp. 184–194. (See review by D. Melnikov: 'Von Hassel's Bellicose Credo' in INTERNATIONAL AFFAIRS (Moscow). 1964. No. 3. pp. 74–77)
von Hassel, Kai-Uwe. ORGANISING WESTERN DEFENCE. Foreign Affairs. Vol. 43. No. 2. April 1965. pp. 209–216
Haviland, H. Field, Jr. BUILDING A POLITICAL COMMUNITY. International Organisation. Vol. 17. No. 3. Summer 1963. pp. 733–752
Healey, Denis. END OF THE COLD WAR? STRATEGY AND

FOREIGN POLICY. Survey. No. 50. January 1964. pp. 17–22
Heath, Edward. REALISM IN BRITISH FOREIGN POLICY. Foreign
Affairs. Vol. 48. No. 1. October 1969. pp. 39–50
Heldring, J.L. ATLANTIC PARTNERSHIP: EUROPEAN UNITY. (i.e.
nuclear partnership). Survival. Vol. 7. No. 1. January/February 1965.
pp. 30–37
Herter, Christian A. ATLANTICA. (In series 'The U.S. and Europe').
Foreign Affairs. Vol. 41. No. 2. January 1963. pp. 299–309
Heusinger, Adolf Ernst. VIETNAM AND THE U.S. ROLE IN EUROPE.
(An assessment of U.S. involvement, de Gaulle's tactics and the
nuclear strategy of the West). Atlantic Community Quarterly. Vol. 3.
No. 4. Winter 1965–66. pp. 496–498
Hinterhof, Eugene. PROBLEMS ALONG NATO'S FLANKS. Orbis.
Vol. 8. No. 3. Fall 1964. pp. 607–623
Hoag, Malcolm W. NUCLEAR POLICY AND FRENCH INTRAN-
SIGENCE. Foreign Affairs. Vol. 41. No. 2. January 1963. pp. 286–298
Hoffmann, Stanley. DISCORD IN COMMUNITY: THE NORTH
ATLANTIC AREA AS A PARTIAL INTERNATIONAL SYSTEM.
International Organisation. Vol. 17. No. 3. Summer 1963. pp. 521–549
Hoffmann, Stanley. DE GAULLE, EUROPE AND THE ALLIANCE.
International Organisation. Vol. 18. No. 1. Winter 1964. pp. 1–28.
Atlantic Community Quarterly. Vol. 2. No. 2. Summer 1964.
pp. 262–275
Hogg, Quintin. BRITAIN LOOKS FORWARD. (i.e. after the Conservative
defeat of 1964). Foreign Affairs. Vol. 43. No. 3. April 1965. pp. 409–
425
Holmes, John W. FEARFUL SYMMETRY: THE DILEMMAS OF CON-
SULTATION AND CO-ORDINATION IN NATO. International
Organisation. Vol. 22. No. 4. Autumn 1968. pp. 821–840
Hooson, Emlyn. THE REFORM OF NATO. (Preliminary Report to
NATO Parliamentarians' Conference. New York. October 1965).
Atlantic Community Quarterly. Vol. 3. No. 4. Winter 1965–66
Hooson, Emlyn. NATO'S FUTURE. Survival. Vol. 8. No. 6. June 1966.
pp. 182–185. (Reprint from Atlantic Community Quarterly. Winter
1966)
Horelick, Arnold L. THE CUBAN MISSILE CRISIS: an analysis of
Soviet calculations and behaviour. World Politics. Vol. 16. No. 3.
April 1964. pp. 363–389
Huizinga, J.H. WHICH WAY EUROPE? (i.e. under President de Gaulle).
Foreign Affairs. Vol. 43. No. 3. April 1965. pp. 436–446

Humphrey, Hubert H. THE NEED FOR COMMON EFFORT. Atlantic Community Quarterly. Vol. 3. No. 4. Winter 1965–66. (Common policies re. strategy, trade, monetary system, by the Vice-President)

Hunter, Robert E. THE FUTURE OF SOVIET-AMERICAN DETENTE. The World Today. Vol. 24. No. 7. July 1968. pp. 281–290

Iklé, Fred Charles. WHEN THE FIGHTING HAS TO STOP: THE ARGUMENTS ABOUT ESCALATION. World Politics. Vol. 19. No. 4. July 1967. pp. 692–708

Ionescu, Ghita. ACTION AND REACTION IN THE SOVIET BLOC. (Prior to Czechoslovakia 1968). The World Today. Vol. 24. No. 5. May 1968. pp. 179–188

Ivanov, K. LESSONS FOR THE FUTURE: (re. Czechoslovakia 1968). International Affairs (Moscow). 1968. No. 10. pp. 3–10

Jackson, Henry M. THE DECISIVE AREA. (Excerpt from the Senate Sub-committee Report). Atlantic Community Quarterly. Vol. 4. No. 1. Spring 1966. pp. 25–36

Jackson, Senator Henry M. THE UNITED STATES AND EUROPE. Atlantic Community Quarterly. Vol. 6. No. 3. Fall 1968. pp. 343–347

Javits, Jacob K. THE UNITED STATES AND EUROPE – AFTER VIET-NAM. Atlantic Community Quarterly. Vol. 6. No. 3. Fall 1968. pp. 361–368

Johnson, Lyndon B. OUR VIEW OF NATO. (i.e. the presidential view). Atlantic Community Quarterly. Vol. 4. No. 2. Wummer 1966. pp. 156–160

Johnson, Lyndon B. LBJ AND EUROPE (speech to editorial writers). Survival. Vol. 8. No. 12. December 1966. pp. 378–379

Johnson, Lyndon B. MAKING EUROPE WHOLE: AN UNFINISHED TASK. Atlantic Community Quarterly. Vol. 4. No. 4. Winter 1966–67. pp. 487–494

Kahn, Herman and Pfaff, William. OUR ALTERNATIVES IN EUROPE. (i.e. following French withdrawal from NATO military structures). Foreign Affairs. Vol. 44. No. 4. July 1966. pp. 587–600

Kaplan, Morton A. OLD REALITIES AND NEW MYTHS. (A critique of J.W. Fulbright's 'Old Myths and New Realities'. New York: Random House 1964). World Politics. Vol. 17. No. 2. January 1965. pp. 334–367

Karjalaiven, Ahti. CONFERENCE ON EUROPEAN SECURITY. (Views of the Finnish Foreign Minister). International Affairs (Moscow). 1969. No. 9. pp. 12–13

Katerinich, V. NATO AND EUROPEAN WAR DANGER. International Affairs (Moscow). 1968. No. 9. pp. 21–27

Kennan, George F. POLYCENTRISM AND WESTERN POLICY. Foreign Affairs. Vol. 42. No. 2. January 1964. pp. 171–183. Survival. Vol. 6. No. 3. May/June 1964. pp. 98–104

Kennedy, John F. and Macmillan, Harold. THE NASSAU COMMUNIQUE, 21 DECEMBER 1962. Survival. Vol. 5. No. 2. March/April 1963. pp. 46–47

Kennedy, John F. EUROPE AND THE UNITED STATES. Atlantic Community Quarterly. Vol. 1. No. 3. Fall 1963. pp. 305–315. (The president's view)

Khrushchev, N. ON PEACE AND PEACEFUL CO-EXISTENCE. International Affairs (Moscow). 1964. No. 6. pp. 3–7

Khvostov, V. THE USSR AND EUROPEAN SECURITY. International Affairs (Moscow). 1968. No. 2. pp. 3–7

Kirk, Peter. RETHINKING NATO. The World Today. Vol. 22. No. 1. January 1966. pp. 28–31

Kissinger, Henry A. STRAINS ON THE ALLIANCE. Foreign Affairs. Vol. 41. No. 2. January 1963. pp. 261–285

Kissinger, Henry A. THE UNITED STATES AND NASSAU. Survival. Vol. 5. No. 3. May/June 1963. pp. 109–125. (See also letter by Anthony Verrier to the Editor, Survival. Vol. 5. No. 4. July/August 1963. pp. 191–192)

Kissinger, Henry A. COALITION DIPLOMACY IN A NUCLEAR AGE. Foreign Affairs. Vol. 42. No. 4. July 1964. pp. 525–545. Survival. Vol. 6. No. 5. September/October 1964. pp. 206–216. Atlantic Community Quarterly. Vol. 2. No. 3. Fall 1964. pp. 434–449

Kissinger, Henry A. WHAT ABOUT THE FUTURE? (i.e. how to move from tutelage to equality in U.S.-European relations). Atlantic Community Quarterly. Vol. 4. No. 3. Fall 1966. pp. 317–330

Kissinger, Henry A. WHAT KIND OF ATLANTIC PARTNERSHIP? Atlantic Community Quarterly. Vol. 7. No. 1. Spring 1969. pp. 18–39

Kleiman, Robert. A POLICY FOR ATLANTIC PARTNERSHIP. (i.e. following French veto of British entry to EEC). Atlantic Community Quarterly. Vol. 2. No. 2. Summer 1964. pp. 222–229

Knapp, Wilfrid. COLD WAR ORIGINS. Survey. No. 58. January 1966. pp. 153–158

Knapp, Wilfrid. THE COLD WAR REVISED. International Journal. Vol. 23. No. 3. Summer 1968. pp. 344–356

Kohn, Hans. NATIONALISM IN THE ATLANTIC COMMUNITY.

Atlantic Community Quarterly. Vol. 3. No. 3. Fall 1965. pp. 293–313

Kolkowicz, Roman. THE WARSAW PACT: ENTANGLING ALLIANCE. Survey. No. 70/71. Winter/Spring 1969. pp. 86–101

Kosygin, Alexei. SOVIET FOREIGN POLICY REVIEWED: speech to the Supreme Soviet. Autumn 1966. Survival. Vol. 8. No. 10. October 1966. pp. 320–326

Kovrig, Bennett. SPHERES OF INFLUENCE: A REASSESSMENT. Survey. No. 70/71. Winter/Spring 1969. pp. 102–120

Kressler, Diane A. GERMANY, NATO AND EUROPE. Orbis. Vol. 10. No. 1. Spring 1966. pp. 223–239

Krippendorff, Ekkehart. BEYOND THE ODER-NEISSE: A CRITIQUE OF BONN'S OSTPOLITIK. Survey. No. 61. October 1966. pp. 47–55

Kryukov, P. and Novoseltsev, Y. BUDENSOME LEGACY. (Adenauer's foreign policy). International Affairs (Moscow). 1963. No. 12. pp. 9–16

Kuzmin, E. SOVEREIGNTY AND NATIONAL SECURITY. International Affairs (Moscow). 1966. No. 12. pp. 16–20

Lange, Halvard. EUROPEAN INTEGRATION AND ATLANTIC PARTNERSHIP. (A Norwegian view). Atlantic Community Quarterly. Vol. 1. No. 4. Winter 1963–64. pp. 512–517

Lavergne, B. ANY FUTURE FOR NATO? International Affairs (Moscow). 1966. No. 5. pp. 31–34

Lemin, I. IMPAIRED ALLIANCE: THE PROBLEM OF 'SPECIAL RELATIONS' WITH U.S.A. International Affairs (Moscow). 1965. No. 5. pp. 48–55

Lemin, I. U.S.A. – BRITAIN – EUROPE. International Affairs (Moscow). 1967. No. 2. pp. 31–39

Lendvai, Paul. SOVIET HEGEMONY AND DETENTE WITH THE WEST. Survey. No. 77. Autumn 1970. pp. 75–92

Levgold, Robert. EUROPEAN SECURITY CONFERENCE. Survey. No. 76. Summer 1970. pp. 41–52

Lieber, Robert J. THE FRENCH NUCLEAR FORCE: A STRATEGIC AND POLITICAL EVALUATION. International Affairs. Vol. 42. No. 3. July 1966. pp. 421–431

Lippmann, Walter. HOW MANY DRIVERS AT THE NUCLEAR WHEEL. (An American view in the aftermath of Cuba). Atlantic Community Quarterly. Vol. 1. No. 1. March 1963. pp. 37–41. (See also a French reply: Raymond Aron: 'The American Atomic Monopoly and Europe' in Atlantic Community Quarterly. Vol. 1.

No. 1. pp. 41–45)
Lodge, John Davis. CAN NATO BE RESTORED? Orbis. Vol. 10. No. 3. Fall 1966. pp. 724–736
Luard, Evan. CONCILIATION AND DETERRENCE: A COMPARISON OF POSTWAR STRATEGIES IN THE INTERWAR AND POSTWAR PERIODS. World Politics. Vol. 19. No. 2. January 1967. pp. 167–189
Lukaszewski, Jerzy. WESTERN INTEGRATION AND THE PEOPLE'S DEMOCRACIES. Foreign Affairs. Vol. 46. No. 2. January 1968. pp. 377–387
Lucas, Joseph M.A.H. INDEPENDENCE OR INTERDEPENDENCE. International Affairs. Vol. 40. No. 1. January 1964. pp. 1–10. Atlantic Community Quarterly. Vol. 2. No. 1. Spring 1964. pp. 10–20
McQuade, Lawrence C. NATO'S NON-NUCLEAR NEEDS. International Affairs. Vol. 40. No. 1. January 1964. pp. 11–21
Mackintosh, Malcolm. SOVIET MOTIVES IN CUBA. Survival. Vol. 5. No. 1. January/February 1963. pp. 16–18
Mackintosh, Malcolm. SOVIET FOREIGN POLICY. The World Today. Vol. 24. No. 4. April 1968. pp. 145–150
Macmillan, Harold. THE JUSTIFICATION OF NASSAU. (Speech to the House of Commons, 30 January 1963). Survival. Vol. 5. No. 2. March/April 1963. pp. 48–49
Mally, Gerhard. PROPOSALS FOR INTEGRATING THE ATLANTIC COMMUNITY. Orbis. Vol. 9. No. 2. Summer 1965. pp. 378–392
Mally, Gerhard. A 'FORWARD STRATEGY' FOR ATLANTICA. (A plea for parallel moves towards European union and Atlantic cooperation). Atlantic Community Quarterly. Vol. 3. No. 3. Fall 1965. pp. 318–325
Mansfield, Mike; Dodd, Thomas J. and Javits, Jacob K. THE GREAT DEBATE ON EUROPE. (Senate debate on Mansfield Resolution to reduce U.S. Forces in Europe). Atlantic Community Quarterly. Vol. 5. No. 1. Spring 1967. pp. 12–34
Marushkin, B. KENNEDY'S EUROPEAN FRONTIERS. International Affairs (Moscow). 1963. No. 1. pp. 41–47
Matveyev, V. ANOTHER NATO MOBILISATION? International Affairs (Moscow). 1966. No. 2. pp. 52–55
Matveyev, V. WAYS OF ENSURING PEACE IN EUROPE. International Affairs (Moscow). 1966. No. 9. pp. 3–7
Matveyev, V. EUROPEAN SECURITY AND NATO. International Affairs (Moscow). 1970. No. 2/3. pp. 88–92
Maudling, Reginald. EUROPE AND THE ATLANTIC COMMUNITY.

Atlantic Community Quarterly. Vol. 4. No. 1. Spring 1966.
pp. 48–56
Maudling, Reginald. THE REAL THREAT TO THE WEST. Atlantic Community Quarterly. Vol. 5. No. 3. Fall 1967. pp. 344–347
Melnikov, D. VON HASSEL'S BELLICOSE CREDO. International Affairs (Moscow). 1964. No. 3. pp. 74–77. (See Kai-Uwe von Hassel: 'Detente through firmness' in FOREIGN AFFAIRS. Vol. 42. No. 2. January 1964. pp. 184–194)
Melnikov, D. EUROPEAN FRONTIERS ARE FINAL. International Affairs (Moscow). 1966. No. 9. pp. 8–13
Mendl, Wolf. THE BACKGROUND OF FRENCH NUCLEAR POLICY. International Affairs. Vol. 41. No. 1. January 1965. pp. 22–36
Mendl, Wolf. FRENCH POLICY IN EUROPE. The World Today. Vol. 23. No. 1. January 1967. pp. 23–29
Mendl, Wolf. PERSPECTIVES OF CONTEMPORARY FRENCH DEFENCE POLICY. The World Today. Vol. 24. No. 2. February 1968. pp. 50–58 ·
Mendl, Wolf. FRENCH DEFENCE POLICY. Survival. Vol. 10. No. 4. April 1968. pp. 115–116
Merchant, Livingston T. EVOLVING UNITED STATES RELATIONS WITH THE ATLANTIC COMMUNITY. International Organisation. Vol. 17. No. 3. Summer 1963. pp. 610–627
Merchant, Livingston T. NORTH AMERICA AND THE ATLANTIC COMMUNITY. Atlantic Community Quarterly. Vol. 2. No. 4. Winter 1964–65. pp. 522–527. (Disarray of NATO caused by disproportion of power, esp. nuclear; proposes limited political union *via* a real Atlantic Community)
Mikhailov, V. BONN BETWEEN PAST AND PRESENT. International Affairs (Moscow). 1966. No. 10. pp. 20–26
Mikhailov, V. BONN: THE OLD ROAD. International Affairs (Moscow). 1967. No. 8. pp. 38–47
Mikoyan, Sergo. NATO, THE SOVIET UNION AND EUROPEAN SECURITY. (A Soviet view). Atlantic Community Quarterly. Vol. 7. No. 3. Fall 1969. pp. 342–351
Miller, Lynn H. THE CONTEMPORARY SIGNIFICANCE OF THE DOCTRINE OF THE JUST WAR. World Politics. Vol. 16. No. 2. January 1964. pp. 254–286
Modrzhinskaya, Y. QUIET ANTI-COMMUNISM. (A Soviet critique of Western view on detente). Survival. Vol. 10. No. 11. November 1967. pp. 363–370. (Reprint from INTERNATIONAL AFFAIRS

(Moscow). August 1967)
Montias, John Michael. COMMUNIST RULE IN EASTERN EUROPE.
Foreign Affairs. Vol. 43. No. 2. April 1965. pp. 331–348
Morgan, Carlyle. NATO: A NEW DESIRE TO EXIST. (i.e. after
Czechoslovakia 1968). Atlantic Community Quarterly. Vol. 7.
No. 1. Spring 1969. pp. 53–59
Moynihan, Daniel P. THE NATO COMMITTEE ON CHALLENGES
OF MODERN SOCIETY. Atlantic Community Quarterly. Vol. 7.
No. 4. Winter 1969–70. pp. 530–538
Mulley, Frederick W. NATO'S NUCLEAR PROBLEMS: CONTROL
OR CONSULTATION. Orbis. Vol. 8. No. 1. Spring 1964. pp. 21–
35. Atlantic Community Quarterly. Vol. 2. No. 3. Fall 1964.
pp. 450–468. Survival. Vol. 7. No. 1. January/February 1965.
pp. 22–29
Munk, Frank. THE ATLANTIC COMMUNITY AND WORLD
COMMUNITY. Atlantic Community Quarterly. Vol. 2. No. 1.
Spring 1964. pp. 53–61
Murarka, Dev. RUSSIAN REALPOLITIK. Survival. Vol. 8. No. 10.
October 1966. pp. 318–319
NATO Parliamentarians' Conference. October 1965. THE REFORM
OF NATO – THE CONFERENCE DEBATE. Atlantic Community
Quarterly. Vol. 3. No. 4. Winter 1965–66. pp. 464–478
Nixon, Richard. THE TIME TO SAVE NATO. (Broadcast, 13 October
1968 – when Republican candidate). Atlantic Community Quarterly.
Vol. 6. No. 4. Winter 1968–69. pp. 479–485
Nixon, Richard. FACING THE TRUTH OF OUR TIMES. (NATO –
PAST AND FUTURE). Atlantic Community Quarterly. Vol. 7.
No. 2. Summer 1969. pp. 203–209
Norstad, Lauris. THE FUTURE OF THE ATLANTIC COMMUNITY.
International Organisation. Vol. 17. No. 3. Summer 1963. pp. 804–
812. Atlantic Community Quarterly. Vol. 1. No. 3. Fall 1963.
pp. 346–354. (The view of SACEUR)
Norstad, Lauris. EUROPEAN UNIFICATION AND ATLANTIC
UNITY. Atlantic Community Quarterly. Vol. 2. No. 2. Summer
1964. pp. 186–191
Norstad, Lauris. THE CONTROL OF NUCLEAR WEAPONS.
Survival. Vol. 6. No. 6. November/December 1964. pp. 278–279.
(Reprint from U.S. News and World Report, 5 October 1964)
Norstad, Lauris. A PROBLEM OF THE ALLIANCE. (Norstad's
proposals for a NATO nuclear force, without an owner veto).

Atlantic Community Quarterly. Vol. 4. No. 1. Spring 1966. pp. 57–65.

Norstad, Lauris. DEFENDING EUROPE WITHOUT FRANCE. Atlantic Community Quarterly. Vol. 4. No. 2. Summer 1966. pp. 178–189

North Atlantic Council. COMMUNIQUE AND ANNEXE (THE HARMEL REPORT). December 1967. Survival. Vol. 10. No. 2. February 1968. pp. 62–64

Novoseltsev, Y. EUROPEAN SECURITY AND WORLD PEACE. International Affairs (Moscow). 1965. No. 2. pp. 3–8

Olson, William C. PUBLIC OPINION, THE ATLANTIC COMMUNITY AND EUROPEAN INTEGRATION. Atlantic Community Quarterly. Vol. 6. No. 3. Fall 1968

Orlik, I. and Razmerov, V. EUROPEAN SECURITY AND RELATIONS BETWEEN THE TWO SYSTEMS. International Affairs (Moscow). 1967. No. 5. pp. 3–8

Osgood, Robert E. KINDS OF COUNTERFORCE. Survival. Vol. 5. No. 1. January/February 1963. pp. 23–26

Osipov, V. PRECARIOUS BALANCE IN WESTERN EUROPE. International Affairs (Moscow). 1968. No. 9. pp. 44–49

Osipov, V. NATO – 20 YEARS OF TENSION AND HOSTILITY. International Affairs (Moscow). 1969. No. 4. pp. 59–61

Owen, Henry. NATO STRATEGY: WHAT IS PAST IS PROLOGUE. Foreign Affairs. Vol. 43. No. 4. July 1965. pp. 682–690

Patijn, C.L. THE FUTURE OF THE ATLANTIC ALLIANCE. (A Dutch view). Atlantic Community Quarterly. Vol. 6. No. 4. Winter 1968–69. pp. 512–520

Pavlov, O. PROLETARIAN INTERNATIONALISM AND DEFENCE OF SOCIALIST GAINS. International Affairs (Moscow). 1968. No. 10. pp. 11–16

Perlo, Victor. ALLIANCE OF MILITARISTS AND ARMS MANUFACTURERS. International Affairs (Moscow). 1969. No. 9. pp. 19–25

Pfaltzgraff, Robert L., Jr. ALTERNATIVE DESIGNS FOR THE ATLANTIC ALLIANCE. Orbis. Vol. 9. No. 2. Summer 1965. pp. 358–377

Pierre, Andrew J. IMPLICATIONS OF THE WESTERN RESPONSE (to Czechoslovakia 1968). Atlantic Community Quarterly. Vol. 7. No. 1. Spring 1969. pp. 59–76

Quaroni, Pietro. 'OPEN DOOR TO THE EAST' SWINGS SHUT. Atlantic Community Quarterly. Vol. 6. No. 4. Winter 1968–69.

pp. 508–512. (A sombre Italian view of detente)
Ranger, Robert. NATO'S REACTION TO CZECHOSLOVAKIA: THE STRATEGY OF AMBIGUOUS RESPONSE. The World Today. Vol. 25. January 1969. pp. 19–26
Reid, Escott. THE BIRTH OF THE NORTH ATLANTIC ALLIANCE. International Journal. Vol. 22. No. 3. Summer 1967. pp. 426–440
von Riekhoff, Harald. THE CHANGING FUNCTION OF NATO. International Journal. Vol. 21. No. 2. Spring 1966. pp. 157–172
von Riekhoff, Harald. NATO WITHOUT FRANCE. International Journal. Vol. 23. No. 2. Spring 1968. pp. 281–286
Rockefeller, Nelson A. FEDERAL UNION OF THE FREE. Atlantic Community Quarterly. Vol. 2. No. 4. Winter 1964–65. pp. 564–570. (A plea for a federal political structure for the N.A. area as the first step towards an eventual 'Union of the Free')
de Rose, François. ATLANTIC RELATIONSHIPS AND NUCLEAR PROBLEMS (A French view). Foreign Affairs. Vol. 41. No. 3. April 1963. pp. 479–490. Atlantic Community Quarterly. Vol. 1. No. 2. Summer 1963. pp. 187–198. Survival. Vol. 5. No. 4. July/August 1963. pp. 156–161
Rostow, Eugene V. THE ATLANTIC DEBATE – FISSION OR FUSION. Survival. Vol. 5. No. 4. July/August 1963. pp. 166–171
Rostow, Eugene V. THE ROAD BEFORE US. Atlantic Community Quarterly. Vol. 5. No. 2. Summer 1967. pp. 161–173. (A plea for interdependence as opposed to isolationism, by the Under-Secretary of State)
Rostow, Eugene V. PROSPECTS FOR THE ALLIANCE. Atlantic Community Quarterly. Vol. 3. No. 1. Spring 1965. pp. 34–42. (The case for institutional arrangements to promote alliance solidarity)
Rostow, Eugene V. THE NEXT STAGE OF THE ALLIANCE. Atlantic Community Quarterly. Vol. 5. No. 4. Winter 1967–68. pp. 475–485. (The view of the then Under-Secretary of State)
Rostow, Eugene V. EUROPE AND THE UNITED STATES – THE PARTNERSHIP OF NECESSITY. Atlantic Community Quarterly. Vol. 6. No. 2. Summer 1968. pp. 216–228
Rostow, Eugene V. THE FUTURE OF THE ATLANTIC COMMUNITY. Atlantic Community Quarterly. Vol. 7. No. 4. Winter 1969–70. pp. 467–480
Rothstein, Robert L. NEW PERSPECTIVES ON NATO. International Organisation. Vol. 24. No. 3. Summer 1970. pp. 566–577. (Review article on: Francis A. Beer: 'Integration and Disintegration in NATO:

processes of Alliance cohesion and prospects for Atlantic Community'. Columbus: Ohio State University Press. 1969; William T.R. Fox and Annette Baker Fox: 'NATO and the range of American Choice'. New York: Columbia University Press. 1967)

Rusk, Dean. DON'T DISMANTLE THE DAM. Atlantic Community Quarterly. Vol. 4. No. 2. Summer 1966. pp. 166–172. (Secretary of State giving U.S. views re. NATO and Vietnam to a French audience)

Sathyamurthy, T.V. FROM CONTAINMENT TO INTERDEPENDENCE. World Politics. Vol. 20. No. 1. October 1967. pp. 142–177

Schaltzel, J. Robert. THE NUCLEAR PROBLEM AND ATLANTIC INTERDEPENDENCE. (An American view). Atlantic Community Quarterly. Vol. 1. No. 4. Winter 1963–64. pp. 561–569

Schaltzel, J. Robert. THE NECESSARY PARTNERSHIP (i.e. the Atlantic partnership). Foreign Affairs. Vol. 44. No. 3. April 1966. pp. 417–433

Schlesinger, Arthur, Jr. END OF THE COLD WAR? CO-EXISTENCE VERSUS PEACE. Survey. No. 50. January 1964. pp. 10–16

Schlesinger, Arthur. ORIGINS OF THE COLD WAR. Foreign Affairs. Vol. 46. No. 1. October 1967. pp. 22–52

Schmidt, Adolph W. THE ATLANTIC COMMUNITY. (A survey of American opinion). Atlantic Community Quarterly. Vol. 1. No. 2. Summer 1963. pp. 219–230

Schmidt, Helmut. THE BREZHNEV DOCTRINE. Survival. Vol. 11. No. 10. October 1969. pp. 307–313

Segni, Antonio. A GOAL OF BASIC IMPORTANCE. Atlantic Community Quarterly. Vol. 2. No. 1. Spring 1964. pp. 5–9. (Italian president's view of the Atlantic Community, stressing Art. II of North Atlantic Treaty)

Seton-Watson, Hugh. THE COLD WAR IN RETROSPECT – THE KHRUSHCHEV ERA. Survey. No. 58. January 1966. pp. 187–195

Shakhov, V. HOW TO SOLVE EUROPE'S VITAL PROBLEMS. International Affairs (Moscow). 1970. No. 1. pp. 11–15

Sherman, Michael. GUARANTEES AND NUCLEAR SPREAD. International Journal. Vol. 21. No. 4. Autumn 1966. pp. 484–490

Shub, Anatole. LESSONS OF CZECHOSLOVAKIA. Foreign Affairs. Vol. 47. No. 2. January 1969. pp. 266–280

Shulman, Marshall D. 'EUROPE' VERSUS 'DETENTE'. Foreign Affairs. Vol. 45. No. 3. April 1967. pp. 389–402

Shulman, Marshall D. A EUROPEAN SECURITY CONFERENCE. Survival. Vol. 11. No. 12. December 1969. pp. 373–381

Shvedkov, Y. WEST EUROPEAN POLITICAL FORCES AND EUROPEAN SECURITY. International Affairs (Moscow). 1968. No. 3. pp. 8–13

Singer, J. David. FROM DETERRENCE TO DISARMAMENT. International Journal. Vol. 16. No. 4. Autumn 1961. pp. 307–326

Slobodenko, A. NATO STRATEGY TODAY. International Affairs (Moscow). 1964. No. 6. pp. 41–45

Slobodenko, A. FRANCO-AMERICAN STRATEGY DISPUTE. International Affairs (Moscow). 1965. No. 1. pp. 37–41

Slobodenko, A. NATO 'REORGANISES'. International Affairs (Moscow). 1968. No. 2. pp. 36–41

Sommer, Theo. FOR AN ATLANTIC FUTURE. Foreign Affairs. Vol. 43. No. 1. October 1964. pp. 112–125. (A European view of the 'current' future)

Sommer, Theo. BONN CHANGES COURSE. Foreign Affairs. Vol. 45. No. 3. April 1967. pp. 477–491. (i.e. foreign policy after the Grand Coalition of 1966)

Sovetov, A. 'PEACE STRATEGY' AND THE 'ATLANTIC COMMUNITY'. International Affairs (Moscow). 1963. No. 9. pp. 24–30

Sovetov, A. ROAD TO A DETENTE: POSSIBILITY AND REALITY. International Affairs (Moscow). 1964. No. 1. pp. 3–11

Spaak, Paul-Henri. HOLD FAST. Foreign Affairs. Vol. 41. No. 4. July 1963. pp. 611–620. (i.e. the Western alliance in the face of French rejection of British membership of EEC and France's nuclear policy)

Spaak, Paul-Henri. A NEW EFFORT TO BUILD EUROPE. Foreign Affairs. Vol. 43. No. 2. January 1965. pp. 199–208

Spaak, Paul-Henri. CHAOS IN EUROPE. Atlantic Community Quarterly. Vol. 4. No. 2. Summer 1966. pp. 211–215. (An attack on President de Gaulle's policy re. NATO)

Spaak, Paul-Henri. THE ALLIANCE MUST GO ON. Atlantic Community Quarterly. Vol. 5. No. 2. Summer 1967. pp. 199–209. (Analysis of the current state and the prospects of the alliance)

Spaak, Paul-Henri. THE INDISPENSABLE ALLIANCE. (i.e. a survey from 1949 to 1967). Atlantic Community Quarterly. Vol. 5. No. 4. Winter 1967–68. pp. 497–504

Spaak, Paul-Henri. THE FUNDAMENTAL REALITY. (*Tour d'horizon* after Czechoslovakia 1968). Atlantic Community Quarterly. Vol. 6. No. 4. Winter 1968–69. pp. 485–493

Spinelli, Altiero. EUROPE AND THE NUCLEAR MONOPOLY. Atlantic Community Quarterly. Vol. 2. No. 4. Winter 1964–65. pp. 588–599. (An Italian plea for the 'Atlanticisation' of the American nuclear

force)
Spinelli, Altiero. SOME ASPECTS OF NUCLEAR INTERDEPENDENCE. Atlantic Community Quarterly. Vol. 3. No. 3. Fall 1965. pp. 335–339. (An Italian contribution to creating a supranational apparatus for an alliance nuclear policy)
de Staercke, André. 'AS TACITUS SAID'. (NATO: PAST AND FUTURE) Atlantic Community Quarterly. Vol. 7. No. 2. Summer 1969. pp. 212–216
Stanley, Timothy W. DECENTRALISING NUCLEAR CONTROL IN NATO. Orbis. Vol. 7. No. 1. Spring 1963
Stanley, Timothy W. PATTERNS FOR THE FUTURE. Atlantic Community Quarterly. Vol. 3. No. 2. Summer 1965. pp. 188–196. (Three arguments on Europe's need of NATO and OECD)
Stanley, Timothy W. and Whitt, Darnell M. DETENTE IN THE 1970'S. Atlantic Community Quarterly. Vol. 8. No. 3. Fall 1970. pp. 313–325
Starobin, J.R. COMMUNISM IN WESTERN EUROPE. Foreign Affairs. Vol. 44. No. 1. October 1965. pp. 62–77
Starobin, J.R. THE ORIGINS OF THE COLD WAR: THE COMMUNIST DIMENSION. Foreign Affairs. Vol. 47. No. 4. July 1969. pp. 681–696
Stehlin, Paul. NECESSITY AND POSSIBILITY WITHIN THE ALLIANCE. Atlantic Community Quarterly. Vol. 5. No. 4. Winter 1967–68. pp. 485–497. (Political issues, by a SHAPE general)
Stikker, Dirk U. NATO – THE SHIFTING WESTERN ALLIANCE. Atlantic Community Quarterly. Vol. 3. No. 1. Spring 1965. pp. 7–17. (A critique of French, British and U.S. practice in NATO by the Secretary General)
Stikker, Dirk U. NATIONALISM THREATENS ATLANTIC CO-OPERATION. Atlantic Community Quarterly. Vol. 6. No. 2. Summer 1968. pp. 228–231
Stikker, Dirk U. EFFECT OF POLITICAL FACTIONS ON THE FUTURE STRENGTH OF NATO. Atlantic Community Quarterly. Vol. 6. No. 3. Fall 1968. pp. 331–343
Strauss, Franz Josef. AN ALLIANCE OF CONTINENTS. International Affairs. Vol. 41. No. 2. April 1965. pp. 191–203
Strausz-Hupé, Robert. THE REAL COMMUNIST THREAT. International Affairs. Vol. 41. No. 4. October 1965. pp. 611–623
Strausz-Hupé, Robert. THE WORLD WITHOUT NATO. Orbis. Vol. 10. No. 1. Spring 1966. pp. 79–90. Atlantic Community Quarterly. Vol. 4. No. 2. Summer 1966. pp. 189–197. (The case for the view

that NATO contributes to general security)
Syed, Anwar. WALTER LIPPMANN ON EUROPE AND THE ATLANTIC COMMUNITY. Orbis. Vol. 7. No. 2. Summer 1963. pp. 308–335
Tatu, Michel. EUROPEAN SECURITY CONFERENCE: IT MIGHT ACTUALLY TAKE PLACE (A French view). Atlantic Community Quarterly. Vol. 8. No. 3. Fall 1970. pp. 309–313
Teplensky, B. SOME ASPECTS OF U.S. GLOBAL STRATEGY. International Affairs (Moscow). 1970. No. 5. pp. 70–75
Tunkin, G. A NON-AGGRESSION PACT: AN IMPORTANT STEP TOWARDS DETENTE. International Affairs (Moscow). 1963. No. 10. pp. 9–14
U.S. Department of State. THE U.S. REPLY TO THE FRENCH AIDE-MEMOIRE OF MARCH 1966 ON THE REMOVAL OF NATO FACILITIES IN FRANCE. April 1966. Survival. Vol. 8. No. 6. June 1966. pp. 186–187
Various. THE SPECTRUM OF IMPOTENCE: STATEMENTS ON THE CZECHOSLOVAKIA CRISIS 1968. Survival. Vol. 10. No. 10. pp. 314–315. October 1968.
Various. CZECHOSLOVAKIA (1968). Survival. Vol. 10. No. 11. pp. 350–377. November 1968.
Vasilyev, V. SOME FACTORS IN INTERNATIONAL LIFE TODAY. (inc. NATO nuclear strategy). International Affairs (Moscow). 1970. No. 5. pp. 55–61
Vidyasova, L. NATO ON THE EVE OF 1969. International Affairs (Moscow). 1968. No. 10. pp. 17–24
Warsaw Pact. DECLARATION ON STRENGTHENING PEACE AND SECURITY IN EUROPE. Bucharest, July 1966. Survival. Vo. 8. No. 9. September 1966. pp. 289–293
Warsaw Pact. THE KARLOVY VARY CONFERENCE. (On European Security). April 1967. Official Statement. Survival. Vol. 9. No. 7. July 1967. pp. 208–213
Warsaw Pact. CALL FOR A EUROPEAN CONFERENCE, March 1969. Survival. Vol. 11. No. 5. May 1969. pp. 159–161
Warsaw Pact. DECLARATION OF MINISTERS OF FOREIGN AFFAIRS OF WARSAW PACT, Prague, October 1969. Survival. Vol. 11. No. 12. December 1969. pp. 394–395
Wilcox, Francis O. THE ATLANTIC COMMUNITY AND THE UNITED NATIONS. International Organisation. Vol. 17. No. 3. Summer 1963. pp. 683–708

Windsor, Philip. RECENT DEVELOPMENTS IN NATO. The World
Today. Vol. 22. No. 6. June 1966. pp. 227–234
Windsor, Philip. NATO AND EUROPEAN DETENTE. The World
Today. Vol. 23. No. 9. September 1967. pp. 361–369
Windsor, Philip. NATO CONFRONTS ITS FUTURE. The World Today.
Vol. 24. No. 3. March 1968. pp. 121–126
Windsor, Philip. THE BOUNDARIES OF DETENTE. The World Today.
Vol. 25. No. 6. June 1969. pp. 255–264
Wolfe, Thomas W. THE WARSAW PACT IN EVOLUTION. Survival.
Vol. 8. No. 7. July 1966. pp. 217–221. (Reprint from THE WORLD
TODAY. May 1966)
Worsthorne, Peregrine. TRUST AMERICA MORE. (REFLECTIONS
ON THE SKYBOLT CANCELLATION). Survival. Vol. 5. No. 2.
March/April 1963. pp. 52–53. (Reprint from THE SUNDAY
TELEGRAPH. 6 January 1963)
Yarmolinsky, Adam. THE ATLANTIC ALLIANCE. Survival. Vol. 11.
No. 2. February 1969. pp. 57–62. (Reprint from INTERPLAY.
December 1968)
Yefinov, D. A PEACE TREATY AND EUROPEAN SECURITY. International Affairs (Moscow). 1963. No. 3. pp. 3–8
Yuryev, N. A DANGEROUS ANACHRONISM. (i.e. NATO). International Affairs (Moscow). 1968. No. 1. pp. 34–37
Yuryev, N. EUROPEAN SECURITY: A DICTATE OF OUR TIMES.
International Affairs (Moscow). 1970. No. 8. pp. 3–7
Zappo, Ciro Elliott. NUCLEAR TECHNOLOGY, MULTIPOLARITY
AND INTERNATIONAL STABILITY. World Politics. Vol. 18.
No. 4. July 1966. pp. 579–606
Zavyalov, L. WHO FORMULATES POLICY IN AMERICA TODAY?
(i.e. a Soviet view of 'the military-political complex'). International
Affairs (Moscow). 1970. No. 5. pp. 48–54
Zhukov, Y. THE PROBLEMS OF EUROPEAN PEACE AND
SECURITY. International Affairs (Moscow). 1965. No. 6. pp. 3–9
Zhukov, Y. NATO: WHAT NOW? (A 20th anniversary article). International Affairs (Moscow). 1969. No. 7. pp. 84–89

Military and Strategic Aspects

Ailleret, General C. THE STRATEGIC THEORY OF 'FLEXIBLE
RESPONSE'. Atlantic Community Quarterly. Vol. 2. No. 3. Fall

1964. pp. 413–428
Ailleret, General C. FLEXIBLE RESPONSE: A FRENCH VIEW. Survival. Vol. 6. No. 6. November/December 1964. pp. 258–265. (Trans. from REVUE DE DEFENSE NATIONALE. August/September 1964)
Ailleret, General C. THE CHARACTER OF STRATEGY. Survival. Vol. 7. No. 3. May/June 1965. pp. 109–117. (Trans. from REVUE DE DEFENSE NATIONALE. February 1965)
Ailleret, General C. FRENCH STRATEGY – DIRECTED DEFENCE. Survival. Vol. 10. No. 2. February 1968. pp. 38–43. (Trans. from REVUE DE DEFENSE NATIONALE. December 1967)
Amme, Carl H., Jr. ARMS CONTROL CONCEPTS AND THE MILITARY BALANCE IN EUROPE. Orbis. Vol. 8. No. 4. Winter 1965. pp. 832–853
Anon. FALLEX 62. Survival. Vol. 5. No. 1. January/February 1963. pp. 19–22. (Trans. from DER SPIEGEL. 10 October 1962)
Anon. THE FRENCH ARMY: YESTERDAY AND TOMORROW. Survival. Vol. 5. No. 2. March/April 1963. pp. 64–70
Anon. THE FRENCH ARMY. Survival. Vol. 6. No. 2. March/April 1964. pp. 67–68. (Reprint from THE FINANCIAL TIMES. 17 December 1965)
Anon. WESTERN EUROPE'S DEFENCE. (The Economist. 10 February 1968). Survival. Vol. 10. No. 4. April 1968. pp. 115–117. (See also Alain Enthoven; letter to the Editor, Survival. Vol. 10. No. 9. September 1968. p. 308)
Anon. NATO STRATEGY – SOVIET VIEW. (Trans. from RED STAR). Survival. Vol. 10. No. 8. August 1968. pp. 256–259
Baldwin, Hanson. SOVIET SUBMARINES. Survival. Vol. 7. No. 1. January/February 1965. pp. 41–45
Beaufre, André. THE SHARING OF NUCLEAR RESPONSIBILITIES – A PROBLEM IN NEED OF SOLUTION. International Affairs. Vol. 41. No. 3. July 1965. pp. 411–419
Beglov, S. THE METARMORPHOSES OF LABOUR'S NUCLEAR STRATEGY. International Affairs (Moscow). 1965. No. 7. pp. 57–62
Berry, John A. FORCE DE FRAPPE. Atlantic Community Quarterly. Vol. 5. No. 4. Winter 1967–68. pp. 569–278. (An American assessment of hazards and values of French nuclear force)
Biryuzov, Marshal S. TRAINING THE SOVIET FORCES. Survival. Vol. 6. No. 4. July/August 1964. pp. 188–192
Brodie, Bernard. CONVENTIONAL CAPABILITIES IN EUROPE. Survival. Vol. 5. No. 4. July/August 1963. pp. 148–155. (Reprint

from THE REPORTER. 23 May 1963)

Brodie, Bernard. THE McNAMARA PHENOMENON. World Politics. Vol. 7. No. 4. July 1965. pp. 672–686

Brown, Harold. PLANNING OUR MILITARY FORCES. (i.e. U.S. forces). Foreign Affairs. Vol. 45. No. 2. January 1967. pp. 277–290

Brown, Neville. TOWARDS THE SUPER-POWER DEADLOCK. (A survey of the development of deterrent forces). The World Today. Vol. 22. No. 9. September 1966. pp. 366–374

Brzezinski, Zbigniev. MOSCOW AND THE M.L,F.: HOSTILITY AND AMBIVALENCE. Foreign Affairs. Vol. 43. No. 1. October 1964. pp. 126–134

Buchan, Alastair. THE MULTILATERAL FORCE – A STUDY IN ALLIANCE POLITICS. International Affairs. Vol. 40. No. 4. October 1964. pp. 619–637

Bull, Hedley. LIMITED AND NUCLEAR WAR. Survival. Vol. 5. No. 2. March/April 1963. pp. 54–57

Bull, Hedley. STRATEGIC STUDIES AND ITS CRITICS. World Politics. Vol. 20. No. 4. July 1968. pp. 593–606

Bundy, McGeorge. TO CAP THE VOLCANO. (i.e. A.B.M. and SALT). Foreign Affairs. Vol. 48. No. 1. October 1969. pp. 1–20

Cabanier, Admiral. FRENCH POLARIS. Survival. Vol. 6. No. 2. March/April 1964. pp. 64–66

Carey, Roger. BRITISH THINKING ON TACTICAL NUCLEAR DETERRENCE IN EUROPE. The World Today. Vol. 25. No. 4. April 1969. pp. 172–177

de Carmoy, Guy. FORCE DE FRAPPE: A TRIPLE DEBATE. Atlantic Community Quarterly. Vol. 2. No. 2. Summer 1964. pp. 278–284. (A French survey of the atomic debate and its consequences: the McNamara Doctrine, the French deterrent and the future of the alliance)

Chuikov, Marshal. SOVIET LAND FORCES IN NUCLEAR WAR. Survival. Vol. 6. No. 2. March/April 1964. pp. 86–89. (Trans. from IZVESTIYA. 21 December 1963)

Chalfont, Alun. THE BRITISH ARMY IN GERMANY. Survival. Vol. 6. No. 1. January/February 1964. pp. 37–38. (Reprint from THE TIMES. 17 October 1963)

Coffey, J.I. A NATO NUCLEAR DETERRENT? Orbis. Vol. 8. No. 3. Summer 1965. pp. 584–594

Cottrell, Alvin J. SOVIET VIEWS OF U.S. OVERSEAS BASES. Orbis. Vol. 7. No. 1. Spring 1963. pp. 77–95

Dawson, Raymond H. and Nicholson, George E., Jr. NATO AND THE SHAPE TECHNICAL CENTER. International Organisation. Vol. 21. No. 3. Summer 1967. pp. 565–591

Dobias, F. and Magler, O. THEORY AND PRACTICE OF WESTERN MILITARY INTEGRATION. International Affairs (Moscow). 1964. No. 12. pp. 31–36

Dougherty, James E. ZONAL ARMS LIMITATION IN EUROPE. Orbis. Vol. 7. No. 3. Fall 1963. pp. 478–517

Dubrovia, V. THE ARMS RACE IN THE NATO COUNTRIES. International Affairs (Moscow). 1963. No. 7. pp. 71–77

Edmonds, Martin and Skitt, John. CURRENT SOVIET MARITIME STRATEGY AND NATO. International Affairs. Vol. 45. No. 1. January 1969. pp. 28–43

Emmet, Christopher. THE U.S. PLAN FOR A NATO NUCLEAR DETERRENT. Orbis. Vol. 7. No. 2. Summer 1963. pp. 265–277

Enthoven, Alain C. AMERICAN DETERRENT POLICY. Survival. Vol. 5. No. 3. May/June 1963. pp. 94–101

Enthoven, Alain C. and Smith, K. Wayne. WHAT FORCES FOR NATO? AND FROM WHOM? Foreign Affairs. Vol. 48. No. 1. October 1969. pp. 80–96

Erickson, John. THE 'MILITARY FACTOR' IN SOVIET POLICY. International Affairs. Vol. 39. No. 2. April 1963. pp. 214–216

Erickson, John. DETENTE, DETERRENCE AND 'MILITARY SUPERIORITY': A SOVIET DILEMMA. The World Today. Vol. 21. No. 8. August 1965. pp. 337–345

Erler, Fritz. PARTNERS IN STRATEGY. (A German contribution to the nuclear debate). Atlantic Community Quarterly. Vol. 2. No. 2. Summer 1964. pp. 292–302

Fourquet, General M. FRENCH STRATEGIC CONCEPTS: THE ROLE OF THE FORCES. (Address at the Institut des Hautes Etudes de Défense Nationale. March 1969). Survival. Vol. 11. No. 7. July 1969. pp. 206–211

Gallois, General Pierre M. U.S. STRATEGY AND THE DEFENCE OF EUROPE. Orbis. Vol. 7. No. 2. Summer 1963. pp. 226–249

Gallois, Pierre M. THE RAISON D'ETRE OF FRENCH DEFENCE POLICY. International Affairs. Vol. 39. No. 4. October 1963. pp. 497–510. Atlantic Community Quarterly. Vol. 1. No. 4. Winter 1963–64. pp. 541–555. (A notable contribution to French nuclear strategic thought). (See also, for a critique of above, Theo Sommer: 'How many fingers on how many triggers?'. ATLANTIC COMMUNITY

QUARTERLY. Vol. 1. No. 4. Winter 1963–64. pp. 556–560)
Gasteyger, Curt. MODERN WARFARE AND SOVIET STRATEGY. Survey. No. 57. October 1965. pp. 46–59
Gerasimov, G. THE FIRST STRIKE THEORY. International Affairs (Moscow). 1965. No. 3. pp. 39–45
Gilpatric, Roswell L. OUR DEFENCE NEEDS: THE LONG VIEW. Foreign Affairs. Vol. 42. No. 3. April 1964. pp. 366–378. Survival. Vol. 6. No. 3. May/June 1964. pp. 129–135
Goldberg, Alfred. THE ATOMIC ORIGINS OF THE BRITISH NUCLEAR DETERRENT. International Affairs. Vol. 40. No. 3. July 1964. pp. 409–429
Goldberg, Alfred. THE MILITARY ORIGINS OF THE BRITISH NUCLEAR DETERRENT. International Affairs. Vol. 40. No. 4. October 1964. pp. 600–619
Goldmann, Kjell. STRATEGIC DOCTRINES AND THE FUTURE OF NATO: SOME REFLECTIONS. Co-operation and Conflict. Vol. 1. No. 1. 1966. pp. 1–10
Goodman, Elliot B. FIVE NUCLEAR OPTIONS FOR THE WEST. Atlantic Community Quarterly. Vol. 2. No. 4. Winter 1964–65. pp. 571–587
Goodman, Elliot R. THE DUYNSTEE PLAN. (i.e. proposals from Western European Union re. nuclear sharing, MLF, ANF). Atlantic Community Quarterly. Vol. 3. No. 3. Fall 1965. pp. 340–346
Gordon Walker, Patrick. VOICES IN OPPOSITION – TO THE MLF. Survival. Vol. 6. No. 1. January/February 1964. pp. 24–25
Gott, Richard. THE EVOLUTION OF THE INDEPENDENT BRITISH DETERRENT. International Affairs. Vol. 39. No. 2. April 1963. pp. 238–252
Grosser, Alfred. FRENCH STRATEGY – DOUBTS ABOUT DEFENCE. Survival. Vol. 10. No. 2. February 1965. pp. 43–44
Hackett, General Sir John. LETTER TO 'THE TIMES'. 6 FEBRUARY 1968. (A plea for 'peace-keeping by military stabilisation' not unilateral force reductions). Atlantic Community Quarterly. Vol. 6. No. 2. Summer 1968. pp. 291–293
Haroche, C. AMERICAN BASES IN EUROPE. International Affairs (Moscow). 1966. No. 7. pp. 32–38
Hartley, Anthony. THE BRITISH BOMB. Survival. Vol. 6. No. 4. July/August 1964. pp. 170–181. (Reprint from ENCOUNTER. May 1964)
Healey, Denis. BRITAIN'S DEFENCE REVIEW: Press briefing by

Secretary of State for Defence, Denis Healey, 4 August 1965. Survival. Vol. 7. No. 4. July 1965. pp. 229–231

Healey, Denis. ON EUROPEAN DEFENCE. (Address to the 6th International Wehrkunde Meeting, Munich, February 1969). Survival. Vol. 11. No. 4. April 1969. pp. 110–115

Heymont, Irving. THE NATO NUCLEAR BILATERAL FORCES. Orbis. Vol. 9. No. 4. Winter 1966. pp. 1025–1041

Hill, R.J. FRENCH STRATEGY AFTER DE GAULLE. International Journal. Vol. 23. No. 2. Spring 1968. pp. 244–253

Hoag, Malcolm W. RATIONALIZING NATO STRATEGY. World Politics. Vol. 17. No. 1. October 1964. pp. 121–142

Hoffman, Fred S. NATO'S MOBILE FORCES. Atlantic Community Quarterly. Vol. 4. No. 2. Summer 1966. pp. 242–248

Holifield, Chet. NUCLEAR CONTROL IN NATO. (A plan for a larger German voice in NATO nuclear strategy). Atlantic Community Quarterly. Vol. 3. No. 4. Winter 1965–66. pp. 496–498

Houn, Franklin W. NUCLEAR DETERRENCE: THE SOVIET POSITION. Orbis. Vol. 8. No. 4. Winter 1965. pp. 922–936

Johnson, Christopher. FRANCE'S DETERRENT. Survival. Vol. 5. No. 2. March/April 1964. pp. 60–62. (Reprint from THE FINANCIAL TIMES. 31 January 1963)

Kaysen, Carl. KEEPING THE STRATEGIC BALANCE. Foreign Affairs. Vol. 46. No. 4. July 1968. pp. 665–675. Survival. Vol. 10. No. 9. pp. 278–283. September 1968

Kaysen, Carl. AMERICAN MILITARY POLICY. Survival. Vol. 11. No. 2. February 1969. pp. 51–56

Knorr, Klaus. FAILURES IN NATIONAL INTELLIGENCE ESTIMATES: THE CASE OF THE CUBAN MISSILES. World Politics. Vol. 16. No. 3. April 1964. pp. 455–467

Kolodziej, Edward A. FRENCH STRATEGY EMERGENT: GENERAL ANDRE BEAUFRE – A CRITIQUE. World Politics. Vol. 19. No. 3. April 1967. pp. 417–442

Larionov, V. THE DOCTRINE OF 'FLEXIBLE' AGGRESSION. International Affairs (Moscow). 1963. No. 7. pp. 46–51

Legault, Albert. ATOMIC WEAPONS FOR GERMANY. International Journal. Vol. 21. No. 4. Autumn 1966. pp. 447–469

Lemnitzer, General Lyman L. COLLECTIVE DEFENCE – THE BASIS OF MILITARY SECURITY. Atlantic Community Quarterly. Vol. 6. No. 2. Summer 1968. pp. 238–245

Lemnitzer, Lyman L. 'THE MOST FORMIDABLE CONVENTIONAL

ARMED FORCES IN THE WORLD TODAY'. (A plea for an overhaul of NATO after Czechoslovakia 1968). Atlantic Community Quarterly. Vol. 6. No. 4. Winter 1968–69. pp. 501–508

Lomov, N. ON GUARD OVER PEACE. (i.e. Soviet armed forces). International Affairs (Moscow). 1968. No. 2. pp. 8–13

McNamara, Robert S. SPECTRUM OF DEFENCE: (Address to the Economic Club of New York. 18 November 1968). Survival. Vol. 6. No. 1. January/February 1964. pp. 2–7

McNamara, Robert S. AMERICAN STRATEGY NOW: Statement to the House Armed Services Committee. 18 February 1965. Survival. Vol. 7. No. 3. May/June 1965. pp. 98–107

McNamara, Robert S. STATEMENT BEFORE THE SENATE SUBCOMMITTEE ON DEPARTMENT OF DEFENCE APPROPRIATIONS. FEBRUARY 1966. Survival. Vol. 8. No. 5. May 1966. pp. 138–146

McNamara, Robert S. REPORT TO THE SENATE ARMED SERVICES COMMITTEE. FEBRUARY 1968. Survival. Vol. 10. No. 4. April 1968. pp. 106–114

Malinovsky, Marshal R.Y. SOVIET DEFENCE POLICY. (Speech by the Minister of Defence to the 23rd Party Congress). Survival. Vol. 8. No. 7. July 1966. pp. 232–235

Malmgren, H.B. A FORWARD-PAUSE DEFENSE FOR EUROPE. Orbis. Vol. 8. No. 3. Fall 1964. pp. 595–606

Maratov, M. NON-PROLIFERATION AND NATO NUCLEAR PLANS. International Affairs (Moscow). 1966. No. 1. pp. 18–23

Martin, L.W. BALLISTIC MISSILE DEFENCE: THE GREAT DEBATE (A European viewpoint). Survival. Vol. 11. No. 8. August 1969

Messmer, Pierre. OUR MILITARY POLICE. (Condensation of 'Notre politique militaire', Revue de Defense Nationale. Paris. May 1963). Atlantic Community Quarterly. Vol. 1. No. 2. Summer 1963. pp. 185–186

Messmer, Pierre. THE ATOM, CAUSE AND MEANS OF AN AUTONOMOUS MILITARY POLICY. (i.e. current French defence policy). Atlantic Community Quarterly. Vol. 6. No. 2. Summer 1968. pp. 270–278

Miksche, F.O. THE NUCLEAR DETERRENT AND WESTERN STRATEGY. Orbis. Vol. 8. No. 2. Summer 1964. pp. 221–237

Moulton, Harland B. THE McNAMARA GENERAL WAR STRATEGY. Orbis. Vol. 8. No. 2. Summer 1964. pp. 238–254

Mulley, Frederick W. NUCLEAR WEAPONS: CHALLENGE TO

NATIONAL SECURITY. Orbis. Vol. 7. No. 1. Spring 1963. pp. 32–40
NATO Young Political Leaders. COLLECTIVE USE OF NUCLEAR WEAPONS – A SYMPOSIUM. Atlantic Community Quarterly. Vol. 4. No. 1. Spring 1966. pp. 66–72
Nelin, Y. NATO'S NEW 'FIRE BRIGADE'. (re. establishment of a standing naval force by NATO in the Mediterranean). International Affairs (Moscow). 1969. No. 3. pp. 56–58
Newton, William M. SOVIET AIMS AND WEAKNESSES. (A bleak reappraisal of Warsaw Pact rearmament, esp. naval). Atlantic Community Quarterly. Vol. 6. No. 3. Fall 1968. pp. 321–331
Nixon, Richard. BALLISTIC MISSILE DEFENCE. Survival. Vol. 11. No. 5. May 1969. pp. 146–149
Orvik, Nils. BASE POLICY – THEORY AND PRACTICE. Co-operation and Conflict. Vol. 2. 1967. pp. 188–204
Pechorkin, V. ABOUT 'ACCEPTABLE' WAR. International Affairs (Moscow). 1963. No. 3. pp. 20–25
Possony, Stefan T. TOWARDS NUCLEAR ISOLATIONISM. Orbis. Vol. 6. No. 4. Winter 1963. pp. 623–644
Read, Thornton. NUCLEAR TACTICS FOR DEFENDING A BORDER. World Politics. Vol. 15. No. 3. April 1963. pp. 390–402
Richardson, Elliot L. and Mansfield, Senator Mike. AMERICAN FORCE IN EUROPE – THE PROS. AND CONS. Atlantic Community Quarterly. Vol. 8. No. 1. Spring 1970. pp. 5–17
Robison, David. A EUROPEAN CO-ORDINATED FORCE. Orbis. Vol. 9. No. 3. Fall 1965. pp. 655–676
Rostow, Eugene V. A NEW START FOR THE ALLIANCE. Atlantic Community Quarterly. Vol. 1. No. 2. Summer 1963. pp. 207–210. (An American plea for a revised form of the Baruch plan for military atomic co-operation)
Rusk, Dean. MLF. Survival. Vol. 5. No. 6. November/December 1963. pp. 251–252
Rybkin, Lt.-Col. E. WAR AND POLICY. Survival. Vol. 8. No. 1. January 1966. pp. 12–16. (Abridgment of article in ARMED FORCES COMMUNIST. September 1965)
Samartsev, A. NUCLEAR-FREE ZONES ARE A VITAL NECESSITY. International Affairs (Moscow). 1964. No. 5. pp. 35–39
Schroeder, Gerhard. INTEGRATED DEFENCE. Atlantic Community Quarterly. Vol. 4. No. 2. Summer 1966. pp. 226–228. (The official German view on de Gaulle's policy on NATO)
Schwarz, Urs. THE CITIZEN ARMY IN THE ATOMIC AGE. Survival.

Vol. 7. No. 4. July 1965. pp. 232–235
Shestov, V. NUCLEAR RUBICON. (i.e. NATO nuclear strategy).
International Affairs (Moscow). 1969. No. 6. pp. 61–64
Shtemenko, Col.-General S.M. SOVIET GROUND FORCES IN
MODERN WAR. Survival. Vol. 5. No. 4. July/August 1963. pp. 180–
183. (Trans. from RED STAR. 3 January 1963)
Shvedkov, Y. BASES IN PENTAGON'S STRATEGY. International
Affairs (Moscow). 1964. No. 5. pp. 56–61
Slessor, Sir John. CONTROL OF NUCLEAR STRATEGY. Foreign
Affairs. Vol. 42. No. 1. October 1963. pp. 96–106. Atlantic
Community Quarterly. Vol. 1. No. 4. Winter 1963–64. pp. 530–540
Slessor, Sir John. MULTILATERAL OR MULTINATIONAL: AN
ALTERNATIVE TO THE MLF. Atlantic Community Quarterly.
Vol. 2. No. 2. Summer 1964. pp. 285–291. (A British plea for a
completely NATO nuclear force)
Slessor, Sir John. ATLANTIC NUCLEAR POLICY. International
Journal. Vol. 20. No. 2. Spring 1965. pp. 143–157. Atlantic
Community Quarterly. Vol. 3. No. 1. Spring 1965. pp. 56–63. (A
case for alliance interdependence, esp. an Atlantic nuclear strike
force)
Smeeton, Vice-Admiral M.R. OCEANS TO DEFEND. Survival. Vol. 5.
No. 3. May/June 1963. pp. 131–134. (Reprint from NATO
LETTER. March 1963)
Smirnov, Vice-Admiral. SOVIET NAVY IN THE MEDITERRANEAN.
Survival. Vol. 11. No. 2. February 1969. pp. 65–66. (Reprint from
RED STAR. 12 November 1968)
Sokolovsky, Marshal V.D. and Cherednichenko, Major-General M.I.
THE MILITARY REVOLUTION. Survival. Vol. 6. No. 6. November/
December 1964. pp. 280–283. (Abridged from RED STAR)
Sokolovsky, Marshal V.D. and Cherednichenko, Major-General M.I.
SOVIET MILITARY STRUCTURE. Survival. Vol. 7. No. 4. July
1965. pp. 236–241. (Trans. and abridged from MILITARY-
HISTORICAL JOURNAL. March 1965)
Sokolovsky, Marshal.V.D. and Cherednichenko, Major-General M.I.
CURRENT MILITARY STRATEGY. Survival. Vol. 8. No. 8.
August 1966. pp. 266–270. (Reprint from ARMED FORCES
COMMUNIST. April 1966)
Sommer, Theo. HOW MANY FINGERS ON HOW MANY TRIGGERS?
Atlantic Community Quarterly. Vol. 1. No. 4. Winter 1963–64.
pp. 556–560. (A German critique of the theories of General Gallois)

Sosnovy, Timothy. SOVIET MILITARY BUDGETS. Foreign Affairs.
Vol. 42. No. 1. April 1964. pp. 487–496. Survival. Vol. 6. No. 4.
July/August 1964. pp. 182–187. (See also R.R. Neild: Letter to
the Editor. Survival. Vol. 6. No. 5. September/October 1964.
p. 248)

Speidel, General Hans. THE ESSENTIAL BASIS OF DETENTE. Atlantic
Community Quarterly. Vol. 7. No. 4. Winter 1969–70. pp. 506–510

Stanley, Timothy W. NATO'S STRATEGIC DOCTRINE. Survival.
Vol. 11. No. 11. November 1969. pp. 342–349. (Reprint from
Orbis. Spring 1969)

Stehlin, General Paul. THE EVOLUTION OF WESTERN DEFENCE.
Foreign Affairs. Vol. 42. No. 1. October 1963. pp. 70–83

Steinhoff, General Johannes. NATO CRISIS: A MILITARY VIEW.
Survival. Vol. 8. No. 11. November 1966. pp. 365–371

Stone, Jeremy J. BOMBER DISARMAMENT. World Politics. Vol. 17.
No. 1. October 1964. pp. 13–39

Talensky, M. A NATO NUCLEAR FORCE IS A DANGEROUS
VENTURE. International Affairs (Moscow). 1963. No. 5. pp. 22–26

Talensky, *et al.* NUCLEAR WEAPONS AND THE WEST. International
Affairs (Moscow). 1964. No. 9. pp. 53–66

Timofeyev, K. THE ROLE OF NAVIES IN IMPERIALIST POLICY.
International Affairs (Moscow). 1969. No. 11. pp. 40–44

Ward, Chester C. THE 'NEW MYTHS' AND 'OLD REALITIES' OF
NUCLEAR WAR. Orbis. Vol. 8. No. 2. Summer 1964. pp. 255–291

Weinstein, Adelbert. FRENCH STRATEGIC CONCEPTS: ONLY
TOWARDS THE EAST. (A German comment on the view of General
Fourquet). Survival. Vol. 11. No. 7. July 1969. pp. 211–212

Whetten, Lawrence L. MILITARY ASPECTS OF THE SOVIET
OCCUPATION OF CZECHOSLOVAKIA. The World Today. Vol. 25.
No. 2. February 1969. pp. 60–68

Wilson, Harold. EXTRACTS FROM HANSARD. 16 DECEMBER 1964:
speech by the Prime Minister on Britain and the Atlantic Nuclear
Force. Survival. Vol. 7. No. 2. March/April 1965. pp. 52–54

Wolfe, Thomas W. SHIFTS IN SOVIET STRATEGIC THOUGHT.
Foreign Affairs. Vol. 42. No. 3. April 1964. pp. 475–486

Wolfe, Thomas W. SOME NEW DEVELOPMENTS IN THE SOVIET
MILITARY DEBATE. Orbis. Vol. 8. No. 3. Fall 1964. pp. 550–562

Wolfe, Thomas W. SOVIET MILITARY POLICY. Survival. Vol. 10.
No. 1. January 1968. pp. 2–9. (Reprint from CURRENT HISTORY.
October 1967)

Wolfe, Thomas W. THE PROJECTION OF SOVIET POWER. (The Soviet naval presence in the Mediterranean). Survival. Vol. 10. No. 5. May 1968. pp. 159–165. pp. 117–122. (Reprint from INTERPLAY. March 1968)

Wolfers, Arnold. INTEGRATION IN THE WEST: THE CONFLICT OF PERSPECTIVES. International Organisation. Vol. 17. No. 3. Summer 1963. pp. 753–770. Atlantic Community Quarterly. Vol. 1. No. 4. Winter 1963–64. pp. 586–605. (A penetrating analysis of West European moves towards integration and their disturbing effect upon relations with the U.S.A.)

Yakubovsky, I.I. SOVIET GROUND FORCES. Survival. Vol. 9. No. 10. October 1967. pp. 327–328. (Reprint from RED STAR. 21 July 1967)

Yeremenko, A. ABSURD PLANS, RIDICULOUS HOPES. (i.e. the MLF). International Affairs (Moscow). 1963. No. 6. pp. 15–18

Yermashov, I. FOREIGN BASES: SOURCE OF TENSION. International Affairs (Moscow). 1963. No. 1. pp. 11–19

Yevgenyev, I. BEHIND THE SCREEN OF NATO NUCLEAR FORCES. International Affairs (Moscow). 1964. No. 1. pp. 23–28

Zakharov, Marshal M. SCIENCE AND MILITARY LEADERSHIP. Survival. Vol. 7. No. 2. March/April 1965. pp. 85–89. (Trans. from RED STAR. 4 February 1965)

SECTION IV

THE ONSET OF DETENTE: 1970–1977

Arid as were the years of confrontation, they were tolerable because of the familiarity of the issues they brought in their train. The process of detente, however, was and remains unfamiliar at best and hazardous at worst. Thus, the SALT talks between the super-powers had to be rendered palatable to the allies of the United States, their reactions varying from cautious approval to anxiety lest a bargain be struck at their expense in Western Europe. With the departure of General de Gaulle, the style and some of the content of French policy changed; Britain was admitted to the European Community and the use of the term 'Anglo-Saxon' as a denigratory description of British and American policies and attitudes was dropped. On the other hand, Dr. Kissinger's call for a new Atlantic charter and his designation of 1973 as 'the year of Europe' awakened little enthusiasm in European hearts. The responses of the Atlantic allies to the Arab oil-embargo were uncoordinated and as the world economic depression began to deepen, the provisions of article 2 of the North Atlantic treaty which pledged them to eliminate conflict in their international economic policies and to encourage economic collaboration remained a dead letter.

New issues arose to trouble the Alliance; the hostility of the Greeks and the Turks over Cyprus drove a wedge between Turkey and the United States while impelling Greece to contract out of the NATO military command structure. Portugal entered what one commentator has described as its 'revolution of carnations', and both there and in Italy a new term entered the political vocabulary – 'Eurocommunism'. Small wonder, then, that a feature of the books, papers and articles described in the section which follows is the uncertainty and the novelty of the issues being discussed. Together with this goes a readiness to take a longer and harder look at the overall costs of defence during a period when perceptions of threat were beginning to reflect a preoccupation with the economic as opposed to the political aspects of international society. At the same time, such scrutiny was not limited to simple introspection, as indicated by the growing number of highly informed studies of the changing military capabilities of the Warsaw Pact and notably on the growth and the role of the Soviet blue-water navy. The Conference on Security and Co-operation in Europe not only came and went in this period, its consequences were subsequently reviewed at Belgrade; but the discussions on mutual and balanced force reductions in Vienna continue without fruitful issue. In such an environment, the continued appearance of perceptive and critical studies of the Atlantic Alliance is to be welcomed as an indication of its significance; it is to be hoped that they serve to confirm that in the midst of the hesitations evidently associated with detente the allies remain, in the words of the preamble to the founding treaty of their association, 'resolved to unite their efforts for collective defence and for the preservation of peace and security'.

Books

Economic and Social Aspects

Aubrey, Henry G. ATLANTIC ECONOMIC CO-OPERATION: THE CASE OF THE OECD. New York, Washington: Praeger for the Council on Foreign Relations; London: Pall Mall. 1967

Clayton, James L. THE ECONOMIC IMPACT OF THE COLD WAR: SOURCES AND READINGS. New York: Harcourt, Brace and World, Inc.. 1970

Dean, Robert W. WEST GERMAN TRADE WITH THE EAST: THE POLITICAL DIMENSION. New York: Praeger. 1974

Hollander, Paul. SOVIET AND AMERICAN SOCIETY: A COMPARISON. New York: Oxford University Press. 1973

Kennedy, Gavin. THE ECONOMICS OF DEFENCE. London: Faber and Faber. 1975

Pisar, Samuel. CO-EXISTENCE AND COMMERCE: GUIDELINES FOR TRANSACTIONS BETWEEN EAST AND WEST. London: Allen Lane, The Penguin Press. 1971

Proxmire, Senator William. REPORT FROM WASTELAND: AMERICA'S MILITARY INDUSTRIAL COMPLEX. New York: Praeger. 1970

Rosen, Steven (ed.). TESTING THE THEORY OF THE MILITARY-INDUSTRIAL COMPLEX. Lexington, Mass: Lexington Books, D.C. Heath. 1973

Sarkesian, Sam C. (ed.). THE MILITARY-INDUSTRIAL COMPLEX: A REASSESSMENT. Beverly Hills and London: SAGE publications. 1972

Treml, Vladimir G. and Hardt, John P. (eds.). SOVIET ECONOMIC STATISTICS. Durham, N. Carolina: Duke University Press. 1972

Weidenbaum, Murray L. THE ECONOMICS OF PEACETIME DEFENCE. London: Pall Mall. 1974

Legal Aspects

Ellert, Robert B. NATO 'FAIR TRIAL' SAFEGUARDS: PRECURSOR TO AN INTERNATIONAL BILL ON PROCEDURAL RIGHTS. The Hague: Nijhoff. 1963. (See review by G.I.A.D. Draper in INTERNATIONAL AFFAIRS. Vol. 40. No. 3. July 1964. p. 501)

Stambuk, George. AMERICAN MILITARY FORCES ABROAD: THEIR IMPACT ON THE WESTERN STATE SYSTEM. Columbus: Ohio State University Press. 1963

National and Regional Aspects

Assembly of Western European Union. TEN YEARS OF SEVEN-POWER EUROPE. Paris: Western European Union. 1964

Bender, Peter. EAST EUROPE IN SEARCH OF SECURITY. London: Chatto and Windus for the International Institute for Strategic Studies. 1972; Baltimore: Johns Hopkins Press. 1975

Birnbaum, Karl E. EAST AND WEST GERMANY: A MODUS VIVENDI. Farnborough: Saxon House; Lexington, Mass.: Lexington Books, D.C. Heath. 1973

Borcier, Paul. EIGHT YEARS WORK FOR EUROPEAN DEFENCE: A POLITICAL SURVEY. Paris: Western European Union. 1964

Brinton, Crane. THE AMERICANS AND THE FRENCH. Cambridge, Mass.: Harvard University Press; London: Oxford University Press.

1968. (See review by Thomas Barman in INTERNATIONAL AFFAIRS. Vol. 45. No. 1. January 1969. pp. 137–138)

Bromke, Adam and Rakowska-Harmstone, Teresa (eds.). THE COMMUNIST STATES IN DISARRAY. 1965–1971. Minneapolis: University of Minnesota Press. 1972

Brzezinski, Zbigniev K. THE SOVIET BLOC: UNITY AND CONFLICT. Cambridge, Mass.: Harvard University Press; London: Oxford University Press. 1967

Buchan, Alastair. EUROPE'S FUTURES, EUROPE'S CHOICES: MODELS OF WESTERN EUROPE IN THE 1970'S. London: Chatto and Windus for the Institute for Strategic Studies; New York: Columbia University Press. 1969. (See review by Y. Login: 'Six recipes for the future' in INTERNATIONAL AFFAIRS (Moscow). 1970. No. 8. pp. 102–104)

Burrows, Sir Bernard and Irwin, Christopher. THE SECURITY OF WESTERN EUROPE: TOWARDS A COMMON DEFENCE POLICY. London: Charles Knight. 1972

Campbell, John C. AMERICAN POLICY TOWARDS COMMUNIST EASTERN EUROPE: THE CHOICES AHEAD. Minneapolis: University of Minnesota Press; London: Oxford University Press. 1965

de Carmoy, Guy. THE FOREIGN POLICIES OF FRANCE 1944–1968. Chicago: University of Chigago Press. 1970

Cordier, Sherwood S. BRITAIN AND THE DEFENCE OF WESTERN EUROPE IN THE 1970'S. New York: Exposition Press. 1973

Cottrell, Alvin J. and Theberge, James D. (eds.). THE WESTERN MEDITERRANEAN: ITS POLITICAL, ECONOMIC AND STRATEGIC IMPORTANCE. New York: Praeger. 1973; London: Pall Mall. 1974

Crollen, Luc. PORTUGAL, THE U.S. AND NATO. Louvain: Louvain University Press. 1973

Crozier, Brian. DE GAULLE. New York: Charles Scribner's Sons. 1973. (See review by D. Bruce Marshall: 'De Gaulle and the shaping of French foreign policy' in ORBIS. Vol. 19. No. 1. Spring 1975. pp. 255–264)

Czerwinski, E.J. and Piekalkiewicz, J. (eds.). THE SOVIET INVASION OF CZECHOSLOVAKIA: ITS EFFECTS ON EASTERN EUROPE. New York: Praeger; London: Pall Mall. 1972

Dobell, Peter C. CANADA'S SEARCH FOR NEW ROLES: FOREIGN POLICY IN THE TRUDEAU ERA. London: Oxford University

Press for the Royal Institute of International Affairs. 1972
Dulles, Eleanor Lansing. ONE GERMANY OR TWO. Stanford: Hoover Institution, Stanford University Press. 1970
Eayrs, James. IN DEFENCE OF CANADA: PEACEMAKING AND DETERRENCE. Toronto: University of Toronto Press; London: Oxford University Press. 1973
Edmonds, Robin. SOVIET FOREIGN POLICY 1962–1973. London: Oxford University Press. 1975
Frankel, Joseph. BRITISH FOREIGN POLICY 1954–1973. London: Oxford University Press for the Royal Institute of International Affairs. 1975
Galtung, Johan (ed.). CO-OPERATION IN EUROPE. New York: Humanities Press. 1971. (Essays with special reference to European security)
de Gaulle, Charles. MEMOIRS OF HOPE: RENEWAL AND ENDEAVOUR. New York: Simon and Schuster. 1972
Goldmann, Kjell. TENSION AND DETENTE IN BIPOLAR EUROPE. Stockholm: Esselte Studium, Scandinavian University Books. 1974
Gray, Colin S. CANADIAN DEFENCE PRIORITIES: A QUESTION OF RELEVANCE. Toronto: Clarke, Irwin. 1972
Grondal, Benedikt. ICELAND: FROM NEUTRALITY TO NATO MEMBERSHIP. Oslo: Universitetsforlaget. 1971
Grosser, Alfred. GERMANY IN OUR TIME: A POLITICAL HISTORY OF THE POST-WAR YEARS. New York: Praeger. 1971
Harris, George S. TROUBLED ALLIANCE: TURKISH-AMERICAN PROBLEMS IN HISTORICAL PERSPECTIVE 1945–1964. Washington, D.C.: American Enterprise Institute for Public Policy Research; Stanford: Hoover Institution. 1972
Holst, Johan J. (ed.). FIVE ROADS TO NORDIC SECURITY. Oslo: Universitetsforlaget. 1973
Jordan, Robert S. (ed.). EUROPE AND THE SUPERPOWERS: PERCEPTIONS OF EUROPEAN INTERNATIONAL POLITICS. Boston, Mass.: Allyn and Bacon. 1971
Kaiser, Karl and Morgan, Roger (eds.). BRITAIN AND WEST GERMANY: CHANGING SOCIETIES AND THE FUTURE OF FOREIGN POLICY. London: Oxford University Press for the Royal Institute of International Affairs. 1971
King, Robert R. and Dean, Robert W. (eds.). EAST EUROPEAN PERSPECTIVES ON EUROPEAN SECURITY AND CO-OPERATION. London: Pall Mall; New York: Praeger. 1975

Kintner, William R. and Klaiber, Wolfgang. EASTERN EUROPE AND EUROPEAN SECURITY. New York: Dunellen. 1971

Kintner, William R. (ed.) and Foster, Richard B. NATIONAL STRATEGY IN A DECADE OF CHANGE. Lexington, Mass.: Lexington Books, D.C. Heath. 1973. (See review by P. Podlesny in INTERNATIONAL AFFAIRS (Moscow). 1975. No. 3. pp. 146–147)

Klaiber, Wolfgang, et al. ERA OF NEGOTIATIONS: EUROPEAN SECURITY AND FORCE REDUCTIONS. Lexington: Lexington Books, D.C. Heath. 1973

Kohl, Wilfrid. FRENCH NUCLEAR DIPLOMACY. Princeton: Princeton University Press. 1971; London: Oxford University Press. 1972

Kolodziej, Edward A. THE UNCOMMON DEFENCE AND CONGRESS 1945–1963. Columbus: Ohio State University Press. 1966

Kolodziej, Edward A. FRENCH INTERNATIONAL POLICY UNDER DE GAULLE AND POMPIDOU. Ithaca: Cornell University Press. 1974. (See review by D. Bruce Marshall: 'De Gaulle and the shaping of French foreign policy' in ORBIS. Vol. 19. No. 1. Spring 1975. pp. 255–264)

Kovrig, Bennett. THE MYTH OF LIBERATION: EAST-CENTRAL EUROPE IN U.S. DIPLOMACY AND POLITICS SINCE 1941. Baltimore: Johns Hopkins Press; Toronto: Copp Clarke. 1973

Kulski, W.W. DE GAULLE AND THE WORLD: THE FOREIGN POLICY OF THE FIFTH FRENCH REPUBLIC. Syracuse: Syracuse University Press. 1966

Landes, David (ed.). WESTERN EUROPE: THE TRIALS OF PARTNERSHIP. Lexington, Mass.: Lexington Books, D.C. Heath. 1977

Lippmann, Heinz. HONECKER AND THE NEW POLITICS OF EUROPE. London: Angus and Robertson. 1973

Macdonald, R. St. J. THE ARCTIC FRONTIER. University of Toronto Press in association with the Canadian Institute of International Affairs and the Arctic Institute of North America; London: Oxford University Press. 1966

Maclean, Donald. BRITISH FOREIGN POLICY SINCE SUEZ. London: Hodder and Stoughton. 1970. (A critique by the celebrated defector)

Mally, Gerhard. THE EUROPEAN COMMUNITY IN PERSPECTIVE. Lexington, Mass.: Lexington Books for the Atlantic Council of the United States. 1973.

Mally, Gerhard (ed.). THE NEW EUROPE AND THE UNITED STATES.

Farnborough: Saxon House. 1974

Merkl, Peter H. GERMAN FOREIGN POLICIES, WEST AND EAST: ON THE THRESHOLD OF A NEW EUROPEAN ERA. Santa Barbara: American Bibliographical Center-Clio Press. 1974

Morgan, Roger. THE UNITED STATES AND WEST GERMANY 1945-1973: A STUDY IN ALLIANCE POLITICS. London: Oxford University Press for Royal Institute of International Affairs and Harvard Center for International Affairs. 1974

Morse, Edward L. FOREIGN POLICY AND INTERDEPENDENCE IN GAULLIST FRANCE. Princeton: Princeton University Press. 1973

Nash, Henry T. AMERICAN FOREIGN POLICY: RESPONSE TO A SENSE OF THREAT. Homewood, Ill.: The Dorsey Press. 1973

Nunnerly, David. PRESIDENT KENNEDY AND BRITAIN. New York: St. Martin's Press. 1972

Pickles, Dorothy. THE UNEASY ENTENTE: FRENCH FOREIGN POLICY AND FRANCO-BRITISH MISUNDERSTANDINGS. London: Oxford University Press for the Royal Institute of International Affairs. 1966

Radvanyi, Janos. HUNGARY AND THE SUPERPOWERS: THE 1956 REVOLUTION AND REALPOLITIK. Stanford: Hoover Institution Press. 1972

Remington, Robin Alison. THE WARSAW PACT: CASE STUDIES IN COMMUNIST CONFLICT RESOLUTION. Cambridge, Mass.: M.I.T. Press. 1971

Roberts, Henry L. EASTERN EUROPE: POLITICS, REVOLUTION AND DIPLOMACY. New York: Knopf. 1970

Rosi, Eugene J. (ed.). AMERICAN DEFENCE AND DETENTE: READINGS IN NATIONAL SECURITY POLICY. New York: Dodd, Mead & Co. 1973

Rostow, Eugene V. PEACE IN THE BALANCE: THE FUTURE OF AMERICAN FOREIGN POLICY. New York: Simon and Schuster. 1972

Schopflin, George (ed.). THE SOVIET UNION AND EASTERN EUROPE: a handbook. London: Anthony Blond. 1970

Seabury, Paul and Wildavsky, Aaron (eds.). U.S. FOREIGN POLICY: PERSPECTIVES AND PROPOSALS FOR THE 1970'S. New York: McGraw-Hill. 1969

Shears, David. THE UGLY FRONTIER. London: Chatto and Windus. 1971. (Discusses the permanence of the boundary between West and East Germany)

Solberg, Carl. RIDING HIGH: AMERICA IN THE COLD WAR. New York: Mason and Lipscomb. 1973. (A discussion of the interrelationship between domestic affairs and foreign policy)

Spanier, John. AMERICAN FOREIGN POLICY SINCE WORLD WAR II. New York: Praeger. 1973

Szulc, Tad. CZECHOSLOVAKIA SINCE WORLD WAR II. New York: The Viking Press. 1971

Thorardson, Bruce. TRUDEAU AND FOREIGN POLICY: A STUDY IN DECISION MAKING. London and Toronto: Oxford University Press. 1972. (Includes an account of reduced Canadian effort in NATO)

U.S. Senate; Committee on Armed Services. EUROPEAN DEFENCE CO-OPERATION. Washington, D.C.: U.S.G.P.O. 1976

Vali, Ferenc A. BRIDGE ACROSS THE BOSPHOROUS: THE FOREIGN POLICY OF TURKEY. Baltimore: Johns Hopkins Press. Toronto: Capp Clark. 1971

Vali, Ferenc A. THE TURKISH STRAITS AND NATO. Stanford: Hoover Institution Press. 1972

Walton, Richard J. COLD WAR AND COUNTER-REVOLUTION: THE FOREIGN POLICY OF JOHN F. KENNEDY. New York: Viking. 1972

Warnock, John W. PARTNER TO BEHEMOTH: THE MILITARY POLICY OF A SATELLITE CANADA. Toronto: New Press. 1970

Watson, Alan. EUROPE AT RISK. London: George C. Harrap and Co. Ltd. 1972

Werth, Alexander. RUSSIA: THE POST-WAR YEARS. New York: Taplinger. 1971

Wettig, Gerhard. COMMUNITY AND CONFLICT IN THE GERMAN CAMP: THE SOVIET UNION, EAST GERMANY AND THE GERMAN PROBLEM 1965-1972. London: Hurst. 1975

Whetten, Lawrence L. GERMANY'S OSTPOLITIK: RELATIONS BETWEEN THE FEDERAL REPUBLIC AND THE WARSAW PACT COUNTRIES. London: Oxford University Press for Royal Institute of International Affairs. 1971

Whetten, Lawrence L. CONTEMPORARY AMERICAN FOREIGN POLICY: MINIMAL DIPLOMACY, DEFENSIVE STRATEGY AND DETENTE MANAGEMENT. Lexington, Mass.: Lexington Books, D.C. Heath. 1974

Williams, Geoffrey and Williams, Alan Lee. CRISIS IN EUROPEAN DEFENCE: THE NEXT 10 YEARS. London: Charles Knight & Co.

1974. (See also review article by T. Belashchenko: 'Atlanticist's Alarms'. in INTERNATIONAL AFFAIRS (Moscow). 1975. No. 9. pp. 125–127)
Windsor, Philip. GERMANY AND THE MANAGEMENT OF DETENTE. London: Chatto and Windus for the Institute for Strategic Studies. 1971
Wolfe, James H. INDIVISIBLE GERMANY: ILLUSION OR REALITY? The Hague: Nijhoff. 1963
Wolfe, Thomas W. SOVIET POWER AND EUROPE. Baltimore: Johns Hopkins Press. 1970
Woods, William. POLAND: PHOENIX IN THE EAST. Harmondsworth: Pelican Books. 1972

Politico-Military Aspects

Acheson, Dean. THIS VAST EXTERNAL REALM. New York: Norton. 1973. (Essays and addresses on foreign affairs 1953–1971)
Alting von Geusau, F.A.M. (ed.). NATO AND SECURITY IN THE SEVENTIES. Leyden: Sijthoff; Lexington, Mass.: Lexington Books, D.C. Heath. 1971. (See reveiw by D.V. Bendall in SURVIVAL. Vol. 13. No. 11. November 1971. pp. 394–395. Also review by L. Khodorkova: 'Inauspicious conclusions' in INTERNATIONAL AFFAIRS (Moscow). 1973. No. 3. pp. 114–115)
Andren, Nils and Birnbaum, Karl. BEYOND DETENTE: PROSPECTS FOR EAST-WEST CO-OPERATION AND SECURITY IN EUROPE. Leyden: Sijthoff. 1976
Arbatov, Georgi. THE WAR OF IDEAS IN CONTEMPORARY INTERNATIONAL RELATIONS: THE IMPERIALIST DOCTRINE, METHODS AND ORGANISATION OF FOREIGN POLITICAL PROPAGANDA. Moscow: Progress Publishers. 1973
Aron, Raymond. THE IMPERIAL REPUBLIC: THE UNITED STATES AND THE WORLD. 1945–1973. Englewood Cliffs: Prentice-Hall. 1974
Atlantic Institute. THE ATLANTIC PAPERS: POLITICAL AND STRATEGIC STUDIES. New York: Dunellen. 1970. (A compendium of studies previously published separately)
Barnet, Richard J. ROOTS OF WAR. New York: Atheneum. 1972. (A 'revisionist' study which argues that American business interests influence but do not determine U.S. foreign policy)

Beer, Francis A. (ed.). ALLIANCES: LATENT WAR COMMUNITIES IN THE CONTEMPORARY WORLD. New York: Holt Rinehart and Winston. 1970

Bletz, Donald F. THE ROLE OF THE MILITARY PROFESSIONAL IN U.S. FOREIGN POLICY. London: Pall Mall; New York: Praeger. 1972

Bloomfield, Lincoln P. IN SEARCH OF AMERICAN FOREIGN POLICY: THE HUMANE USE OF POWER. New York: Oxford University Press. 1974

Braeman, J. (ed.), *et al.* TWENTIETH CENTURY AMERICAN FOREIGN POLICY. Columbus: Ohio State University Press. 1971

Brandon, Henry. THE RETREAT OF AMERICAN POWER: NIXON'S AND KISSINGER'S FOREIGN POLICY — AND ITS EFFECTS. London: The Bodley Head. 1973

Brezhnev, Leonid. ON THE POLICY OF THE SOVIET UNION AND THE INTERNATIONAL SITUATION. Garden City: Doubleday. 1973

Brown, Lord George. IN MY WAY. London: Victor Gollancz. 1971; Harmondsworth: Pelican. 1972. (The colourful political biography of a colourful Labour Foreign Secretary of the sixties)

Brzezinski, Zbigniev and Huntington, Samuel P. POLITICAL POWER: U.S.A./U.S.S.R. London: Chatto and Windus for the Russian Institute and the Institute of War and Peace Studies, Columbia University. 1964

Buchan, Alastair. POWER AND EQUILIBRIUM IN THE 1970'S. New York: Praeger. 1972. (The Russell C. Leffingwell Lectures 1972. Published for the Council on Foreign Relations)

Buchan, Alastair. THE END OF THE POST-WAR ERA: A NEW BALANCE OF WORLD POWER. London: Weidenfeld and Nicolson. 1974

Burgess, W. Randolph and Huntley, James Robert. EUROPE AND AMERICA: THE NEXT TEN YEARS. New York: Walker & Co. 1970

Chace, James and Ravenal, Earl C. (eds.). ATLANTIS LOST: U.S.-EUROPEAN RELATIONS AFTER THE COLD WAR. New York: New York University Press for the Council on Foreign Relations. 1976

Deutsch, Karl W. ARMS CONTROL AND THE ATLANTIC ALLIANCE. New York: Wiley. 1967

Clemens, Walter C., Jr. THE SUPERPOWERS AND ARMS CONTROL:

FROM COLD WAR TO INTERDEPENDENCE. Lexington, Mass.: Lexington Books. 1973

Donovan, John C. THE COLD WARRIORS: A POLICY-MAKING ELITE. Lexington, Mass.: Lexington Books, D.C. Heath. 1974

Eriksen, Bjarne. THE COMMITTEE SYSTEM OF THE NATO COUNCIL. Oslo: Universitetsforlaget. 1967

Foster, Richard B. (ed.), *et al.* STRATEGY FOR THE WEST: AMERICAN-ALLIED RELATIONS IN TRANSITION. New York: Crane, Russak. 1974

Fox, William T.R. and Schilling, Warner R. (eds.). EUROPEAN SECURITY AND THE ATLANTIC SYSTEM. New York: Columbia University Press. 1973. (See review by V. Kulish: 'Turning a blind eye on new trends' in INTERNATIONAL AFFAIRS (Moscow). No. 9. 1974. pp. 126–129)

Gallagher, Matthew P. and Spielmann, Karl F. SOVIET DECISION-MAKING FOR DEFENCE: A CRITIQUE OF U.S. PERSPECTIVES ON THE ARMS RACE. London: Pall Mall. 1973

Gamson, William A. and Modigliani, André. UNTANGLING THE COLD WAR: A STRATEGY FOR TESTING RIVAL THEORIES. Boston: Little, Brown. 1971

Gehlen, Michael P. THE POLITICS OF CO-EXISTENCE. Bloomington: Indiana University Press. 1967

Geiger, Theodore. THE FORTUNES OF THE WEST: THE FUTURE OF THE ATLANTIC NATIONS. Bloomington: Indiana University Press. 1973

Gelber, Lionel. CRISIS IN THE WEST: AMERICAN LEADERSHIP AND THE GLOBAL BALANCE. London: Macmillan. 1975

Godson, Joseph (ed.). TRANSATLANTIC CRISIS: EUROPE AND AMERICA IN THE 1970'S. London: Alcove Press Ltd. 1974. (A series of articles from INTERNATIONAL HERALD TRIBUNE, April–June 1974 to commemorate the silver jubilee of the Atlantic Alliance)

Goodman, Eliot R. THE FATE OF THE ATLANTIC COMMUNITY. New York: Praeger for the Atlantic Council of the United States. Lavalette: Academic Market Place. 1975

Graubard, Stephen R. KISSINGER: PORTRAIT OF A MIND. New York: W.W. Norton. 1973

Gregg, Robert W. and Kegley, Charles W., Jr. (eds.). AFTER VIETNAM: THE FUTURE OF AMERICAN FOREIGN POLICY. Garden City: Doubleday & Co. 1971

Griffith, William E. COLD WAR AND CO-EXISTENCE: RUSSIA, CHINA AND THE UNITED STATES. Englewood Cliffs: Prentice-Hall. 1971

Gromyko, Anatole Andreievitch. THROUGH RUSSIAN EYES: PRESIDENT KENNEDY'S 1,036 DAYS. Washington: International Library. 1973

Halle, L.J. THE COLD WAR AS HISTORY. London: Chatto and Windus. 1971

Hanak, H. (ed.). SOVIET FOREIGN POLICY SINCE THE DEATH OF STALIN. London: Routledge and Kegan Paul. 1972

Hanreider, Wolfram (ed.). THE UNITED STATES AND WESTERN EUROPE: POLITICAL, ECONOMIC AND STRATEGIC PERSPECTIVES. Cambridge, Mass.: Winthrop. 1974

Harriman, W. Averell. AMERICA AND RUSSIA IN A CHANGING WORLD. New York: Doubleday. 1971. (See review by Y. Mikhailov, 'Ex-Diplomat on Soviet-American relations' in INTERNATIONAL AFFAIRS (Moscow). 1971. No. 6. pp. 102–104)

Hayter, William. RUSSIA AND THE WORLD: A STUDY OF SOVIET FOREIGN POLICY. London: Secker and Warburg. 1970

Head, Richard G. and Rokke, Erwin J. (eds.). AMERICAN DEFENCE POLICY. Baltimore: Johns Hopkins Press. 1973

Hill-Norton, Admiral of the Fleet Sir Peter. NO SOFT OPTIONS. London: C. Hurst. 1978

Holst, Johan J. and Nehrlich, Uwe. BEYOND NUCLEAR DETERRENCE: NEW AIMS, NEW ARMS. New York: Crane, Russak. 1977

Horton, Frank B. (ed.), *et al.* COMPARATIVE DEFENCE POLICY. Baltimore: Johns Hopkins Press. 1974

Jacobsen, C.G. SOVIET STRATEGY – SOVIET FOREIGN POLICY: MILITARY CONSIDERATIONS AFFECTING SOVIET POLICY-MAKING. Glasgow: The University Press, Robert Maclehose & Co. Ltd. 1972

Kaiser, Karl. EUROPE AND THE UNITED STATES: THE FUTURE OF THE RELATIONSHIP. Washington, D.C.: Columbia Books. 1973

Kaplan, Morton A. THE RATIONALE FOR NATO. Washington, D.C.: American Enterprise Institute for Public Policy Research; Stanford: The Hoover Institution, Stanford University Press. 1973

Kaplan, Morton A. NATO AND DISSUASION. Chicago: Center for Policy Study, University of Chicago. 1974

Kiep, Walther L. A NEW CHALLENGE FOR WESTERN EUROPE: A VIEW FROM BONN. New York: Mason and Lipscomb. 1974. (A plan by a leading member of the CDU for a revitalised Western Alliance)

Kintner, William R. and Pfaltzgraff, Robert L. (eds.). SALT: IMPLICATIONS FOR ARMS CONTROL IN THE 1970'S. Pittsburgh: University of Pittsburgh Press. 1973

Kohler, Foy D., *et al.* SOVIET STRATEGY FOR THE SEVENTIES: FROM COLD WAR TO PEACEFUL CO-EXISTENCE. Coral Gables: Center for Advanced International Studies, University of Miami. 1973

Kolko, Joyce and Gabriel. THE LIMITS OF POWER: THE WORLD AND U.S. FOREIGN POLICY 1945–1954. New York: Harper and Row. 1972. (A study by two leading revisionist historians)

Korbel, Josef. DETENTE IN EUROPE: REAL OR IMAGINARY? Princeton: Princeton University Press. 1971. London: Oxford University Press. 1972

Kulski, W.W. THE SOVIET UNION IN WORLD AFFAIRS: A DOCUMENTATED ANALYSIS 1964–1972. Syracuse: Syracuse University Press. 1973

Landau, David. KISSINGER: THE USES OF POWER. London: Robson. 1974

Leifer, Michael (ed.). CONSTRAINTS AND ADJUSTMENTS IN FOREIGN POLICY. London: Allen and Unwin. 1972. (Contains a useful essay on NATO)

Ludz, Peter Christian, *et al.* DILEMMAS OF THE ATLANTIC ALLIANCE. (Atlantic Institute Studies I). New York: Praeger. 1975

Mally, Gerhard. INTERDEPENDENCE. Lexington, Mass.: Lexington Books for the Atlantic Council of the United States. 1976

Mensonides, Louis J. and Kuhlman, James A. THE FUTURE OF INTER-BLOC RELATIONS IN EUROPE. New York: Praeger. 1974; London: Pall Mall. 1975

Miller, Lynn H. and Pruessen, Ronald W. (eds.). REFLECTIONS ON THE COLD WAR: A QUARTER CENTURY OF AMERICAN FOREIGN POLICY. Philadelphia: Temple University Press. 1974. (9 essays, originally lectures at Temple University 1970–1971)

Moulton, Harland B. FROM SUPERIORITY TO PARITY: the United States and the strategic arms race 1961–1971. Westport, Conn.: Greenwood Press. 1973

Nalin, Y. and Nikolayev, A. THE SOVIET UNION AND EUROPEAN SECURITY. Moscow: Progress Publishers. 1973

Neustadt, Richard E. ALLIANCE POLITICS. New York: Columbia University Press. 1970

Osgood, Robert E. ALLIANCES AND AMERICAN FOREIGN POLICY. Baltimore: Johns Hopkins Press; London: Oxford University Press. 1968
Osgood, Robert E., *et al.* AMERICA AND THE WORLD: FROM THE TRUMAN DOCTRINE TO VIETNAM. Baltimore: Johns Hopkins Press. 1970
Owen, David. THE POLITICS OF DEFENCE. London: Jonathan Cape. 1972. (A study by a future British foreign secretary)
Parker, W.H. THE SUPERPOWERS: THE UNITED STATES AND THE SOVIET UNION COMPARED. London: Macmillan. 1972
Pfaltzgraff, Robert L., Jr. THE ATLANTIC COMMUNITY: A COMPLEX IMBALANCE. New York: Van Nostrand Rinhold for the Foreign Policy Research Institute, University of Pennsylvania. 1970
Pick, Otto and Critchley, Julian. COLLECTIVE SECURITY. London: Macmillan. 1974
Pipes, Richard (ed.). SOVIET STRATEGY IN EUROPE. New York: Crane, Russak. 1975; London: Macdonald and Jane's. 1976
Pranger, Robert (ed.). DETENTE AND DEFENCE. Washington, D.C.: American Enterprise Institute. 1976
Rapoport, Anatol. THE BIG TWO: SOVIET-AMERICAN PERCEPTIONS OF FOREIGN POLICY. New York: Pegasus. 1971. (Emphasises game-theory methodology)
Roberts, Chalmers M. THE NUCLEAR YEARS: THE ARMS RACE AND ARMS CONTROL. 1945–1970. New York: Praeger. 1970
Schaetzel, J. Robert. THE UNHINGED ALLIANCE: AMERICA AND THE EUROPEAN COMMUNITY. New York: Harper and Row for the Council on Foreign Relations. 1975. (A plea for a revitalised U.S. commitment to Europe)
Schilling, Warner R., *et al.* AMERICAN ARMS AND A CHANGING EUROPE: DILEMMAS OF DETERRENCE AND DISARMAMENT. New York: Columbia University Press. 1974
Schmidt, Helmut. THE BALANCE OF POWER. London: William Kimber. 1971
Stanley, Timothy W. A CONFERENCE ON EUROPEAN SECURITY? PROBLEMS, PROSPECTS AND PITFALLS. Washington, D.C.: The Atlantic Council of the United States. 1970
Stanley, Timothy W. and Whitt, Darnell M. DETENTE DIPLOMACY: THE U.S. AND EUROPEAN SECURITY IN THE 1970'S. Cambridge, Mass.: The University Press of Cambridge; New York: Dunellen for the Atlantic Council of the United States. 1970; London: Martin

Robertson. 1973
Steibel, Gerald L. DETENTE: PROMISES AND PITFALLS. New York: Crane, Russak. 1975
Terchek, Ronald J. THE MAKING OF THE TEST-BAN TREATY. The Hague: Nijhoff. 1970
Twitchett, K.J. (ed.). INTERNATIONAL SECURITY. London: Oxford University Press for the Royal Institute of International Affairs. 1971
Ulam, Adam B. THE RIVALS: AMERICA AND RUSSIA SINCE WORLD WAR II. New York: The Viking Press. 1971
Urban, G.R. (ed.). DETENTE. London: Maurice Temple Smith. 1976
Vayrynen, Raimo. TWO APPROACHES TO EUROPEAN SECURITY: ARMS CONTROL AND CO-OPERATION. Tampere: Tampere Peace Research Institute. 1974. (A Finnish view)
Vigor, P.H. THE SOVIET VIEW OF WAR, PEACE AND NEUTRALITY. London: Routledge & Kegan Paul. 1975
Weeks, Albert L. THE OTHER SIDE OF CO-EXISTENCE. New York: Pitman. 1970. (An analysis of Soviet foreign policy vis-à-vis the United States)
Whetten, Lawrence (ed.). THE POLITICAL IMPLICATIONS OF SOVIET MILITARY POWER. London: Macdonald and Jane's. 1977
Wyle, Frederick S. U.S., EUROPE, SALT AND STRATEGY. Chicago: Center for Policy Study, Chicago University Press. 1971
Yost, Charles. THE CONDUCT AND MISCONDUCT OF FOREIGN AFFAIRS: REFLECTIONS ON U.S. FOREIGN POLICY SINCE WORLD WAR II. New York: Random House. 1972
Zimmerman, William. SOVIET PERSPECTIVES ON INTERNATIONAL RELATIONS 1945–1967. Princeton: Princeton University Press for the Russian Institute and the Institute of War and Peace Studies, Columbia University; London: Oxford University Press. 1969

Military-Strategic Aspects

Baylis, John (ed.), *et al.* CONTEMPORARY STRATEGY, THEORIES AND POLICIES. London: Croom Helm. 1975
Bertram, Christoph and Holst, Johan Jorgen (eds.). NEW STRATEGIC FACTORS IN THE NORTH ATLANTIC. Guildford, Surrey: IPC Science and Technology Press; Oslo: Universitetsforlaget. 1977
Buchan, Alastair (ed.). PROBLEMS OF MODERN STRATEGY. London:

Chatto and Windus. 1970. (A selection of papers presented at the 10th annual I.S.S. Conference, Oxford, 1968)

Eller, Ernest McNeill. THE SOVIET SEA CHALLENGE: THE STRUGGLE FOR CONTROL OF THE WORLD'S OCEANS. New York: Cowles Book Co., Inc. 1971

Enthoven, Alain C. and Smith, K. Wayne. HOW MUCH IS ENOUGH? New York: Haper and Row. 1971. (Concerning the balance of forces in Europe)

Fairhall, David. RUSSIA LOOKS TO THE SEA: A STUDY OF THE EXPANSION OF SOVIET MARITIME POWER. London: André Deutsch. 1971

Goldhamer, Herbert. THE SOVIET SOLDIER. New York: Crane Russak. 1975

Gorshkov, Admiral Sergi C. RED STAR RISING AT SEA. Annapolis, Md: United States Naval Institute. 1974

Gouré, Leon, et al. THE ROLE OF NUCLEAR FORCES IN CURRENT SOVIET STRATEGY. Washington, D.C.: Center for Advanced International Studies, University of Miami. 1974

Grechko, Andrey. THE ARMED FORCES OF THE SOVIET STATE. Washington, D.C.: U.S. Air Force. 1976

Kaplan, Morton A. (ed.). SALT: PROBLEMS AND PROSPECTS. Morristown, N.J.: General Learning Press. 1973

Lawrence, R.D. and Record, J. U.S. FORCE STRUCTURE IN NATO: AN ALTERNATIVE. (Studies in Defence Policy, The Brookings Institution). Washington: Brookings Institution. 1974; London: Allen and Unwin. 1975

Legault, Albert and Lindsey, George. THE DYNAMICS OF THE NUCLEAR BALANCE. Ithaca: Cornell University Press. 1974. (A–Z of the strategic arms race)

Lomov, Col.-General N.A. (ed.). SCIENTIFIC-TECHNICAL PROGRESS AND THE REVOLUTION IN MILITARY AFFAIRS. (Soviet Military Thought Series No. 3.) Moscow: Soviet Ministry of Defence Publishing House. 1973; Washington, D.C.: U.S.G.P.O. 1974

MccGuire, Michael (ed.). SOVIET NAVAL DEVELOPMENTS: CAPABILITY AND CONTEXT. New York: Praeger; London: Pall Mall. 1973

MccGuire, Michael and McDonnell, John (eds.). SOVIET NAVAL INFLUENCE: DOMESTIC AND FOREIGN DIMENSIONS. New York: Praeger. 1977

MccGuire, Michael (ed.), et al. SOVIET NAVAL POLICY: OBJECTIVES

AND CONSTRAINTS. New York: Praeger; London: Pall Mall. 1975
Morris, Eric. THE RUSSIAN NAVY: MYTH AND REALITY. London: Hamish Hamilton. 1977
Newhouse, J. (ed.). U.S. TROOPS IN EUROPE: ISSUES, COSTS AND CHOICES. Washington, D.C.: Brookings Institution. 1971; London: Allen and Unwin. 1972. (See review by A. Utkin: 'U.S. troops in Europe: Policy and finance' in INTERNATIONAL AFFAIRS (Moscow). 1972. No. 7. pp. 89–90)
Newhouse, J. COLD DAWN: THE STORY OF SALT. New York: Holt, Rinehart and Winston. 1973
Northedge, F.S. (ed.). THE USE OF FORCE IN INTERNATIONAL RELATIONS. London: Faber. 1974
Paul, Roland A. AMERICAN MILITARY COMMITMENTS ABROAD. New Brunswick: Rutgers University Press. 1973
Perrett, Bryan. NATO ARMOUR. London: Ian Allen. 1971
Polmar, Norman. SOVIET NAVAL POWER: CHALLENGE FOR THE 1970'S. London: Macdonald and Jane's; New York: Crane, Russak. 1974
Record, Jeffrey. U.S. NUCLEAR WEAPONS IN EUROPE: ISSUES AND ALTERNATIVES. Washington, D.C.: Brookings Institution. 1974
Record, Jeffrey. SIZING UP THE SOVIET ARMY. Oxford: Blackwell for the Brookings Institution. 1976
Roberts, Adam. NATIONS IN ARMS. London: Chatto and Windus for the International Institute for Strategic Studies. 1976. (Territorial defence in Yugoslavia and Sweden, as models for NATO)
SIPRI (Stockholm International Peace Research Institute). FORCE REDUCTIONS IN EUROPE. Stockholm: Almqvist and Wiksell. 1974
Sokolovsky, V.D. (edited by Harriet Fast Scott). SOVIET MILITARY STRATEGY. New York: Crane, Russak. 1975
Sukovic, Olga. FORCE REDUCTIONS IN EUROPE. Stockholm: Stockholm International Peace Research Institute. 1974
Swedish Ministry of Defence. PROSPECTS OF MUTUAL REDUCTIONS IN EUROPE. Stockholm: Ministry of Defence. 1976
Tanmen, Ronald L. MIRV AND THE ARMS RACE: AN INTERPRETATION OF DEFENCE STRATEGY. New York: Praeger. 1973
Theberge, James (ed.). SOVIET SEAPOWER IN THE CARIBBEAN: POLITICAL AND STRATEGIC IMPLICATIONS. New York: Praeger; London: Pall Mall. 1972
Tillema, Herbert K. APPEAL TO FORCE: AMERICAN MILITARY

INTERVENTION IN THE ERA OF CONTAINMENT. New York: Crowell. 1973
Whetten, Lawrence L. (ed.). THE FUTURE OF SOVIET MILITARY POWER. London: Macdonald and Jane's. 1976
Willrich, Mason and Rhinelander, John B. (eds.). SALT: THE MOSCOW AGREEMENTS AND BEYOND. New York: Free Press. 1974

Reports, Papers and Pamphlets

Economic Aspects

Kaldor, Mary. EUROPEAN DEFENCE INDUSTRIES – NATIONAL AND INTERNATIONAL IMPLICATIONS. (Occasional Papers. 1st Series. No. 8.). Brighton: Institute for the Study of International Organisation, University of Sussex. 1972
Wolf, Charles, Jr. 'OFFSETS', STANDARDISATION AND TRADE LIBERALISATION IN NATO. (Rand Paper, P-5779). Santa Monica: Rand Corporation. October 1976

National and Regional Aspects

Archer, Clive (ed.). SECURITY IN NORTHERN EUROPE. Aberdeen: Centre for Nordic Studies, University of Aberdeen. 1976
Baker, Steven. ITALY AND THE NUCLEAR OPTION. Santa Monica: Seminar on Arms Control and Foreign Policy. May 1974
Bark, Dennis L. AGREEMENT ON BERLIN: A STUDY OF THE 1970–1972 QUADRIPARTITE NEGOTIATIONS. (AEI-Hoover policy studies). Washington, D.C.: American Enterprise Institute for Public Policy Research. 1974
Bellini, James. FRENCH DEFENCE POLICY. London: R.U.S.I. 1974
Brown, Neville. EUROPEAN SECURITY 1972–1980. London: R.U.S.I. 1972
Conant, Melvin A. A PERSPECTIVE OF DEFENCE: THE CANADIAN-UNITED STATES COMPACT. ('Behind the Headlines'. Vol. 33. No. 4.). Toronto: Canadian Institute of International Affairs. October 1974

Cromwell, William C. THE EUROGROUP AND NATO. (Monograph No. 18). Philadelphia: Foreign Policy Research Institute, University of Pennsylvania. 1974

Danish Strategic Study Group. DENMARK BETWEEN THE SUPERPOWERS. Copenhagen: Danish Foreign Policy Society. 1977

Gray, Colin S. CANADA AND NORAD: A STUDY IN STRATEGY. Toronto: Canadian Institute of International Affairs. 1972

Holst, Johan J. and Urban, G.R. NORWAY IN THE EVOLVING PROCESS OF EUROPEAN SECURITY. (NUP1/N-72, June 1974). Oslo: Norsk Utenrikspolitik Institutt. 1974

Janczewski, George H. DETENTE AND EASTERN EUROPE. Washington, D.C.: Strategic Research Group, National War College. 1975

Ludz, Peter Christian. TWO GERMANYS IN ONE WORLD. (Atlantic Papers 1973. No. 3). Paris: Atlantic Institute for International Affairs. 1973

Norwegian Atlantic Committee. NORWAY AND THE ATLANTIC TIES. Oslo: Norwegian Atlantic Committee. 1976

Orvik, Nils. EUROPE'S NORTHERN CAP AND THE SOVIET UNION. (Occasional Papers in International Affairs. No. 6). Cambridge, Mass.: Center for International Affairs, Harvard University. 1963

Rees, David. SOUTHERN EUROPE: NATO'S CRUMBLING FLANK. (Conflict Studies. No. 60). London: Institute for the Study of Conflict. August 1975

Sherman, Michael E. A SINGLE SERVICE FOR CANADA? Adelphi Paper No. 39. July 1967. London: I.S.S.

Smart, Ian. FUTURE CONDITIONAL: THE PROSPECT FOR ANGLO-FRENCH NUCLEAR CO-OPERATION. Adelphi Paper No. 78. August 1971. London: I.S.S.

Ulstein, Egil. NORDIC SECURITY. Adelphi Paper No. 81. November 1971. London: I.I.S.S.

Vannicelli, Primo. ITALY, NATO AND THE EUROPEAN COMMUNITY. (Harvard Studies in International Affairs. No. 31). Cambridge, Mass.: Center for International Affairs, Harvard University. 1974

Windsor, Philip. GERMANY AND THE MANAGEMENT OF DETENTE. (Studies in International Security. 15). London: Chatto and Windus for the I.S.S. 1971

Politico-Military Aspects

Binkin, Martin. SUPPORT COSTS IN THE DEFENSE BUDGET: THE SUBMERGED ONE-THIRD. Washington, D.C.: The Brookings Institution. 1972

Bluhm, Georg R. DETENTE AND MILITARY RELAXATION IN EUROPE: A GERMAN VIEW. Adelphi Paper. No. 40. September 1967. London: I.S.S.

Buchan, Alastair. THE FUTURE OF NATO. (International Conciliation No. 565). New York: Carnegie Endowment for International Peace. 1967

Buchan, Alastair. EUROPE AND AMERICA: FROM ALLIANCE TO COALITION. (Atlantic Papers 1973. No. 4). Paris: Atlantic Institute for International Affairs.

Bull, Hedley. STRATEGY AND THE ATLANTIC ALLIANCE: A CRITIQUE OF UNITED STATES DOCTRINE. (Policy Memo. No. 29). Princeton, N.J.: Center of International Studies, Woodrow Wilson School of Public and International Affairs, Princeton University. 1964

Burt, Richard. DEFENCE BUDGETING: THE BRITISH AND AMERICAN CASES. Adelphi Paper No. 112. Winter 1974—75. London: I.I.S.S.

Caldwell, Lawrence T. SOVIET ATTITUDES TO SALT. Adelphi Paper No. 75. February 1971. London: I.S.S.

Caldwell, Lawrence T. SOVIET SECURITY INTERESTS IN EUROPE AND MBFR. Los Angeles: University of Southern California Arms Control and Foreign Policy Seminar. January 1974

Caldwell, Lawrence T. SOVIET-AMERICAN RELATIONS: ONE-HALF DECADE OF DETENTE PROBLEMS AND ISSUES. (Atlantic Papers 1975. No. 5). Paris: Atlantic Institute for International Affairs

Caldwell, Lawrence T. SOVIET SECURITY INTERESTS IN EUROPE AND MFR. (Research Paper No. 72). Santa Monica: California Seminar on Arms Control and Foreign Policy. April 1976

Cliffe, Trevor. MILITARY TECHNOLOGY AND THE EUROPEAN BALANCE. Adelphi Paper No. 89. August 1972. London: I.I.S.S.

Coffey, J.I. NEW APPROACHES TO ARMS REDUCTION IN EUROPE. Adelphi Paper No. 105. Summer 1974. London: I.I.S.S.

Coffey, J.I. ARMS CONTROL, TACTICAL NUCLEAR FORCES AND EUROPEAN SECURITY. (Occasional Paper No. 2). Pittsburgh: Center for Arms Control and International Security Studies, University Center for International Studies. 1976

Collier, David S. and Glaser, Kurt (eds.). THE CONDITIONS FOR PEACE IN EUROPE: PROBLEMS OF DETENTE AND SECURITY.

(Foundation for Foreign Affairs, Series 13). Washington, D.C.: Public Affairs Press in co-operation with the Foundation for Foreign Affairs. 1969

Crean, G. EUROPEAN SECURITY – THE CSCE FINAL ACT: TEXT AND COMMENTARY. Toronto: Canadian Institute of International Affairs. September 1976

Cromwell, William C. (ed.), *et ql.* POLITICAL PROBLEMS OF ATLANTIC PARTNERSHIP. (Studies in Contemporary European Issues No. 3). Brussels: College of Europe. 1969

Crozier, Brian (ed.). EUROPEAN SECURITY AND THE SOVIET PROBLEM. London: Institute for the Study of Conflict. 1971. (A very sceptical view of ECSC)

Dougherty, James and Pfaltzgraff, Diane. EUROCOMMUNISM AND THE ATLANTIC ALLIANCE. Cambridge, Mass.: Institute for Foreign Policy Analysis. January 1977

Erickson, John. RUSSIAN AIMS, INTENTIONS AND CAPABILITIES. London: R.U.S.I. October 1970

Europe-America Conference. NEW ROLES AND RELATIONSHIPS IN THE NEXT DECADE. Amsterdam: Europe-America Conference. March 1973

Federal German Ministry of Defence. THE SECURITY OF THE FEDERAL REPUBLIC OF GERMANY AND THE DEVELOPMENT OF THE FEDERAL ARMED FORCES. (Defence White Paper 1975/ 1976). Bonn: Federal Ministry of Defence. 1976

Gittings, John and Gott, Richard. NATO'S FINAL DECADE. London: CND (Campaign for Nuclear Disarmament). 1964

Goldstein, Walter. THE DILEMMA OF BRITISH DEFENCE: THE IMBALANCE BETWEEN COMMITMENTS AND RESOURCES. (The Social Science Program of the Mershon Center for Education in National Security, Ohio State University. Pamphlet Series, No. 3). Columbus: Ohio State University Press. 1966

Gorgey, Lazslo. BONN'S EASTERN POLICY 1964–1971: EVOLUTION AND LIMITATIONS. (International Relations Series, No. 3). Hamden, Conn.: Archon for The Institute of International Studies, University of South Carolina. 1972

Greenwood, David. BUDGETING FOR DEFENCE. London: R.U.S.I. 1972

Hadley, Guy. TRANSATLANTIC PARTNERSHIP AND PROBLEMS: AN ENQUIRY INTO RELATIONS BETWEEN WESTERN EUROPE AND THE UNITED STATES. Tunbridge Wells: Free Trade

Association Trust. 1974

Harrison, Michael. WESTERN EUROPE TO THE EXTREME LEFT: IMPLICATIONS FOR ATLANTIC RELATIONS. (Occasional Paper No. 17). Bologna: Johns Hopkins University Center. January 1977

Hartley, A. AMERICAN FOREIGN POLICY IN THE NIXON ERA. Adelphi Paper No. 110. Winter 1974–1975. London: I.I.S.S.

Heisenberg, Wolfgang. THE ALLIANCE AND EUROPE: PART I: CRISIS STABILITY IN EUROPE AND NUCLEAR WEAPONS. Adelphi Paper No. 96. Summer 1973. London: I.I.S.S.

Heyhoe, D.C.R. THE ALLIANCE AND EUROPE: PART VI: THE EUROPEAN PROGRAMME GROUP. Adelphi Paper No. 129. Winter 1976–1977. London: I.I.S.S.

Hill, R.J. POLITICAL CONSULTATION IN NATO. (ORAE Memorandum No. 64). Ottawa: O.R.A.E., Department of National Defence. March 1975

Hoffman, Stanley, et al. FORCE IN MODERN SOCIETIES: ITS PLACE IN INTERNATIONAL POLITICS. Adelphi Paper No. 102. Winter 1973. London: I.I.S.S.

Holtzel, Michael (ed.). HELSINKI, BELGRADE AND DETENTE. Berlin: Aspen Institute. October 1976

Huntley, James R. MAN'S ENVIRONMENT AND THE ATLANTIC ALLIANCE. Brussels: NATO Information Service 1971. (Concerning the work of the Committee on the Challenges of Modern Society)

Joshua, Wynfred and Hahn, Walter P. NUCLEAR POLITICS: AMERICA, FRANCE AND BRITAIN. (The Washington Papers 1, No. 9). Beverly Hills: SAGE Publications. 1973

Kaplan, Morton A. THE RATIONALE FOR NATO: EUROPEAN COLLECTIVE SECURITY – PAST AND FUTURE. Stanford: Hoover Institution; Washington, D.C.: American Enterprise Institute for Public Policy Research. 1973

Kaplan, Morton A. NATO AND DISSUASION. Chicago: Center for Policy Study, University of Chicago. 1974

Knorr, Klaus. A NATO NUCLEAR FORCE: THE PROBLEM OF MANAGEMENT. (Policy Memorandum, No. 26). Princeton, Center of International Studies, Woodrow Wilson School of Public and International Affairs, Princeton University. 1963

Kohler, Foy D., et al. SOVIET STRATEGY FOR THE SEVENTIES: FROM COLD WAR TO PEACEFUL CO-EXISTENCE. Miami: Center for Advanced International Studies, University of Miami. 1974

Kohn, Hans. NATIONALISM IN THE ATLANTIC COMMUNITY.

(Monograph Series, No. 3). Philadelphia: Foreign Policy Research Institute, University of Pennsylvania. 1965

Kolkowicz, Roman (ed.). THE WARSAW PACT. Arlington, Virginia: International and Social Division, Institute for Defense Analysis. 1969

Korbonski, Andrzej. THE WARSAW PACT. (International Conciliation. No. 573. May 1969). New York: Carnegie Endowment for International Peace. 1969

Kronenberg, Vernon J. ALL TOGETHER NOW: THE ORGANISATION OF THE DEPARTMENT OF NATIONAL DEFENCE IN CANADA. (Wellesley Paper 1973. No. 3). Toronto: Canadian Institute of International Affairs. 1973

Kudryatsev, Vladimir. PEACE PROGRAMME FOR EUROPE. Moscow: Novosti Press Agency. 1972

MccGuire, Michael. THE SOVIET UNION IN EUROPE AND THE NEAR EAST: HER CAPABILITIES AND INTENTIONS. London: R.U.S.I. 1971

Meeker, Thomas A. THE MILITARY-INDUSTRIAL COMPLEX: A SOURCE GUIDE TO THE ISSUES OF DEFENCE SPENDING AND POLICY CONTROL. (Political Issues Series, Center for the Study of Armament and Disarmament). Los Angeles: California State University. 1973

Meissner, Boris. THE BREZHNEV DOCTRINE. (East European Monograph No. 2). Kansas City: Government Research Bureau, Park College. December 1970

Mendershausen, Horst. THE ATLANTIC DEFENCE RELATIONSHIPS: CORE, TROUBLES, PROSPECTS. (Rand Paper P5262). Santa Monica: Rand Corporation. July 1974

Mendershausen, Horst. OUTLOOK ON WESTERN SOLIDARITY: POLITICAL RELATIONS IN THE ATLANTIC ALLIANCE SYSTEM. (R-1512-PR). Santa Monica: Rand Corporation. June 1976

Moscow News Editorial Board. EUROPEAN SECURITY: A SPECTRUM OF OPINIONS. Moscow: Moscow News. 1972

Nerlich, Uwe. THE ALLIANCE AND EUROPE: PART V: NUCLEAR WEAPONS AND EAST-WEST NEGOTIATION. Adelphi Paper No. 120. Winter 1975–1976. London: I.I.S.S.

Netherlands Institute for Peace Questions. NUCLEAR WEAPONS FOR WESTERN EUROPE? The Hague: Netherlands Institute for Peace Questions. 1974

Netherlands Institute for Peace Questions. SHOULD THE WEST PROMISE NEVER TO BE THE FIRST TO USE NUCLEAR

WEAPONS? The Hague: Netherlands Institute for Peace Questions. 1974

Neuman, H.J. NUCLEAR WEAPONS FOR WESTERN EUROPE. (Paper prepared for the Netherlands Ministry of Foreign Affairs). The Hague: Netherlands Institute for Peace Questions. November 1974

Northedge, F.S. EAST-WEST RELATIONS: DETENTE AND AFTER. (Monograph Series, No. 4. Institute of Administration). Ife, Nigeria: University of Ife Press. 1975

Nunn, Senator Sam. POLICY, TROOPS AND THE NATO ALLIANCE. (Report to the Senate Committee on Armed Services, April 1974). Washington, D.C.: U.S.G.P.O. 1974

Palmer, Michael. THE PROSPECTS FOR A EUROPEAN SECURITY CONFERENCE. London: R.I.I.A./P.E.P. 1971

Petrov, Vladimir. U.S. – SOVIET DETENTE: PAST AND FUTURE. Washington, D.C.: American Enterprise Institute for Public Policy Research. 1975

Pugwash Conference. EUROPEAN SECURITY, DISARMAMENT AND OTHER PROBLEMS. (Proceedings of the 23rd Conference). Anlanko, Finland: Pugwash Conference. 1973

Rosecrance, Richard (ed.). THE FUTURE OF THE INTERNATIONAL STRATEGIC SYSTEM. London and San Francisco: Chandler Publishing Co. 1972

Rosecrance, Richard. STRATEGIC DETERRENCE RECONSIDERED. Adelphi Paper No. 116. Spring 1977. London: I.I.S.S.

Ruehl, Lothar. THE NINE AND NATO. (The Atlantic Papers 1974. No. 2). Paris: Atlantic Institute for International Affairs

Serfaty, Simon. AMERICA AND EUROPE IN THE 1970'S: INTEGRATION OR DISINTEGRATION? (Research Paper Series No. 8, Institute of Foreign Policy Research). Bologna: Johns Hopkins University. February 1974

Slocombe, Walter. THE POLITICAL IMPLICATIONS OF STRATEGIC PARITY. Adelphi Paper No. 77. May 1971. London: I.S.S.

Sloss, Leon. NATO REFORM: PROSPECTS AND PRIORITIES. (Washington Papers. Vol. 3. No. 30). Beverly Hills and London: SAGE Publications for the Center for Strategic and International Studies, Georgetown University, Washington D.C. 1975

Trezise, Philip H. THE ATLANTIC CONNECTION: PROSPECTS, PROBLEMS AND POLICIES. Washington, D.C.: The Brookings Institution. 1975

Vandevanter, E., Jr. COMMON FUNDING IN NATO. (Memorandum

RM-5282 PR). Santa Monica: Rand Corporation. 1967
Vincent, R.J. MILITARY POWER AND POLITICAL INFLUENCE. Adelphi Paper No. 119. Autumn 1975. London: I.I.S.S.
W.E.U. (Western European Union). A EUROPEAN ARMAMENTS POLICY. Paris: W.E.U. May 1977
Wolfe, Thomas W. ROLE OF THE WARSAW PACT IN SOVIET POLICY. (Rand paper P-4975). Santa Monica: Rand Corporation. 1975

Military and Strategic Aspects

Adomeit, Hannes. SOVIET RISK-TAKING AND CRISIS BEHAVIOUR: FROM CONFRONTATION TO CO-EXISTENCE? Adelphi Paper No. 101. Autumn 1973. London: I.I.S.S.
Bertram, Christoph. MUTUAL FORCE REDUCTIONS IN EUROPE: THE POLITICAL ASPECTS. Adelphi Paper No. 84. January 1972. London: I.I.S.S.
Booth, Ken. THE MILITARY INSTRUMENT IN SOVIET POLICY, 1917–1972. London: R.U.S.I. 1973
British Atlantic Committee. THE SECURITY OF NORTH SEA OIL AND THE OVERALL SOVIET NAVAL THREAT. Paris: Atlantic Treaty Association. 1976
British Council of Churches. THE BRITISH NUCLEAR DETERRENT: RESOLUTION AND REPORT OF A WORKING GROUP, October 1963. London: S.C.M. Press. 1963
Bull, Hedley, *et al.* POWER AT SEA: PART I: THE NEW ENVIRONMENT. Adelphi Paper No. 122. Spring 1976. London: I.I.S.S.
Burt, Richard. NEW WEAPONS TECHNOLOGIES: DEBATE AND DIRECTIONS. Adelphi Paper No. 126. Autumn 1976. London: I.I.S.S.
Canby, Steven L. DAMPING NUCLEAR COUNTERFORCE INCENTIVES: CORRECTING NATO'S INFERIORITY IN CONVENTIONAL MILITARY STRENGTH. Santa Monica: California Arms Control and Foreign Policy Seminar. August 1974
Canby, Steven. THE ALLIANCE AND EUROPE: PART IV: MILITARY DOCTRINE AND TECHNOLOGY. Adelphi Paper No. 109. Winter 1974–1975. London: I.I.S.S.
Davis, Lynn Etheridge. LIMITED NUCLEAR OPTIONS: DETERRENCE AND THE NEW AMERICAN DOCTRINE. Adelphi Paper No. 121. Winter 1975–1976. London: I.I.S.S.

Digby, James F. PRECISION-GUIDED WEAPONS. Adelphi Paper No. 118. Summer 1975. London: I.I.S.S.

Facer, Roger. THE ALLIANCE AND EUROPE: PART III: WEAPONS PROCUREMENT IN EUROPE – CAPABILITIES AND CHOICES. Adelphi Paper No. 108. Winter 1974. London: I.I.S.S.

Fischer, Robert Lucas. DEFENDING THE CENTRAL FRONT: THE BALANCE OF FORCES. Adelphi Paper No. 127. Autumn 1976. London: I.I.S.S.

de Gara, John P. NUCLEAR PROLIFERATION AND SECURITY. (International Conciliation No. 578). New York: Carnegie Foundation for International Peace. May 1970

Gard, Major-General Robert G., Jr., *et al.* FORCE IN MODERN SOCIETIES: THE MILITARY PROFESSION. Adelphi Paper No. 103. Winter 1973. London: I.I.S.S.

Goure, Leon and others. THE ROLE OF NUCLEAR FORCES IN CURRENT SOVIET STRATEGY. Washington: Center for Advanced International Studies, University of Miami. 1974

Greenwood, Ted. RECONNAISSANCE, SURVEILLANCE AND ARMS CONTROL. Adelphi Paper No. 88. June 1972. London: I.I.S.S.

Holloway, David. TECHNOLOGY, MANAGEMENT AND THE SOVIET MILITARY ESTABLISHMENT. Adelphi Paper No. 76. April 1971. London: I.S.S.

Holloway, David. THE SOVIET APPROACH TO MBFR. (The Waverley Papers, Series 1, Occasional paper 5). Edinburgh: The University of Edinburgh. March 1975

Holst, Johan J. POWER AT SEA: PART II: SUPER-POWERS AND NAVIES. Adelphi Paper No. 123. Spring 1976. London: I.I.S.S.

Howard, Michael. POWER AT SEA: PART III: COMPETITION AND CONFLICT. Adelphi Paper No. 124. Spring 1976. London: I.I.S.S.

Jukes, Geoffrey. THE DEVELOPMENT OF SOVIET STRATEGIC THINKING SINCE 1945. (Canberra Paper No. 14). Canberra: Australian National University Press. 1972

Kemp, Geoffrey. NUCLEAR FORCES FOR MEDIUM POWERS: PART I: TARGETS AND WEAPONS SYSTEMS. Adelphi Paper No. 106. Autumn 1974. London: I.I.S.S.

Kemp, Geoffrey. NUCLEAR FORCES FOR MEDIUM POWERS: PARTS II AND III: STRATEGIC REQUIREMENTS AND OPTIONS. Adelphi Paper No. 107. Autumn 1974. London: I.I.S.S.

Lawrence, Richard and Record, Jeffrey. U.S. FORCE STRUCTURE IN NATO: AN ALTERNATIVE. Washington, D.C.: The Brookings

Institution. 1974

Luttwak, Edward. THE US – USSR NUCLEAR WEAPONS BALANCE. (Washington Papers. Vol. 11. No. 13). Beverly Hills: SAGE Publications for Center for Strategic and International Studies, Georgetown University, Washington, D.C. 1975

Nailor, Peter, *et al.* THE ROLES OF MARITIME FORCES IN THE SECURITY OF WESTERN EUROPE. Southampton: Department of Extra-Mural Studies, University of Southampton. 1972

Newhouse, John (ed.). U.S. TROOPS IN EUROPE: ISSUES, COSTS AND CHOICES. Washington: The Brookings Institution. 1971. (See review by A. Utkin: 'U.S. troops in Europe: policy and finance' in INTERNATIONAL AFFAIRS (Moscow). 1972. No. 7. pp. 89–90)

Phillips, J. EVOLUTION OF NATO DEFENCE STRATEGY. (Monograph on National Security Affairs. August 1974). Providence, Rhode Island: Brown University. 1974

Possony, Stefan T. SOVIET MILITARY DOCTRINE ON THE EVE OF SALT. (Monograph No. 16). Philadelphia: Foreign Policy Research Institute, University of Pennsylvania. 1974

Record, Jeffrey. U.S. NUCLEAR WEAPONS IN EUROPE – ISSUES AND ALTERNATIVES. Washington, D.C.: The Brookings Institution. December 1974

Record, Jeffrey. SIZING UP THE SOVIET ARMY. Washington, D.C.: The Brookings Institution. 1975. (See review by John Erickson in SURVIVAL. Vol. 18. No. 3. May/June 1976. pp. 137–138)

R.U.S.I. (Royal United Services Institute for Defence Studies). A CONVENTIONAL STRATEGY FOR THE CENTRAL FRONT IN NATO. (Report of a Seminar). London: R.U.S.I. 1975

Smart, Ian. MBFR ASSAILED: A CRITICAL VIEW ON THE PROPOSED NEGOTIATIONS. Ithaca: Cornell University Peace Studies Program. 1972

Sukovic, Olga. FORCE REDUCTIONS IN EUROPE. (A SIPRI Monograph). Stockholm: Almqvist and Wiksell; London: Paul Elek; New York: Humanities Press for Stockholm International Peace Research Institute. 1974

Szaz, Z. Michael (ed.). MUTUAL BALANCED FORCE REDUCTIONS AT THE CROSSROADS. Washington, D.C.: American Institute on Problems of European Unity, Inc. 1974

Tucker, Gardiner. TOWARDS RATIONALISING ALLIED WEAPONS PRODUCTION. (Atlantic Paper No. 1. 1976). Paris: Atlantic Institute for International Affairs.

White, William D. U.S. TACTICAL AIR POWER: MISSIONS, FORCES AND COSTS. (Studies in Defence Policy). Washington: The Brookings Institution. 1974

Wolfe, Thomas W. SOVIET ATTITUDES TOWARDS MBFR AND THE USSR'S MILITARY PRESENCE IN EUROPE. Santa Monica: Rand Corporation. April 1972

Wolfe, Thomas W. SOVIET MILITARY CAPABILITIES AND INTENTIONS IN EUROPE. (Rand Paper P-1588). Santa Monica: Rand Corporation. March 1974

Articles

Economic and Social Aspects

Basiuk, Victor. TECHNOLOGY, WESTERN EUROPE'S ALTERNATIVE FUTURES AND AMERICAN POLICY. Orbis. Vol. 15. No. 2. Summer 1971. pp. 485–506

Blaney, Harry C. NATO'S NEW CHALLENGE TO THE PROBLEMS OF MODERN SOCIETY. Atlantic Community Quarterly. Summer 1973. Vol. 11. No. 2. pp. 236–248

Callaghan, Thomas A., Jr. A COMMON MARKET FOR ATLANTIC DEFENCE. Survival. Vol. 17. No. 3. May/June 1975. pp. 129–132. Atlantic Community Quarterly. Vol. 13. No. 2. Summer 1975. pp. 161–168

Callaghan, Thomas A. STANDARDISATION: A PLAN FOR US/EUROPE CO-OPERATION. Atlantic Community Quarterly. Winter 1975–76. Vol. 13. No. 4. pp. 477–486

Korbonski, Andrzej. DETENTE, EAST-WEST TRADE AND THE FUTURE OF ECONOMIC INTEGRATION IN EASTERN EUROPE. World Politics. Vol. 28. No. 4. July 1976. pp. 568–589

Sandler, Todd and Cauley, Jon. ON THE ECONOMIC THEORY OF ALLIANCES. Journal of Conflict Resolution. Vol. 19. No. 2. June 1975. pp. 330–348

Stankiewicz, W. THE CONTRADICTIONS OF MILITARY-INDUSTRIAL INTEGRATION IN WESTERN EUROPE. International Affairs (Moscow). 1972. No. 7. pp. 28–34

Tuthill, John W. ECONOMIC SLOWDOWN AND NATO. Survival.

Vol. 14. No. 2. March/April 1972. pp. 58–61

Vernon, Raymond. APPARATCHIKS AND ENTREPRENEURS: U.S. – SOVIET ECONOMIC RELATIONS. Foreign Affairs. Vol. 52. No. 2. January 1974. pp. 249–262

Institutional Aspects

Bergsten, C. Fred. INTERDEPENDENCE AND THE REFORM OF INTERNATIONAL INSTITUTIONS. International Organisation. Vol. 30. No. 2. Spring 1976. pp. 361–372

Finger, Seymour Maxwell. UNITED STATES POLICY TOWARD INTERNATIONAL INSTITUTIONS. International Organisation. Vol. 30. No. 2. Spring 1976. pp. 347–360

Hartley, Livingston. THE NORTH ATLANTIC ASSEMBLY. Atlantic Community Quarterly. Vol. 13. No. 4. Winter 1975–76. pp. 486–492

Jordan, Robert S. and Newman, Parley W., Jr. THE SECRETARY-GENERAL OF NATO AND MULTINATIONAL POLITICAL LEADERSHIP. International Journal. Vol. 30. No. 4. Autumn 1975. pp. 732–757

Kharlanov, Y. EUROPEAN CROSSROADS. International Affairs (Moscow). 1975. No. 2. pp. 96–102. (A journalist's view of NATO in Brussels)

Kyba, Patrick. CCMS: THE ENVIRONMENTAL CONNECTION. International Journal. Vol. 29. No. 2. Spring 1974. pp. 256–267

McGale, Senator Gale. ATLANTIC UNION RESOLUTION. Atlantic Community Quarterly. Vol. 10. No. 4. 1972–73. pp. 541–543. (A plea for Atlantic federal union)

NATO Information Service. THE EUROGROUP. Atlantic Community Quarterly. Vol. 14. No. 1. Spring 1976. pp. 76–88

Ruehl, Lothar. NATO'S POLITICAL LIMITATIONS. Atlantic Community Quarterly. Vol. 12. No. 4. Winter 1974–75. pp. 463–470. (i.e. the limitations on the roles of the Secretary-General, Chairman of the Military Committee and SACEUR)

Scott, P.H. BEYOND THE EUROGROUP: NEW DEVELOPMENTS IN EUROPEAN DEFENCE. The World Today. Vol. 32. No. 1. January 1976. pp. 31–38

Shtemenko, General Sergei. THE WARSAW PACT SYSTEM. Survival. Vol. 18. No. 4. July/August 1976. pp. 168–170. (Trans. from Za

Rubezhom. 7 May 1976)
West German Ministry of Defence. THE EUROGROUP IN NATO: REPORT BY THE PLANNING STAFF, WEST GERMAN MINISTRY OF DEFENCE. Survival. Vol. 14. No. 5. November/December 1972. pp. 291–293

Zellentin, Gerda. INSTITUTIONS FOR DETENTE AND CO-OPERATION. The World Today. Vol. 29. No. 1. January 1973. pp. 8–15

National and Regional Aspects

Albert, E.H. THE BRANDT DOCTRINE OF TWO STATES IN GERMANY. International Affairs. Vol. 46. No. 2. April 1970. pp. 293–303

Albert, E.H. BONN'S MOSCOW TREATY AND ITS IMPLICATIONS. International Affairs. Vol. 47. No. 2. April 1971. pp. 316–326

Albrecht-Carrié, René. THE NORTH SEA TRIANGLE. Orbis. Vol. 17. No. 4. Winter 1974. pp. 1306–1325

Allison, Graham. COOL IT: THE FOREIGN POLICY OF YOUNG AMERICA. Foreign Policy. No. 1. Winter 1970–71. pp. 144–160

Andersen, K.B. DENMARK AND NATO. The Atlantic Community Quarterly. Fall 1973. Vol. 11. No. 3. pp. 322–327

Are, Giusseppe. ITALY'S COMMUNISTS: FOREIGN AND DEFENCE POLICIES. Survival. Vol. 18. No. 5. September/October 1976. pp. 210–216

Aseyev, I. EUROPE 1972: TIME OF HOPES. International Affairs (Moscow). 1972. No. 10. pp. 16–21

Bahr, Egon. GERMAN OSTPOLITIK AND SUPER-POWER RELATIONS. Survival. Vol. 15. No. 6. November/December 1973. pp. 296–300

Balniel, Lord. EUROPEAN DEFENCE AND EUROPEAN SECURITY. (Paper presented at the 8th International Wehrkunde Conference. Munich. February 1971). Survival. Vol. 13. No. 5. May 1971. pp. 168–172

Bark, Dennis L. THE DILEMMAS OF DETENTE: NEGOTIATION AND AGREEMENT ON BERLIN 1970–1972. Washington: American Enterprise Institute for Public Policy Research. 1974

Barman, Thomas. BRITAIN, FRANCE AND WEST GERMANY: THE CHANGING PATTERN OF THEIR RELATIONSHIP IN

WEST GERMANY. International Affairs. Vol. 46. No. 2. April 1970

Basagni, Fabio and Flynn, Gregory A. ITALY, EUROPE AND WESTERN SECURITY. Survival. Vol. 20. No. 3. May/June 1977. pp. 98–106

Bechtoldt, Heinrich. BERLIN AGREEMENT AND SECURITY CONFERENCE. Aussenpolitik. Vol. 23. No. 1. 1972. pp. 26–35

Bellini, James and Pattie, Geoffrey. BRITISH DEFENCE OPTIONS: A GAULLIST PERSPECTIVE. Survival. Vol. 19. No. 5. September/October 1977. pp. 217–224

Bender, Peter. THE SPECIAL RELATIONSHIP OF THE TWO GERMAN STATES. The World Today. Vol. 29. No. 2. September 1973. pp. 389–397

Bernos, Roger. GAULLIST FOREIGN POLICY IN RETROSPECT. The World Today. Vol. 30. No. 8. August 1974. pp. 345–354

Bertram, Christoph. WEST GERMAN PERSPECTIVES ON EUROPEAN SECURITY: CONTINUITY AND CHANGE. The World Today. Vol. 27. No. 3. March 1971. pp. 115–123

Birnbaum, Karl E. SOVIET POLICY IN NORTHERN EUROPE. Survival. Vol. 12. No. 7. July 1970. pp. 227–232

Bjarnason, Bjorn. THE SECURITY OF ICELAND. Conciliation and Conflict. Vol. 7. Nos. 3/4. 1972. pp. 193–208

Bleek, Wilhelm. FROM COLD WAR TO OSTPOLITIK: TWO GERMANIES IN SEARCH OF SEPARATE IDENTITIES. World Politics. Vol. 29. No. 1. October 1976. pp. 114–129

Brandt, Willy. GERMANY'S 'WESTPOLITIK'. Foreign Affairs. Vol. 50. No. 3. April 1972. pp. 416–426

Brandt, Willy. EUROPE'S NEW SELF-AWARENESS. Survival. Vol. 15. No. 4. July/August 1973. pp. 193–194

Byrnes, Robert F. RUSSIA IN EASTERN EUROPE: HEGEMONY WITHOUT SECURITY. Foreign Affairs. Vol. 49. No. 4. July 1971. pp. 682–697

Caldwell, Lawrence T. THE WARSAW PACT: DIRECTIONS OF CHANGE. Problems of Communism. Vol. 24. September/October 1975. pp. 1–19

Campbell, John C. SOVIET STRATEGY IN THE BALKANS. Problems of Communism. Vol. 23. No. 4. July/August 1974. pp. 1–16

Co-operation and Conflict. (Nordic Journal of International Politics. Oslo: Universitetsforlaget). 1972. Nos. 3–4. (Issue devoted to Nordic security)

Dean, Robert W. BONN-PRAGUE RELATIONS: THE POLITICS OF

RECONCILIATION. The World Today. Vol. 29. No. 4. April 1973. pp. 149–159

Debré, Michel. THE PRINCIPLES OF OUR DEFENCE POLICY. (Speech of French defence minister at the Institut des Hautes Etudes de Défense Nationale, 25 June 1970). Survival. Vol. 12. No. 11. November 1970. pp. 376–383

Debré, Michel. FRANCE'S GLOBAL STRATEGY. Foreign Affairs. Vol. 49. No. 3. April 1971. pp. 395–406

Debré, Michel. THE DEFENSE OF EUROPE AND SECURITY IN EUROPE. Atlantic Community Quarterly. Vol. 11. No. 1. Spring 1973. pp. 93–119

Delarue, Maurice. FRANCE – FOR A EUROPEAN EUROPE. Aussenpolitik. Vol. 25. No. 2. 1974. pp. 134–145

Dobell, Peter C. EUROPE: CANADA'S LAST CHANCE? International Journal. Vol. 27. No. 1. Winter 1971. pp. 113–133

Dobell, W.M. STABILITY IN THE NORTH EAST MEDITERRANEAN. International Journal. Vol. 27. No. 4. Autumn 1972. pp. 546–559. (i.e. Greece and Turkey)

Eggertsson, T. DETERMINANTS OF ICELANDIC FOREIGN RELATIONS. Conciliation and Conflict. 1975. Nos. 1–2. pp. 94–99

Ferreira, Jose Medeiros. PORTUGAL AND NATO. Survival. Vol. 18. No. 5. September/October 1976. pp. 230–232

Fontaine, André. THE REAL DIVISIONS OF EUROPE. Foreign Affairs. Vol. 49. No. 2. January 1971. pp. 302–314

Frelek, Ryszard. POLAND AND THE ALL-EUROPEAN CONFERENCE. International Affairs (Moscow). 1971. No. 7. pp. 31–33

Friedrich, P.J. DEFENCE AND THE FRENCH POLITICAL LEFT. Survival. Vol. 16. No. 4. July/August 1974. pp. 165–171

Fromkin, David. ENTANGLING ALLIANCES. Foreign Affairs. Vol. 48. No. 4. July 1970. pp. 688–700. (A legal and political study of the various alliances of the United States)

Gasteyger, Curt. THE SUPER-POWERS IN THE MEDITERRANEAN. Survival. Vol. 17. No. 6. November/December 1975. pp. 270–275. Atlantic Community Quarterly. Vol. 14. No. 1. Spring 1976. pp. 49–58

Giscard d'Estaing, President Valéry. FRENCH DEFENCE POLICY. (Address to the Institut des Hautes Etudes de Défense Nationale. 1 June 1976). Survival. Vol. 18. No. 5. September/October 1976. pp. 225–230

Golovin, Y. NORDIC EUROPE: SECURITY AND CO-OPERATION.

International Affairs (Moscow). 1971. No. 2. pp. 53–59

Grayson, George W. PORTUGAL AND THE ARMED FORCES MOVEMENT. Orbis. Summer 1975. Vol. 19. No. 2. pp. 335–378

Greenwood, David. THE 1974 (BRITISH) DEFENCE REVIEW IN PERSPECTIVE. Survival. Vol. 17. No. 5. September/October 1975. pp. 223–229

Grishin, A. NATO EXACERBATES THE MEDITERRANEAN SITUATION. International Affairs (Moscow). 1975. No. 1. pp. 89–92

Grosser, Alfred. FRANCE AND GERMANY: LESS DIVERGENT OUTLOOKS? Foreign Affairs. Vol. 48. No. 2. January 1970. pp. 235–244

Guterman, A. SOBER ARGUMENTS ABOUT THE DESTINY OF EUROPE. International Affairs (Moscow). 1971. No. 9. pp. 105–107. (Review article on European security)

Haagerup, Niels, J. DENMARK'S SECURITY POLICY. Survival. Vol. 13. No. 5. May 1971. pp. 172–177

Haagerup, Niels, J. DENMARK'S DEFENCE REFORM. Survival. Vol. 15. No. 4. July/August 1973. pp. 171–177

Hartley, Anthony. EUROPE BETWEEN THE SUPERPOWERS. Foreign Affairs. Vol. 49. No. 2. January 1971. pp. 271–282

Heathcote, Nina. BRANDT'S OSTPOLITIK AND WESTERN INSTITUTIONS. The World Today. Vol. 26. No. 8. August 1970. pp. 334–343

Holmes, John W. CANADA – THE RELUCTANT POWER. Orbis. Vol. 15. No. 1. Spring 1977. pp. 292–304

Holst, Johan Jorgen. THE SOVIET UNION AND NORDIC SECURITY. Conciliation and Conflict. 1971. Nos. 3–4. pp. 137–146

International Journal. Vol. 28. No. 2. Spring 1973. UNITED STATES FOREIGN POLICY

Jacoviello, Alberto. THE ITALIAN SITUATION AND NATO. Survival. Vol. 18. No. 4. July/August 1976. pp. 166–167. (Trans. from L'UNITÀ. 1 March 1976)

Johnston, Admiral Mears, Jr. NATO'S SOUTHERN REGION: PROBLEMS AND PROSPECTS. U.S. Naval Institute Proceedings. Vol. 101. No. 1/863. January 1975. pp. 47–51

Jones, Christopher D. SOVIET HEGEMONY IN EASTERN EUROPE: THE DYNAMICS OF POLITICAL AUTONOMY AND MILITARY INTERVENTION. World Politics. Vol. 29. No. 2. January 1977. pp. 216–241

Jones, W. Treharne. EAST GERMANY UNDER HONECKER. The World Today. Vol. 32. No. 9. September 1976. pp. 339–346

Kaiser, Karl. PROSPECTS FOR WEST GERMANY AFTER THE BERLIN AGREEMENT. The World Today. Vol. 28. No. 1. January 1972. pp. 30–35

Keatinge, Patrick. ODD MAN OUT? IRISH NEUTRALITY AND EUROPEAN SECURITY. International Affairs. Vol. 48. No. 3. July 1972. pp. 438–449

Kennan, George F. AFTER THE COLD WAR: AMERICAN FOREIGN POLICY IN THE 1970'S. Foreign Affairs. Vol. 51. No. 1. October 1972. pp. 210–227

Laloy, Jean. DOES EUROPE HAVE A FUTURE? Foreign Affairs. Vol. 51. No. 1. October 1972. pp. 154–166

Legters, Lyman. A 'SUCCESSFUL' PARTITION: THE CASE OF GERMANY. Intellect. Vol. 103. No. 2363. February 1975. pp. 294–296

Lentner, Howard H. FOREIGN POLICY DECISION MAKING: THE CASE OF CANADA AND NUCLEAR WEAPONS. World Politics. Vol. 29. No. 1. October 1976. pp. 29–66

Leonhard, Wolfgang. THE DOMESTIC POLITICS OF THE NEW SOVIET FOREIGN POLICY. Foreign Affairs. Vol. 52. No. 1. October 1973. pp. 59–74

Libby, Ruthren E. PORTUGAL: A SETBACK FOR NATO. Strategic Review. Vol. 3. No. 2. Spring 1975. pp. 25–29

Livingston, Robert Gerald. EAST GERMANY BETWEEN MOSCOW AND BONN. Foreign Affairs. Vol. 50. No. 2. January 1972. pp. 297–309

Mahncke, Dieter. IN SEARCH OF A MODUS VIVENDI FOR BERLIN: PROSPECTS FOR FOUR-POWER TALKS. The World Today. Vol. 26. No. 4. April 1970. pp. 137–146. Survival. Vol. 12. No. 7. July 1970. pp. 233–239

Mahncke, Dieter. THE BERLIN AGREEMENT: BALANCE AND PROSPECTS. The World Today. Vol. 27. No. 12. December 1971. pp. 511–521

Marshall, D. Bruce. DE GAULLE AND THE SHAPING OF FRENCH FOREIGN POLICY. Orbis. Vol. 19. No. 1. Spring 1975. pp. 255–264

Matveyev, B. IN THE GRIP OF OBSOLETE NOTIONS. (Soviet commentary on a report by the Committee of Experts of the

Governmental Committee on Denmark's Security Policy, 1970).
International Affairs (Moscow). 1972. No. 3. pp. 97–98

McGeehen, Robert and Warnecke, Steven J. EUROPE'S FOREIGN POLICIES: ECONOMICS, POLITICS OR BOTH? Orbis. Vol. 17. No. 4. Winter 1974. pp. 1251–1279

MccGuire, Michael. THE MEDITERRANEAN AND SOVIET NAVAL INTERESTS. International Journal. Vol. 27. No. 4. Autumn 1972. pp. 511–527

Merlini, Cesare. ITALY IN THE ATLANTIC COMMUNITY AND THE ATLANTIC ALLIANCE. The World Today. Vol. 31. No. 4. April 1975. pp. 160–166

Méry, General Guy. FRENCH DEFENCE POLICY. Survival. Vol. 18. No. 5. September/October 1976. pp. 226–228

Mettler, Erich. WHOSE SUCCESS? (The Soviet-West German treaty of August 1970). Survival. Vol. 12. No. 10. October 1970. pp. 325–326

Melton, T.R. NATO'S TROUBLED SOUTHERN FLANK. Strategic Review. Vol. 3. No. 4. Fall 1975. pp. 27–31

Morgan, Roger. WASHINGTON AND BONN: A CASE STUDY IN ALLIANCE POLITICS. International Affairs. Vol. 47. No. 3. July 1971. pp. 489–503

Morgan, Roger. ANGLO-FRENCH RELATIONS TODAY. The World Today. Vol. 27. No. 7. July 1971. pp. 285–290

Morse, Edward L. WESTERN EUROPE: WHY THE MALAISE? Foreign Affairs. Vol. 51. No. 2. January 1973. pp. 367–379

Nerlich, Uwe. WEST EUROPEAN DEFENCE IDENTITY: THE FRENCH PARADOX. The World Today. Vol. 30. No. 5. May 1974. pp. 187–198

Neuman, H.J. THE DUTCH DEFENCE REFORMS. Survival. Vol. 17. No. 1. January/February 1975. pp. 2–8

Northedge, F.S. BRITAIN AS A SECOND-RANK POWER. International Affairs. Vol. 46. No. 1. January 1970. pp. 37–47

Oppermann, Thomas. GERMAN UNITY AND PEACE. Survival. Vol. 13. No. 7. July 1971. pp. 239–243

Orvik, Nils. SEMI-NEUTRALITY AND CANADA'S SECURITY. International Journal. Vol. 29. No. 2. Spring 1974. pp. 186–215

Palmer, Michael and Thomas, David. ARMS CONTROL AND THE MEDITERRANEAN. The World Today. Vol. 27. No. 12. December 1971. pp. 495–502

Palmer, Michael. THE PROSPECTS FOR A EUROPEAN SECURITY

CONFERENCE. Atlantic Community Quarterly. Vol. 9. No. 3. Fall 1971. pp. 293–301

Palmer, Michael. A EUROPEAN SECURITY CONFERENCE: PREPARATION AND PROCEDURE. The World Today. Vol. 28. No. 1. January 1972. pp. 36–46

Palmer, Michael. THE EUROPEAN COMMUNITY AND A SECURITY CONFERENCE. The World Today. Vol. 28. No. 7. July 1972. pp. 296–303

Paterson, W.E. FOREIGN POLICY AND STABILITY IN WEST GERMANY. International Affairs. Vol. 49. No. 3. July 1973. pp. 413–430

Petersen, Nikolaj. DANISH SECURITY POLICY IN THE SEVENTIES: CONTINUITY OR CHANGE? Co-operation and Conflict. 1972. No. 3/4. pp. 139–170

Pierre, Andrew J. THE SALT AGREEMENT AND EUROPE. The World Today. Vol. 28. No. 7. July 1972. pp. 281–288

Porzgen, Hermann. WHY MOSCOW WANTED THE (SOVIET-WEST GERMAN) TREATY (OF AUGUST 1970). Survival. Vol. 12. No. 10. October 1970. pp. 324–325

Possony, Stefan T. THE USSR: BEYOND ITS ZENITH? Orbis. Vol. 15. No. 1. Spring 1971. pp. 87–103. (Soviet policy on German reunification)

Radio Free Europe Research. SIX MONTHS AFTER: THE EAST EUROPEAN RESPONSE TO HELSINKI. Atlantic Community Quarterly. Vol. 14. No. 1. Spring 1976. pp. 59–65

Ranger, Robin. CANADIAN FOREIGN POLICY IN AN AGE OF SUPER-POWER DETENTE. The World Today. Vol. 28. No. 12. December 1972. pp. 546–554

Richards, Ivor. A EUROPEAN DEFENCE POLICY. (Paper presented at the 7th International Wehrkunde Meeting. Munich. February 1970). Survival. Vol. 12. No. 3. March 1970. pp. 75–80

Richardson, Elliot. THE UNITED STATES AND WESTERN EUROPE. Survival. Vol. 12. No. 3. March 1970. pp. 86–90

Ruehl, Lothar. ICELAND'S VITAL VALUE TO NATO STRATEGY. Atlantic Community Quarterly. Vol. 14. No. 1. Spring 1976. pp. 66–68

Sanakoyev, S. USSR – FRG: A TURN TOWARDS NEW RELATIONS. International Affairs (Moscow). 1973. No. 8. pp. 12–17. (i.e. the Moscow-Bonn treaty of 1970)

Sanchez-Gijon, Antonio. SPAIN AND THE ATLANTIC ALLIANCE.

Survival. Vol. 18. No. 6. November/December 1976. pp. 248–253

von Schenk, G. WESTERN EUROPE AND THE NORTHERN MEDITERRANEAN. Aussenpolitik. Vol. 26. No. 2. 1975. pp. 201–212

Schmidt, Helmut. GERMANY IN THE ERA OF NEGOTIATIONS. Foreign Affairs. Vol. 49. No. 1. October 1970. pp. 40–50

Schutz, Klaus. BERLIN IN THE AGE OF DETENTE. The World Today. Vol. 31. No. 1. January 1975. pp. 29–35

Schweigler, Gebhard. A NEW POLITICAL GIANT? WEST GERMAN FOREIGN POLICY IN THE 1970'S. The World Today. Vol. 31. No. 4. April 1975. pp. 134–141

Silvestri, Stefano and Aliboni, Roberto. ITALY'S MEDITERRANEAN ROLE. International Journal. Vol. 27. No. 4. Autumn 1972. pp. 499–510

Sparring, Ake. ICELAND, EUROPE AND NATO. The World Today. Vol. 28. No. 9. September 1972. pp. 393–403

Starnes, John. QUEBEC, CANADA AND THE ALLIANCE. Survival. Vol.19. No. 5. September/October 1977. pp. 212–216

Stewart, Michael. BRITAIN, EUROPE AND THE ALLIANCE. Foreign Affairs. Vol. 48. No. 4. July 1970. pp. 648–659. (The views of the former British Foreign Secretary)

Story, Jonathan. PORTUGAL'S REVOLUTION OF CARNATIONS: PATTERNS OF CHANGE AND CONTINUITY. International Affairs. Vol. 52. No. 3. July 1976. pp. 417–433

Sulzberger, C.L. GREECE UNDER THE COLONELS. Foreign Affairs. Vol. 48. No. 2. January 1970. pp. 300–311

Swanson, Roger Frank. AN ANALYTICAL ASSESSMENT OF THE US-CANADIAN DEFENCE ISSUE AREA. International Organisation. Vol. 28. No. 4. Autumn 1974. pp. 781–802

Ullmann, Marc. SECURITY ASPECTS IN FRENCH FOREIGN POLICY. Survival. Vol. 15. No. 6. November/December 1973. pp. 262–267

Various. THE FUTURE OF DUTCH DEFENCE: REPORT BY THE COMMISSION OF CIVILIAN AND MILITARY EXPERTS. Survival. Vol. 14. No. 6. November/December 1972. pp. 293–300

Vatikiotis, P.J. GREECE AND THE MEDITERRANEAN CRISIS. Survival. Vol. 18. No. 1. January/February 1976. pp. 23–28. (Reprint from Millennium: Journal of International Studies. Vol. 4. No. 1.)

Wagner, Wolfgang. EUROPEAN SECURITY: FOREIGN POLICY AFTER THE CHANGE (i.e. of West German government). Survival.

Vol. 12. No. 2. February 1970. pp. 46–50.
Wagner, Wolfgang. THROUGH DIFFERENT EYES (THE FOUR-POWER NEGOTIATIONS OVER BERLIN). Survival. Vol. 13. No. 7. July 1971. pp. 244–247
Wagner, Wolfgang. TOWARDS A NEW POLITICAL ORDER: GERMAN OSTPOLITIK AND THE EAST-WEST REALIGNMENT. International Journal. Vol. 27. No. 1. Winter 1971. pp. 18–31
Waites, Neville. BRITAIN AND FRANCE: TOWARDS A STABLE RELATIONSHIP. The World Today. Vol. 32. No. 12. December 1976. pp. 451–458
Warnke, Paul C. and Gelb, Leslie H. SECURITY OR CONFRONTATION: THE CASE FOR A (U.S.) DEFENCE POLICY. Foreign Policy. No. 1. Winter 1970–71. Survival. Vol. 13. No. 2. February 1971. pp. 38–48
Warnke, Paul C. APES ON A TREADMILL. Foreign Policy. No. 18. Spring 1975. pp. 12–29. (A critique of U.S. defence spending)
Whetten, Lawrence L. RECENT CHANGES IN EAST EUROPEAN APPROACHES TO EUROPEAN SECURITY. The World Today. Vol. 26. No. 7. July 1970. pp. 277–288
Whetton, Lawrence L. SOVIET STRATEGY – THE MEDITERRANEAN THREAT. Survival. Vol. 12. No. 8. August 1970. pp. 252–258. (Reprint from SURVEY June 1970)
Whetten, Lawrence L. THE PROBLEM OF BERLIN. The World Today. Vol. 27. No. 5. May 1971. pp. 222–227
Whetten, Lawrence L. APPRAISING THE OSTPOLITIK. Orbis. Vol. 15. No. 3. Fall 1977. pp. 856–878
Wilson, Duncan. ANGLO-SOVIET RELATIONS: THE EFFECT OF IDEAS ON REALITY. International Affairs. Vol. 50. No. 3. July 1974. pp. 380–393
Wolfe, Thomas W. THE SOVIET UNION'S STRATEGIC STAKE IN THE GDR. The World Today. Vol. 27. No. 8. August 1971. pp. 340–350
Wyle, Frederick S. THE UNITED STATES AND WEST EUROPEAN SECURITY. Survival. Vol. 14. No. 1. January/February 1972. pp. 8–15
Yugov, L. ITALIAN POLICY AND RELAXATION IN EUROPE. International Affairs (Moscow). 1972. No. 10. pp. 48–52
Yurieva, L. NEW MEMOIRS OF GENERAL DE GAULLE. International Affairs (Moscow). 1971. No. 1. pp. 65–70

Politico-Military Aspects

Allison, Graham; May, Ernest and Yarmolinsky, Adam. LIMITS TO INTERVENTION. Foreign Affairs. Vol. 48. No. 2. January 1970. pp. 245–261

Antonov, A. NATO IN CONDITIONS OF DETENTE. International Affairs (Moscow). 1974. No. 2. pp. 34–41

Antonov, A. SMALL POWERS AND POLICY OF ALIGNMENT. International Affairs (Moscow). 1975. No. 10. pp. 119–122

Arbatov, G.A. A STEP SERVING THE INTERESTS OF PEACE (The Nixon visit to Moscow). Survival. Vol. 14. No. 1. January/February 1972. pp. 16–19

Arbatov, G.A. ON SOVIET-AMERICAN RELATIONS. Survival. Vol. 15. No. 3. May/June 1973. pp. 124–130. (Reprint from KOMMUNIST. No. 3. 1973)

Art, Robert J. WHY WE OVERSPEND AND UNDERACCOMPLISH. Foreign Policy. No. 6. Spring 1972. pp. 95–117. (A critique of U.S. defence spending)

Ball, George W. THE USSR AND THE WEST. 1972. Atlantic Community Quarterly. Vol. 10. No. 2. Summer 1972. pp. 188–194. (A cautious note on detente)

Bark, Dennis L. CHANGING EAST-WEST RELATIONS IN EUROPE: THE BONN-MOSCOW TREATY OF AUGUST 1970. Orbis. Vol. 15. No. 2. Summer 1971. pp. 625–642

Barnet, Richard J. THE ILLUSION OF SECURITY. Foreign Policy. No. 2. Spring 1971. pp. 71–89. (A critique of post-war U.S. defence policy by a former U.S. official)

Beaton, Leonard. THE STRATEGIC AND POLITICAL ISSUES FACING AMERICA, BRITAIN AND CANADA. Atlantic Community Quarterly. Vol. 9. No. 4. Winter 1971–72. pp. 476–493

Bertram, Christoph. INTERNAL PRESSURES ON DEFENCE POLICY. Survival. Vol. 13. No. 1. January 1971. pp. 13–16

Bertram, Christoph. THE POLITICS OF MBFR. The World Today. Vol. 29. No. 1. January 1973. pp. 1–7

van der Beugel, Ernst H. and Kohnstamm, Max. WESTERN EUROPE AND AMERICA IN THE SEVENTIES. Atlantic Community Quarterly. Vol. 10. No. 3. Fall 1972. pp. 295–312

Birnbaum, Karl E. PAN-EUROPEAN PERSPECTIVES AFTER THE BERLIN AGREEMENT (1970). International Journal. Vol. 27. No. 1. Winter 1971. pp. 32–44

Birnbaum, Karl E. THE MEMBER STATES OF THE WARSAW

TREATY ORGANISATION AND CSCE: CURRENT PREOCCU-
PATIONS AND EXPECTATIONS. Co-operation and Conflict. Vol.
9. No. 1. 1974. pp. 29–34

Booth, Ken. SECURITY MAKES STRANGE BEDFELLOWS: NATO'S
PROBLEMS FROM A MINIMALIST PERSPECTIVE. R.U.S.I.
Journal for Defence Studies. Vol. 120. No. 4. December 1975.
pp. 3–14

Brennan, Donald G. SOME FUNDAMENTAL PROBLEMS OF ARMS
CONTROL AND NATIONAL SECURITY. Orbis. Vol. 15. No. 1.
Spring 1977. pp. 218–231

Brosio, Manlio. WILL NATO SURVIVE DETENTE? The World Today.
Vol. 27. No. 6. June 1971. pp. 231–241. Atlantic Community
Quarterly. Vol. 9. No. 2. Summer 1971. pp. 143–156

Brosio, Manlio. AN ACCOUNT OF STEWARDSHIP. Atlantic
Community Quarterly. Vol. 9. No. 4. Winter 1971–72. pp. 451–460

Brosio, Manlio. EUROPE AND THE ATLANTIC ALLIANCE TODAY.
Atlantic Community Quarterly. Vol. 10. No. 3. Fall 1972. pp. 285–
295. (A cautious look at the prospects for a conference on European
security and co-operation)

Brosio, Manlio. CONSULTATION AND THE ATLANTIC ALLIANCE.
Survival. Vol. 16. No. 3. May/June 1974. pp. 115–120. Atlantic
Community Quarterly. Vol. 12. No. 3. Fall 1974. pp. 308–319

Brzezinski, Zbigniew. AMERICA AND EUROPE. Foreign Affairs. Vol.
49. No. 1. October 1970. pp. 11–29

Brzezinski, Zbigniew. THE BALANCE OF POWER DELUSION.
Foreign Policy. No. 7. Summer 1972. pp. 54–59

Brzezinski, Zbigniew. HOW THE COLD WAR WAS PLAYED. Foreign
Affairs. Vol. 51. No. 1. October 1972. pp. 181–209

Brzezinski, Zbigniew. U.S. FOREIGN POLICY: THE SEARCH FOR
FOCUS. Foreign Affairs. Vol. 51. No. 4. July 1973. pp. 708–727

Bundy, William P. INTERNATIONAL SECURITY TODAY. Foreign
Affairs. Vol. 53. No. 1. October 1974. pp. 24–44

Bussmann, Bernard. A EUROPEAN SECURITY CONFERENCE
(Paper presented at the 7th International Wehrkunde meeting).
Munich. February 1970. Survival. Vol. 12. No. 3. March 1970.
pp. 81–85

Bykov, Vladimir L. THE USSR AND SECURITY IN EUROPE. The
Annals of the American Academy of Political and Social Science.
No. 414. July 1974. pp. 96–104

Campbell, John C. SOVIET-AMERICAN RELATIONS: DETENTE

AND DISPUTE. Current History. Vol. 69. No. 109. October 1975. pp. 113–116/146–147/149–151

Camps, Miriam. SOURCES OF STRAIN IN TRANSATLANTIC RELATIONS. International Affairs. Vol. 48. No. 4. October 1972. pp. 559–578

Chace, James. THE CONCEPT OF EUROPE. Foreign Affairs. Vol. 52. No. 1. October 1973. pp. 96–108

Chemenko, K. THE CONFERENCE ON HELSINKI AND INTERNATIONAL SECURITY. International Affairs (Moscow). 1975. No. 11. 1975. pp. 3–14

Cicco, John A. THE ATLANTIC ALLIANCE AND THE ARAB CHALLENGE: THE EUROPEAN PERSPECTIVE. World Affairs. Vol. 137. No. 4. Spring 1975. pp. 303–325

Coffey, J.I. STRATEGIC ARMS LIMITATIONS AND EUROPEAN SECURITY. International Affairs. Vol. 47. No. 4. October 1971. pp. 692–707

Coffey, J.I. DETENTE, ARMS CONTROL AND EUROPEAN SECURITY. International Affairs. Vol. 52. No. 1. January 1976. pp. 39–52

Cogniot, G. THE STRUGGLE FOR EUROPEAN SECURITY AND THE NEW INTRIGUES OF THE ATLANTICISTS. International Affairs (Moscow). 1974. No. 3. pp. 38–46

Conquest, Robert. STALIN'S SUCCESSORS. Foreign Affairs. Vol. 48. No. 3. April 1970. pp. 509–524

Conquest, Robert. A NEW RUSSIA? A NEW WORLD. Foreign Affairs. Vol. 53. No. 3. April 1975. pp. 482–497

Crankshaw, Edward. WHERE KHRUSHCHEV LEFT OFF. (The background to the Soviet-West Germany non-aggression treaty). Survival. Vol. 12. No. 11. November 1970. pp. 374–375. (Reprint from The Observer (London). 23 August 1970)

Curtis, Michael. SOVIET-AMERICAN RELATIONS AND THE MIDDLE EAST CRISIS. Orbis. Vol. 15. No. 1. Spring 1971. pp. 403–427

Dobrosielski, M. PEACEFUL CO-EXISTENCE AND EUROPEAN SECURITY. International Affairs (Moscow). 1972. No. 6. pp. 33–36

Dougherty, James E. ARMS CONTROL IN THE 1970'S. Orbis. Vol. 15. No. 1. Spring 1977. pp. 194–217

Duchêne, François. SALT, THE OSTPOLITIK AND THE POST-COLD WAR CONTEXT. The World Today. Vol. 26. No. 12. December 1970. pp. 500–511

Duchêne, François. A NEW EUROPEAN DEFENCE COMMUNITY.

Foreign Affairs. Vol. 50. No. 1. October 1971. pp. 59–68
Duchêne, François. THE STRATEGIC CONSEQIENCES OF THE ENLARGED EUROPEAN COMMUNITY. Survival. Vol. 15. No. 1. January/February 1973. pp. 2–7. Atlantic Community Quarterly. Vol. 11. No. 2. Summer 1973. pp. 207–218
Duchêne, François. THE FUTURE OF EUROPE: WAYS FORWARD. The World Today. Vol. 27. No. 9. September 1971. pp. 457–462
Ecobescu, Nicolae and Celac, Sergia. SECURITY AND CO-OPERATION IN EUROPE. Survival. Vol. 13. No. 6. June 1971. pp. 203–207
Ehrhardt, Carl A. LESSONS OF THE BRUSSELS NATO SUMMIT. Aussenpolitik. Vol. 26. No. 3. 1975. pp. 270–282
Ehrhardt, Carl A. FRESH IMPETUS FOR EUROPE AND NATO. Aussenpolitik. Vol. 25. No. 3. 1974. pp. 272–281
Ehrhardt, Carl A. DISENCHANTMENT BETWEEN EUROPE AND AMERICA. Aussenpolitik. Vol. 24. No. 4. 1973. pp. 377–392
Ellsworth, Robert. EUROPE, AMERICA AND THE ERA OF NEGOTIATION. Survival. Vol. 13. No. 4. April 1971. pp. 114–122
Frank, Paul. GERMAN OSTPOLITIK IN A CHANGING WORLD. Aussenpolitik. Vol. 23. No. 1. 1972. pp. 14–25
Freymond, Jacques. AN ATLANTICIST OR EUROPEAN EUROPE. The World Today. Vol. 31. No. 5. May 1975. pp. 214–221
Galtung, Johan. EUROPEAN SECURITY AND CO-OPERATION: A SKEPTICAL CONTRIBUTION. Journal of Peace Research. Vol. 12. No. 3. 1975. pp. 165–173
Gasteyger, Curt. WORLD POLITICS ON THE SEVEN SEAS. Survival. Vol. 12. No. 3. March 1970. pp. 92–96
Gasteyger, Curt. EUROPE AND AMERICA AT THE CROSSROADS. Atlantic Community Quarterly. Vol. 10. No. 2. Summer 1972. pp. 154–167. (Anglo-European differences, notably on defence cuts)
Gasteyger, Curt. EUROPE COOL TO U.S. SUGGESTIONS ON REVITALISED CHARTER. Atlantic Community Quarterly. Fall 1973. Vol. 11. No. 3. pp. 319–322
Gati, Charles. WHAT CONTAINMENT MEANT. Foreign Policy. No. 7. Summer 1972. pp. 22–40
Goldmann, Kjell. EAST-WEST TENSION IN EUROPE 1946–1970: A CONCEPTUAL ANALYSIS AND A QUANTITATIVE DESCRIPTION. World Politics. Vol. 26. No. 1. October 1973. pp. 106–125
Goldsborough, James O. FRANCE, THE EUROPEAN CRISIS AND

THE ALLIANCE. Foreign Affairs. Vol. 52. No. 3. April 1974.
pp. 538-555

Goldwater. Barry. THE PERILOUS CONJUNCTURE: SOVIET ASCENDENCY AND AMERICAN ISOLATIONISM. Orbis. Vol. 15. No. 1. Spring 1971. pp. 53-64

Goodpaster, General Andrew J. NEW CHALLENGES, NEW PROBLEMS, NEW DANGERS. Atlantic Community Quarterly. Vol. 10. No. 4. 1972/73. pp. 457-470. (i.e. MBFR, European co-operation and co-ordination)

Gorokhov, A. THE USSR'S STRUGGLE FOR EUROPEAN SECURITY. International Affairs (Moscow). 1971. No. 1. pp. 3-8

Gorokhov, A. PRACTICAL PREPARATIONS FOR AN ALL-EUROPEAN CONFERENCE. International Affairs (Moscow). 1972. No. 11. pp. 3-6

Gray, Colin S. OF BARGAINING CHIPS AND BUILDING BLOCKS: ARMS CONTROL AND DEFENCE POLICY. International Journal. Vol. 28. No. 2. Spring 1973. pp. 266-296

Gray, Colin S. THE URGE TO COMPETE: RATIONALES FOR ARMS RACING. World Politics. Vol. 26. No. 2. January 1974. pp. 207-233

Gray, Colin S. FOREIGN POLICY AND THE STRATEGIC BALANCE. Orbis. Vol. 18. No. 3. Fall 1974. pp. 706-727

Greenhill, Denis. THE FUTURE SECURITY OF WESTERN EUROPE. International Affairs. Vol. 50. No. 1. January 1974. pp. 1-14

von Groll, Gotz. THE FINAL ACT OF THE CSCE. Aussenpolitik. Vol. 26. No. 3. 1975. pp. 247-269

von Groll, Gotz. EAST-WEST TALKS IN HELSINKI. Aussenpolitik. Vol. 23. No. 4. 1972. pp. 371-382

von Groll, Gotz. THE CSCE BUNDESTAG DEBATE. Aussenpolitik. Vol. 25. No. 4. 1974. pp. 375-384

von Groll, Gotz. THE FOREIGN MINISTERS IN HELSINKI. Aussenpolitik. Vol. 24. No. 3. 1973. pp. 255-274

von Groll, Gotz. THE HELSINKI CONSULTATIONS. Aussenpolitik. Vol. 24. No. 2. 1973. pp. 123-129

Halperin, Morton H. THE GOOD, THE BAD AND THE WASTEFUL. Foreign Policy. No. 6. Spring 1972. pp. 69-83. (A critique of U.S. defence spending)

Harlech, Lord. SUEZ SNAFU, SKYBOLT SABU. Foreign Policy. No. 2. Spring 1971. pp. 38-50. (A British perspective on transatlantic conflict issues)

Harned, Joseph W. (ed.), *et al.* CSCE AND NEGOTIATIONS ON

MBFR. Atlantic Community Quarterly. Vol. 11. No. 1. Spring 1978. pp. 7–55

Haroche, Charles. EUROPE: FROM SPLIT TO CO-OPERATION. International Affairs (Moscow). 1970. No. 4. pp. 63–69

Hartman, Arthur. A. U.S. – SOVIET DETENTE: PERCEPTIONS AND PURPOSES. Atlantic Community Quarterly. Vol. 12. No. 3. Fall 1974. pp. 300–308

Haselkorn, Avigdor. THE SOVIET COLLECTIVE SECURITY SYSTEM. Orbis. Vol. 19. No. 1. Spring 1975. pp. 231–254

Hassner, Pierre. THE NEW EUROPE: FROM COLD WAR TO HOT PEACE. International Journal. Vol. 27. No. 1. Winter 1971. pp. 1–17

Hassner, Pierre and Steel, Ronald. 'SPHERES OF WHAT?' AN EXCHANGE. Foreign Policy. No. 6. Spring 1972. pp. 142–152. (See Ronald Steel: 'A spheres of influence policy' in FOREIGN POLICY. No. 5. Winter 1971–72. pp. 107–118)

Hassner, Pierre. HOW TROUBLED A PARTNERSHIP? International Journal. Vol. 29. No. 2. Spring 1974. pp. 166–185. (A silver jubilee survey of NATO)

Hassner, Pierre. DETENTE AND POLITICAL CHANGE IN EUROPE. Survival. Vol. 18. No. 2. March/April 1976. pp. 68–72

Hassner, Pierre. EUROCOMMUNISM AND DETENTE. Survival. Vol. 19. No. 6. November/December 1977. pp. 251–255

Hirsch, Mario. INFLUENCE WITHOUT POWER: SMALL STATES IN EUROPEAN POLITICS. The World Today. Vol. 32. No. 3. March 1976. pp. 112–118

Hoffmann, Stanley. WEIGHING THE BALANCE OF POWER. Foreign Affairs. Vol. 50. No. 4. July 1972. pp. 618–643

Holloway, David. THE WARSAW PACT IN THE ERA OF NEGOTIATION. Survival. Vol. 14. No. 6. November/December 1972. pp. 275–279

Holst, Johan Jorgen. FORCE LIMITATIONS AND EUROPEAN POLITICAL DEVELOPMENT. Conciliation and Conflict. 1973. No. 2. pp. 119–130. Survival. Vol. 15. No. 6. November/December 1973. pp. 283–288

Holst, Johan Jorgen and Melander, Karen Alette. EUROPEAN SECURITY AND CONFIDENCE BUILDING MEASURES. Survival. Vol. 19. No. 4. July/August 1977. pp. 146–154

Holzman, Franklyn D. and Levgold, Robert. THE ECONOMICS AND POLITICS OF EAST-WEST RELATIONS. International Organisation.

Vol. 29. No. 1. Winter 1975. pp. 275–322

Howard, Michael. NATO AND THE YEAR OF EUROPE. Survival. Vol. 16. No. 1. January/February 1974. pp. 21–27. (Reprint from ROUND TABLE. October 1973)

Hudson, George E. SOVIET NAVAL DOCTRINE AND SOVIET POLITICS 1953–1975. World Politics. Vol. 29. No. 1. October 1976. pp. 90–113

Humphrey, Hubert H. THE COURSE OF SOVIET FOREIGN POLICY AND SOVIET-AMERICAN RELATIONS IN THE 1970'S. Orbis. Vol. 15. No. 1. Spring 1971. pp. 65–86

Hunter, Robert E. TROOPS, TRADE AND DIPLOMACY. Atlantic Community Quarterly. Vol. 9. No. 3. Fall 1971. pp. 283–293. (Success in SALT, Britain's entry to EEC, Soviet interest in MBFR, Senate vote on reduction of forces in Europe – a new era?)

Huntington, Samuel P. and Manshell, Warren D. 'X' PLUS 25: INTERVIEW WITH GEORGE KENNAN. Foreign Policy. No. 7. Summer 1972. pp. 3–21. (See X (G.F. Kennan): 'The Sources of Soviet Conduct'. FOREIGN AFFAIRS. Vol. 30. No. 4. July 1947)

Huntley, James R. THE UNITED STATES AND THE EUROPEAN COMMUNITY. Atlantic Community Quarterly. Vol. 10. No. 4. 1972–73. pp. 527–541

I.I.S.S.; Japan Institute of International Affairs; The Brookings Institution. SALT AND MBFR: THE NEXT PHASE. (Report of a Trilateral Conference). Survival. Vol. 17. No. 1. January/February 1975. pp. 14–24

Iklé, Fred Charles. CAN NUCLEAR DETERRENCE LAST OUT THE CENTURY? Foreign Affairs. Vol. 51. No. 2. January 1973. pp. 267–285

International Affairs Editorial Board. EUROPEAN SECURITY SYSTEM: CONTENT AND WAYS OF ENSURING IT. International Affairs (Moscow). 1971. No. 11. pp. 64–88

Janowitz, Morris. THE FUTURE OF NATO. Survival. Vol. 13. No. 12. December 1971. pp. 412–415

Jones, David C. REAPPRAISING THE PROSPECTS FOR NATO. Strategic Review. Vol. 2. No. 4. Fall 1974. pp. 9–12

Kaiser, Karl. EUROPE AND AMERICA: A CRITICAL PHASE. Foreign Affairs. Vol. 52. No. 4. July 1974. pp. 725–741

Kann, Robert A. ALLIANCES VERSUS ENTENTES. World Politics. Vol. 28. No. 4. July 1976. pp. 611–621

Karenin, A. DETENTE AND NEW VARIATIONS OF OLD

DOCTRINES. International Affairs (Moscow). 1975. No. 6. pp. 98–106

Kennan, George F. EUROPE'S PROBLEMS, EUROPE'S CHOICES. Foreign Policy. No. 14. Spring 1974. pp. 3–16. (A devastating critique of current ideas of 'Finlandisation')

Khomutov, N. THE ATLANTIC PARTNERSHIP 25 YEARS LATER. International Affairs (Moscow). 1974. No. 5. pp. 37–45

Kissinger, Henry A. A NEW ATLANTIC CHARTER. Survival. Vol. 15. No. 4. July/August 1973. pp. 188–192. Atlantic Community Quarterly. Vol. 11. No. 2. Summer 1973. pp. 151–161

Kissinger, Henry A. DETENTE: THE AMERICAN VIEW. Survival. Vol. 17. No. 1. January/February 1975. pp. 32–42

Kissinger, Henry A. THE PERMANENT CHALLENGE OF PEACE: U.S. POLICY TOWARDS THE SOVIET UNION. Atlantic Community Quarterly. Vol. 14. No. 1. Spring 1976. pp. 20–36

Kohl, Wilfrid L. THE NIXON-KISSINGER FOREIGN POLICY SYSTEM AND U.S.-EUROPEAN RELATIONS: PATTERNS OF POLICY-MAKING. World Politics. Vol. 28. No. 1. October 1975. pp. 1–43

Kolosov, G. and Madzojewski, S. THE PLANS FOR MILITARY INTEGRATION IN WESTERN EUROPE: THE BRITISH VARIANT. International Affairs (Moscow). 1973. No. 9. pp. 52–58

Komer, Robert W. TEN SUGGESTIONS FOR RATIONALISING NATO. Survival. Vol. 19. No. 2. March/April 1977. pp. 67–72

Kudrin, M. AN IMPORTANT STEP TOWARDS STRENGTHENING PEACE. International Affairs (Moscow). 1973. No. 10. pp. 10–14. (Re. the U.S.-Soviet Agreement on the prevention of nuclear war)

Kupperman, Robert H.; Behr, Robert M. and Jones, Thomas P., Jr. THE DETERRENCE CONTINUUM. Orbis. Vol. 18. No. 3. Fall 1974. pp. 728–749

Lane, Major-General Thomas A. PROSPECTS FOR THE ATLANTIC ALLIANCE. Strategic Review. Vol. 3. No. 1. Winter 1975. pp. 39–45

Lavrov, K. EUROPEAN CONFERENCE: IMPORTANT TASKS OF THE SECOND STAGE. International Affairs (Moscow). 1974. No. 5. pp. 16–23

Legere, Lawrence J. A PRESIDENTIAL PERSPECTIVE. Foreign Policy. No. 6. Spring 1972. pp. 84–94. (A critique of U.S. defence spending)

Leonidov, A. EUROPE AWAITS DECISIONS. International Affairs (Moscow). 1974. No. 9. pp. 98–101. (Re. the European Conference on Security and Co-operation)

Levgold, Robert. THE PROBLEM OF EUROPEAN SECURITY. Problems of Communism. Vol. 23. No. 1. January/February 1974. pp. 13–33

Luns, Joseph. THE FUTURE OF THE ATLANTIC ALLIANCE IN THE LIGHT OF PRESENT EUROPEAN DEVELOPMENTS. Atlantic Community Quarterly. Vol. 10. No. 2. Summer 1972. pp. 194–203

Luns, Joseph. NATO VIEW OF SECURITY CONFERENCE. Atlantic Community Quarterly. Vol. 11. No. 1. Spring 1973. pp. 55–65

Luns, Joseph. NATO'S 25TH BIRTHDAY. Atlantic Community Quarterly. Vol. 12. No. 1. Spring 1974. pp.7–12

Lvov, M. THE EUROPEAN CONFERENCE: EXPERIENCE AND SIGNIFICANCE. International Affairs (Moscow). 1976. No. 4. pp. 41–50. (i.e. The European Conference on Security and Co-operation)

Lyon, Peyton V. BEYOND NATO. International Journal. Vol. 29. No. 2. Spring 1974. pp. 268–278

Mackintosh, Malcolm. SOVIET STRATEGIC POLICY. The World Today. Vol. 26. No.7. July 1970. pp. 269–276

Mackintosh, Malcolm. ERA OF NEGOTIATION? CLUES TO SOVIET POLICY. Survival. Vol. 13. No. 1. January 1971. pp. 25–29. (Reprint from U.S. NEWS AND WORLD REPORT (Washington). 2 November 1970)

Mackintosh, Malcolm. MOSCOW'S VIEW OF THE BALANCE OF POWER. The World Today. Vol. 29. No. 3. March 1973. pp. 108–118

Mackintosh, Malcolm. THE WARSAW PACT TODAY. Survival. Vol. 16. No. 3. May/June 1974. pp. 122–126

Marantz, Paul. PRELUDE TO DETENTE: DOCTRINAL CHANGE UNDER KHRUSHCHEV. International Studies Quarterly. Vol. 19. No. 4. December 1975. pp. 501–528

Mason, Roy. BRITAIN'S SECURITY INTERESTS. Survival. Vol. 17. No. 5. September/October 1975. pp. 217–222

Matveyev, V. PEACEFUL CO-EXISTENCE – HIGHROAD OF INTERNATIONAL DEVELOPMENT. International Affairs (Moscow). 1973. No. 8. pp. 6–11

Matveyev, V. NATO AT THE TIME OF CHANGES. International

Affairs (Moscow). 1975. No. 8. pp. 84–92

Matveyev, V. NATO: BACK TO OLD POSITIONS. International Affairs (Moscow). 1974. No. 9. pp. 102–105. (Soviet critique of NATO's Ottawa declaration, June 1974)

MacNeil, Robert. NATO AND THE PRICE OF PEACE. Atlantic Community Quarterly. Vol. 13. No. 3. Fall 1975. pp. 308–312

Meany, George. DETENTE AND THE WORKINGMAN. Atlantic Community Quarterly. Vol. 14. No. 1. Spring 1976. pp. 37–41. (An attack upon the processes of detente by the president of the AFL-CIO)

Mikhailov, Y. EX-DIPLOMAT ON SOVIET-AMERICAN RELATIONS. (Review article on W. Averell Harriman: 'America and Russia in a changing world'. New York: Doubleday. 1971). International Affairs (Moscow). 1971. No. 6. pp. 102–104

Mikhailov, M. CONCERNING EXCHANGES AND CONTACTS. International Affairs (Moscow). 1973. No. 5. pp. 64–68. (Problems of European security)

Morgan, Roger. EAST-WEST RELATIONS IN EUROPE: POLITICAL PERSPECTIVES. International Affairs. Vol. 49. No. 2. April 1973. pp. 177–189

Morgenthau, Hans J. CHANGES AND CHANCES IN AMERICAN AND SOVIET RELATIONS. Foreign Affairs. Vol. 49. No. 3. April 1971. pp. 429–441

Multan, W. and Towpik, A. WESTERN ARMS CONTROL POLICIES IN EUROPE SEEN FROM THE EAST. Survival. Vol. 16. No. 3. May/June 1974. pp. 127–132

Nacht, Michael L. THE DELICATE BALANCE OF ERROR. Foreign Policy. No. 19. Summer 1975. pp. 163–177. (A critique of two articles by Albert Wohlstetter: 'Is there a strategic arms race?' in Foreign Policy. No. 15. Summer 1974. and 'Rivals but no "race"' in Foreign Policy. No. 16. Fall 1974)

Nau, Henry R. A POLITICAL INTERPRETATION OF THE TECHNOLOGY GAP DISPUTE. Orbis. Vol. 15. No. 2. Summer 1977. pp. 507–527

Nelson, Daniel N. THE EARLY SUCCESS OF OSTPOLITIK: AN EASTERN EUROPEAN PERSPECTIVE. World Affairs. Vol. 138. No. 1. Summer 1975. pp. 32–50

Newhouse, John. WESTERN EUROPE: STUCK FAST. Foreign Affairs. Vol. 51. No. 2. January 1973. pp. 353–366

Nitze, Paul H. SALT: THE STRATEGIC BALANCE BETWEEN HOPE

AND SKEPTICISM. Foreign Policy. No. 17. Winter 1974—75. pp. 136—156

Nixon, Richard M. EUROPE AND THE ATLANTIC ALLIANCE. Atlantic Community Quarterly. Vol. 11. No. 3. Fall 1973. pp. 293—314

Novikov, N. NEW PHASE IN THE STRUGGLE FOR EUROPEAN SECURITY. International Affairs (Moscow). 1972. No. 6. pp. 3—7

Nunn, Senator Sam, *et al.* NATO STRATEGY. Survival. Vol. 19. No. 1. January/February 1977. pp. 30—38

Odom, William E. THE SOVIET MILITARY AND FOREIGN POLICY. Survival. Vol. 17. No. 6. November/December 1975. pp. 276—281

Panofsky, Wolfgang K.H. THE MUTUAL-HOSTAGE RELATIONSHIP BETWEEN AMERICA AND RUSSIA. Foreign Affairs. Vol. 52. No. 1. October 1973. pp. 109—118

Pfaltzgraff, Robert L., Jr. NATO AND EUROPEAN SECURITY: PROSPECTS FOR THE 1970'S. Orbis. Vol. 15. No. 1. Spring 1977. pp. 154—177

Pfaltzgraff, Robert L., Jr. EUROPEAN-AMERICAN DEFENCE BURDEN SHARING. Atlantic Community Quarterly. Vol. 12. No. 2. Summer 1974. pp. 197—205

Pick, Otto. ATLANTIC DEFENCE AND THE INTEGRATION OF EUROPE. Atlantic Community Quarterly. Vol. 10. No. 2. Summer 1972. pp. 174—185

Pierre, Andrew J. NUCLEAR DIPLOMACY: BRITAIN, FRANCE AND AMERICA. Foreign Affairs. Vol. 49. No. 2. January 1971. pp. 283—301

Pierre, Andrew J. AMERICA DOWN, RUSSIA UP; THE CHANGING POLITICAL ROLE OF MILITARY POWER. Foreign Policy. Vol. 4. Fall 1971. pp. 163—187

Pierre, Andrew J. EUROPE AND AMERICA IN A PENTAGONAL WORLD. Survey. Vol. 18. No. 1. 1972. pp. 183—201

Pierre, Andrew J. CAN EUROPE'S SECURITY BE 'DECOUPLED' FROM AMERICA? Foreign Affairs. Vol. 51. No. 4. July 1973. pp. 761—777

Pierre, Andrew J. WHAT HAPPENED TO THE YEAR OF EUROPE? The World Today. Vol. 30. No. 3. March 1974. pp. 110—119

Pipes, Richard. SOVIET FOREIGN POLICY: BACKGROUND AND PROSPECTS. Survey. Vol. 17. No. 4. 1971. pp. 1—9

Polyanov, N. EUROPEAN REALITIES AND PROSPECTS. International

Affairs (Moscow). 1971. No. 9. pp. 3–10. (re. European security)
Polyanov, N. THE OPPONENTS OF DETENTE HAVE NOT SURRENDERED. International Affairs (Moscow). 1976. No. 1. pp. 103–112
Quester, George H. MISSILES IN CUBA, 1970. Foreign Affairs. Vol. 49. No. 3. April 1971. pp. 493–506
Rakhmaninov, Y. TOWARDS LASTING PEACE IN EUROPE. International Affairs (Moscow). 1972. No. 3. pp. 3–8
Rakhmaninov, Y. EUROPE: PRINCIPLES OF SECURITY AND CO-OPERATION. International Affairs (Moscow). 1976. No. 2. pp. 41–50
Repnitsky, V. RECIPES FOR NUCLEAR 'EUROPEANISATION' OF NATO. (Review article on: Andrew J. Pierre: 'Nuclear Politics'. London: Oxford University Press. 1972). International Affairs (Moscow). 1974 No. 4. pp. 92–94
Richardson, J.L. COLD-WAR REVISIONISM: A CRITIQUE. World Politics. Vol. 24. No. 4. July 1972. pp. 579–612
Ritchie, Ronald S. THE ATLANTIC CONDITION. International Journal. Vol. 29. No. 2. Spring 1975. pp. 155–165. (A silver jubilee survey)
Roberts, Chalmers M. THE ABCs OF FBS AND SALT AND MBFR AND CES (ESC). Survival. Vol. 13. No. 9. September 1971. pp. 303–306. (Reprint from THE WASHINGTON POST. 29 May 1971)
Roberts, Chalmers M. HOW CONTAINMENT WORKED. Foreign Policy. No. 7. Summer 1972. pp. 41–53
Rosecrance, Richard and Stein, Arthur. INTERDEPENDENCE: MYTH OR REALITY? World Politics. Vol. 26. No. 1. October 1973. pp. 1–27
Rosecrance, Richard. DETENTE OR ENTENTE. Foreign Affairs. Vol. 53. No. 3. April 1975. pp. 464–481
Rosenfeld, Stephen S. DILEMMAS OF DETENTE: PLURALISM AND POLICY. Foreign Affairs. Vol. 52. No. 2. January 1974. pp. 263–272
Rosenthal, Benjamin S. AMERICA'S MOVE. Foreign Affairs. Vol. 51. No. 2. January 1973. pp. 380–391. (A discussion of U.S. options prior to ECSC)
Rush, Kenneth. THE NATO ALLIANCE: THE BASIS FOR AN ERA OF NEGOTIATION. Atlantic Community Quarterly. Vol. 11. No. 3. Fall 1973. pp. 327–335
Rzhevsky, Y. TOWARDS NORMALISING THE SITUATION IN EUROPE. International Affairs (Moscow). 1972. No. 4. pp. 65–67

Sanakoyev, Sh. SOCIALIST COUNTRIES' STRUGGLE FOR EUROPEAN SECURITY. International Affairs (Moscow). 1972. No. 4. pp. 3–10

Sanakoyev, Sh. PEACE IN EUROPE AND THE CONFRONTATION OF THE TWO SYSTEMS. International Affairs (Moscow). 1972. No. 11. pp. 7–15

Sanakoyev, Sh. USSR – USA RELATIONS: A HISTORIC TURNING POINT. International Affairs (Moscow). 1973. No. 9. pp. 3–10. (re. detente and the SALT agreement)

Schaetzel, J. Robert. SOME EUROPEAN QUESTIONS FOR DR. KISSINGER. Foreign Policy. No. 12. Fall 1973. pp. 66–78. (A comment on Kissinger's proposals that 1973 should see a new 'Atlantic Charter')

Schlesinger, James R. NATO AND MUTUAL SECURITY. Atlantic Community Quarterly. Vol. 13. No. 3. Fall 1975. pp. 302–308

Schlesinger, James R. A TESTING TIME FOR AMERICA. Atlantic Community Quarterly. Vol. 14. No. 1. Spring 1976. pp. 7–19. (A plea for the maintenance of U.S. military capabilities by a former Secretary of Defense)

Schmidt, Helmut. EUROPEAN SECURITY: PERSPECTIVES OF THE ALLIANCE. Survival. Vol. 12. No. 2. February 1970. pp. 43–46

Schwarz, Hans Peter. A DOUBTFUL SERVICE – THE EUROPEAN SECURITY CONFERENCE. Survival. Vol. 13. No. 2. February 1971. pp. 49–55

Schwelien, Joachim. ERA OF NEGOTIATION? HARSH WORDS – FRIENDLY DIALOGUES. Survival. Vol. 13. No. 1. January 1971. pp. 29–31

Shakhov, V. EUROPEAN SECURITY SYSTEM: SOVIET EFFORT. International Affairs (Moscow). 1971. No. 5. pp. 32–37

Shein, V. NATO: THE PRICE OF 'MATURE PARTNERSHIP'. International Affairs (Moscow). 1972. No. 2. pp. 50–56. (re. President Nixon's desire to see Europe shouldering a larger share of the defence burden)

Shulman, Marshall D. WHAT DOES SECURITY MEAN TODAY? Foreign Affairs. Vol. 49. No. 4. July 1971. pp. 607–618

Shulman, Marshall D. TOWARDS A WESTERN PHILOSOPHY OF CO-EXISTENCE. Foreign Affairs. Vol. 52. No. 1. October 1973. pp. 35–58

Shulman, Marshall D. PRIORITIES FOR DETENTE. Survival. Vol. 18. No. 1. January/February 1976. pp. 27–28. Atlantic Community

Quarterly. Vol. 14. No. 1. Spring 1976. pp. 42–44
Sinnreich, Richard H. NATO'S DOCTRINAL DILEMMA. Orbis. Vol. 19. No. 2. Summer 1975. pp. 461–476
Slavyanov, M. and Yuryev, V. CONFERENCE ON SECURITY AND CO-OPERATION IN EUROPE. International Affairs (Moscow). 1974. No. 3. pp. 12–17
Smart, Ian. THE NEW ATLANTIC CHARTER. The World Today. Vol. 29. No. 6. June 1973. pp. 238–243
Smith, Gaddis. THE SHADOW OF JOHN FOSTER DULLES. Foreign Affairs. Vol. 52. No. 2. January 1974. pp. 403–408
Sommer, Theo. DETENTE AND SECURITY: THE OPTIONS. Atlantic Community Quarterly. Vol. 9. No. 1. Spring 1971. pp. 34–50
Sorensen, Theodore C. DILEMMAS OF DETENTE. MOST-FAVORED-NATION AND LESS FAVORITE NATIONS. Foreign Affairs. Vol. 52. NO. 2. January 1974. pp. 273–286
Sovetov, A. PEACEFUL CO-EXISTENCE – A REAL FACTOR IN INTERNATIONAL RELATIONS. International Affairs (Moscow). 1972. No. 9. pp. 9–17
de Staercke, André. WHERE DOES THE ATLANTIC ALLIANCE STAND TODAY? Atlantic Community Quarterly. Vol. 11. No. 4. Winter 1973–74. pp. 448–456
Stanley, Timothy W. THE POLITICAL ECONOMICS OF DEFENCE: BURDEN-SHARING. Atlantic Community Quarterly. Vol. 9. No. 4. Winter 1971–72. pp. 442–451
Steel, Ronald. A SPHERES OF INFLUENCE POLICY. Foreign Policy. No. 5. Winter 1971–72. pp. 107–118. (An American critique of post-war U.S. policy. See also Pierre Hassner and Robert Steel: 'Spheres of what? An exchange' in FOREIGN POLICY. No. 6. Spring 1972. pp. 142–152)
Steinhoff, General Johannes. THE ROAD TO DETENTE. Atlantic Community Quarterly. Vol. 10. No. 4. Winter 1972–73. pp. 446–457
Stone, Jeremy. WHEN AND HOW TO USE SALT. Foreign Affairs. Vol. 48. No. 2. January 1970. pp. 262–271
Svetlov, A. THE SOVIET UNION'S STRUGGLE FOR MILITARY DETENTE. International Affairs (Moscow). 1976. No. 2. pp. 92–101
Svetlov, B. USSR – USA: POSSIBILITIES AND REALITIES. International Affairs (Moscow). 1972. No. 2. pp. 15–20
Tatu, Michel. SOMETHING MORE THAN AN INTERLUDE. Atlantic Community Quarterly. Vol. 9. No. 1. Spring 1971. pp. 50–56. (The future of detente, with especial reference to Berlin)

Tatu, Michel. THE DEVOLUTION OF POWER: A DREAM? Foreign
Affairs. Vol. 53. No. 4. July 1975. pp. 668–682. (On 'United Europe'
and its transatlantic relationships)
Taylor, General Maxwell D. THE LEGITIMATE CLAIMS OF
NATIONAL SECURITY. Foreign Affairs. Vol. 52. No. 3. April 1974.
pp. 577–594
Thomas, John R. SOVIET FOREIGN POLICY AND THE MILITARY.
Survey. Vol. 17. No. 3. 1971. pp. 129–156
Tickell, Crispin. ENLARGED COMMUNITY AND SECURITY
CONFERENCE. Aussenpolitik. Vol. 25. No. 1. 1974. pp. 13–22
Trofimenko, G. FROM CONFRONTATION TO CO-EXISTENCE.
International Affairs (Moscow). 1975. No. 10. pp. 33–41
Trotman, J.H. NATO IN THEORY AND PRACTICE. Survival. Vol. 13.
No. 12. December 1971. pp. 406–411
Ulam, Adam B. and Windsor, Philip. MOSCOW PLAYS THE BALANCE...
BUT EUROPE SHOULDN'T. Foreign Policy. No. 8. Fall 1972.
pp. 86–101. (A commentary on current concepts of the balance of
power)
Unattributed. THE URGENT TASK OF CONSOLIDATING PEACE IN
EUROPE. International Affairs (Moscow). 1971. No. 3. pp. 23–28
Unattributed. TOWARDS AN ALL-EUROPEAN CONFERENCE.
International Affairs (Moscow). 1972. No. 2. pp. 3–6
Unattributed. DETENTE IN CHECK. Atlantic Community Quarterly.
Vol. 14. No. 1. Spring 1976. pp. 45–48. (Reprint from The
Economist. 7 February 1976)
Vernon, Raymond. ROGUE ELEPHANT IN THE FOREST: AN
APPRAISAL OF TRANSATLANTIC RELATIONS. Foreign Affairs.
Vol. 51. No. 3. April 1973. pp. 573–587
Vidyasova, L. THE CONFERENCE ON SECURITY AND CO-
OPERATION IN EUROPE: A SUCCESSFUL BEGINNING. Inter-
national Affairs (Moscow). 1973. No. 9. pp. 11–17
Vysotsky, V. LANDMARK IN THE STRUGGLE FOR DETENTE.
International Affairs (Moscow). 1971. No. 11. pp. 12–16
Wieck, Hans-Georg. THOUGHTS ON SECURITY IN EUROPE.
Aussenpolitik. Vol. 23. No. 3. 1972. pp. 263–270
Windsor, Philip. CURRENT TENSIONS IN NATO. The World Today.
Vol. 26. No. 7. July 1970. pp. 289–295
Windsor, Philip. NATO'S 25 YEARS. The World Today. Vol. 30. No. 5.
May 1974. pp. 181–187
Windsor, Philip. THE STATE OF NATO. The World Today. Vol. 31.

No. 8. August 1975. pp. 318–325

Wohlstetter, Albert. THREATS AND PROMISES OF PEACE: EUROPE AND AMERICA IN THE NEW ERA. Orbis. Vol. 17. No. 4. Winter 1974. pp. 1107–1144

Wolf, Charles., Jr. IS UNITED STATES FOREIGN POLICY BEING MILITARISED? Orbis. Vol. 14. No. 4. Winter 1971. pp. 819–828

Wood, Robert Jefferson. MILITARY ASSISTANCE AND THE NIXON DOCTRINE. Orbis. Vol. 15. No. 1. Spring 1977. pp. 247–274

Wyle, Frederick S. IS EUROPEAN SECURITY NEGOTIABLE? Survival. Vol. 12. No. 6. June 1970. pp. 189–193. (Reprint from THE ROUND TABLE (London). April 1970)

Yarmolinsky, Adam. THE MILITARY ESTABLISHMENT (OR HOW POLITICAL PROBLEMS BECOME MILITARY PROBLEMS). Foreign Policy. No. 1. Winter 1970–71. pp. 78–97

Yefimov, A. EUROPEAN CONFERENCE AND DETENTE IN EUROPE. International Affairs (Moscow). 1975. No. 5. pp. 25–31

Yemelyanov, Y. IMPERIALISM'S NUCLEAR DIPLOMACY. International Affairs (Moscow). 1973. No. 4. pp. 95–96

Yuriev, N. THE FOUNDATIONS OF PEACE AND SECURITY IN EUROPE. International Affairs (Moscow). 1973. No. 10. pp. 15–23. (re. ECSC)

Z. THE YEAR OF EUROPE. Foreign Affairs. Vol. 52. No. 2. January 1974. pp. 237–248

Zakharov, Y. AN IMPORTANT CONDITION FOR DETENTE IN EUROPE. International Affairs (Moscow). 1972. No. 10. pp. 27–33

Zhurkin, V. DETENTE AND INTERNATIONAL CONFLICTS. International Affairs (Moscow). 1974. No. 7. pp. 89–97

Zumwalt, Elmo R. THE LESSONS FOR NATO OF RECENT MILITARY EXPERIENCE. Atlantic Community Quarterly. Vol. 12. No. 4. Winter 1974–75. pp. 463–470. (i.e. military, political and economic considerations of the Arab-Israeli War 1973)

Military – Strategic Aspects

Aaron, David. SALT: A NEW CONCEPT. Foreign Policy. No. 17. Winter 1974–75. pp. 157–165

Arbatov, G.A. THE AMERICAN STRATEGIC DEBATE: A SOVIET VIEW. Survival. Vol. 16. No. 3. May/June 1974. pp. 133–134

Bell, Coral. STRATEGIC PROBLEMS OF THE ATLANTIC. Survival.

Vol. 12. No. 3. March 1970. pp. 98–101

Bolton, David. EUROPEAN DEFENCE – ARMS AND OPTIONS. R.U.S.I. Journal for Defence Studies. Vol. 120. No. 1. March 1975. pp. 38–41

Bracken, Paul. URBAN SPRAWL AND NATO DEFENCE. Survival. Vol. 18. No. 6. November/December 1976. pp. 254–260

Brenner, Michael J. TACTICAL NUCLEAR STRATEGY AND EUROPEAN DEFENCE: A CRITICAL REAPPRAISAL. International Affairs. Vol. 51. No. 1. January 1975. pp. 23–42

Brodie, Bernard. WHY WERE WE SO STRATEGICALLY WRONG? Foreign Policy. No. 5. Winter 1971–72. pp. 151–152. (A reply to: Colin S. Gray: 'What Rand hath wrought'. Foreign Policy. No. 4. Fall 1971. pp. 111–129)

Brown, Neville. AN UNSTABLE BALANCE OF TERROR? The World Today. Vol. 26. No. 1. January 1970. pp. 38–46

Brown, Neville. THE TACTICAL AIR BALANCE IN EUROPE. The World Today. Vol. 28. No. 9. September 1972. pp. 385–392

Burt, Richard. THE SS-20 AND THE EUROSTRATEGIC BALANCE. The World Today. Vol. 33. No. 2. February 1977. pp. 43–51

Burt, Richard. NEW WEAPONS TECHNOLOGIES AND EUROPEAN SECURITY. Orbis. Vol. 19. No. 2. Summer 1975. pp. 514–532

Byers, R.B. CANADIAN DEFENCE: THE ASW DILEMMA. Survival. Vol. 18. No. 4. July/August 1976. pp. 154–161

Canby, Steven L. NATO MUSCLE: MORE SHADOW THAN SUBSTANCE. Foreign Policy. No. 8. Fall 1972. pp. 38–49. (A critique of the current military posture of NATO)

Canby, Steven L. THE WASTEFUL WAYS OF NATO. Survival. Vol. 15. No. 1. January/February 1973. pp. 21–26. (Reprint from FOREIGN POLICY. Fall 1972)

Canby, Steven L. DUMPING NUCLEAR COUNTERFORCE INCENTIVES: CORRECTING NATO'S INFERIORITY IN CONVENTIONAL MILITARY STRENGTH. Orbis. Vol. 19. No. 1. Spring 1975. pp. 47–71

Canby, Steven L. NATO: REASSESSING THE CONVENTIONAL WISDOMS. Survival. Vol. 19. No. 4. July/August 1977. pp. 164–168

Carter, Barry. FLEXIBLE STRATEGIC OPTIONS: NO NEED FOR NEW STRATEGY. Survival. Vol. 17. No. 1. January/February 1975.

pp. 25–31. (Reprint from SCIENTIFIC AMERICAN. May 1974)
Chester, Conrad V. and Wigner, Eugene P. POPULATION VULNER-
ABILITY: THE NEGLECTED ISSUE IN ARMS LIMITATION
AND THE STRATEGIC BALANCE. Orbis. Vol. 18. No. 3. Fall 1974.
pp. 763–769
Chirac, Jacques. THE PURPOSE OF PLUTON. Survival. Vol. 17.
No. 5. September/October 1975. pp. 241–243
von Cleave, William R. and Barnett, Roger W. STRATEGIC ADAP-
TABILITY. Orbis. Vol. 18. Fall 1974. pp. 655–676
Cohen, Samuel T. TACTICAL NUCLEAR WEAPONS AND U.S.
MILITARY STRATEGY. Orbis. Vol. 15. No. 1. Spring 1971.
pp. 178–193
Cohen, S.T. and Lyons, W.C. A COMPARISON OF U.S.-ALLIED AND
SOVIET TACTICAL NUCLEAR FORCE CAPABILITIES AND
POLICIES. Orbis. Vol. 19. No. 1. Spring 1975. pp. 72–92
Colbert, Admiral R.S. THE SHIFTING BALANCE OF POWER AT SEA.
Atlantic Community Quarterly. Vol. 10. No. 4. 1972–73. pp. 470–
480
Collins, John M. MANEUVER TO MASS: THE KEY TO ASSURED
STABILITY. Orbis. Vol. 18. No. 3. Fall 1974. pp. 750–762
Curl, Richard L. STRATEGIC DOCTRINE IN THE NUCLEAR AGE.
Strategic Review. Vol. 3. No. 1. Winter 1975. pp. 45–56
Davison, Michael S. PORTRAIT OF AN ARMY: THE U.S. SEVENTH
ARMY IN EUROPE. Survival. Vol. 14. No. 5. September/October
1972. pp. 220–225
Drischler, Alvin Paul. STANDING NAVAL FORCES FOR NATO: A
PROPOSAL. Survival. Vol. 14. No. 5. September/October 1972.
pp. 226–230
Enthoven, Alain C. U.S. FORCES IN EUROPE: HOW MANY? DOING
WHAT? Foreign Affairs. Vol. 53. No. 3. April 1975. pp. 513–532
Erickson, John. MBFR: FORCE LEVELS AND SECURITY REQUIRE-
MENTS. Strategic Review. Vol. 1. No. 2. Summer 1973. pp. 28–43.
(A study of Soviet attitudes)
Furlong, R.D.M. CAN NATO AFFORD AWACS? International Defence
Review. Vol. 7. No. 5. October 1975. pp. 667–676
Garnett, J.C. BAOR AND NATO. International Affairs. Vol. 46. No. 4.
October 1970. pp. 670–681
Geisenheyner, Stefan. A DEFENSIVE MIX FOR EUROPE: PANDORA,
MEDUSA, DRAGON SEED. Survival. Vol. 13. No. 9. September

1971. pp. 307—309
Gelb, Leslie H. and Halperin, Morton H. WHY WEST EUROPE NEEDS 300,000 G.I.'S. Atlantic Community Quarterly. Vol. 9. No. 1. Spring 1971. pp. 56—61
Geneste, Marc E. THE CITY WALLS: A CREDIBLE DEFENCE DOCTRINE FOR THE WEST. Orbis. Vol. 19. No. 2. Summer 1975. pp. 477—496
Gladwyn, Lord. NUCLEAR WEAPONS AND EUROPE. Survival. Vol. 16. No. 2. March/April 1974. pp. 94—95
Gladwyn, Lord. WESTERN EUROPE'S COLLECTIVE DEFENCE. International Affairs. Vol. 51. No. 2. April 1975. pp. 166—174
Gladwyn, Lord. THE DEFENSE OF WESTERN EUROPE. Foreign Affairs. Vol. 51. No. 3. April 1973. pp. 588—597
Goldhamer, Herbert. THE U.S.-SOVIET STRATEGIC BALANCE AS SEEN FROM LONDON AND PARIS. Survival. Vol. 19. No. 5. September/October 1977. pp. 202—207
Goodpaster, General Andrew J. NATO AND U.S. FORCES: CHALLENGES AND PROSPECTS. Strategic Review. Vol. 2. No. 1. Winter 1974. pp. 6—17
Goodpaster, Andrew J. NATO STRATEGY AND REQUIREMENTS 1975—1985. Survival. Vol. 17. No. 5. September/October 1975. pp. 210—216. Atlantic Community Quarterly. Vol. 13. No. 4. Winter 1975—76. pp. 461—473
Gray, Colin S. WHAT RAND HATH WROUGHT. Foreign Policy. No. 4. Fall 1971. pp. 111—129. (A review of 20 years strategic thought. For a reply, see Bernard Brodie: 'Why were we so strategically wrong?' in FOREIGN POLICY. No. 5. Winter 1971—72. pp. 151—162)
Gray, Colin S. MINI-NUKES AND STRATEGY. International Journal. Vol. 29. No. 2. Spring 1974. pp. 216—241
Gray, Colin S. HOW DOES THE NUCLEAR ARMS RACE WORK? Conciliation and Conflict. 1974. No. 4. pp. 285—296
Gray, Colin S. DETERRENCE AND DEFENCE IN EUROPE: REVISING NATO'S THEATER NUCLEAR POSTURE. Strategic Review. Vol. 3. No. 2. Spring 1975. pp. 58—69
Gray, Colin S. THEATER NUCLEAR WEAPONS: DOCTRINES AND POSTURES. World Politics. Vol. 28. No. 2. January 1976. pp. 300—314
Greenwood, Ted and Nacht, Michael L. THE NEW NUCLEAR DEBATE — SENSE OR NONSENSE? Foreign Affairs. Vol. 52. No. 4. July

1974. pp. 761—780

Hahn, Walter F. NUCLEAR BALANCE IN EUROPE. Foreign Affairs. Vol. 50. No. 3. April 1972. pp. 501—516

Hill, R.J. MBFR. International Journal. Vol. 29. No. 2. Spring 1974. pp. 242—255

Holst, Johan Jorgen. THE SOVIET BUILD UP IN THE NORTH-EAST ATLANTIC. Survival. Vol. 14. No. 1. January/February 1972. pp. 25—28

Holst, Johan Jorgen. ARMS LIMITING AND FORCE ADJUSTING IN THE NORTHERN CAP AREA. Confiliation and Conflict. 1972. No. 2. pp. 113—120

Holst, Johan Jorgen. A STRATEGIC ARMS RACE? WHAT IS REALLY GOING ON? Foreign Policy. No. 19. Summer 1975. pp. 155—169. (A critique of two articles by Albert Wohlstetter: 'Is there a strategic arms race?' in Foreign Policy. No. 15. Summer 1974. and 'Rivals, but no race' in Foreign Policy. No. 16. Fall 1974)

Irwin, Christopher. NUCLEAR ASPECTS OF WEST EUROPEAN DEFENCE INTEGRATION. International Affairs. Vol. 47. No. 4. October 1971. pp. 679—691

Janowitz, Morris. TOWARDS A REDEFINITION OF MILITARY STRATEGY IN INTERNATIONAL RELATIONS. World Politics. Vol. 26. No. 4. July 1974. pp. 473—508

Jones, Christopher D. JUST WARS AND LIMITED WARS: RESTRAINTS ON THE USE OF SOVIET ARMED FORCES. World Politics. Vol. 28. No. 1. October 1975. pp. 44—68

Karber, Phillip A. THE SOVIET ANTI-TANK DEBATE. Survival. Vol. 18. No. 3. May/June 1976. pp. 105—111

Karenin, A. ON THE LIMITATION OF STRATEGIC WEAPONS. International Affairs (Moscow). 1974. No. 10. pp. 13—21

Khlestov, O. MUTUAL FORCE REDUCTION IN EUROPE (THE SOVIET VIEW). Survival. Vol. 16. No. 6. November/December 1974. pp. 293—298. (Reprint from WORLD ECONOMICS and INTER-

Kissinger, Henry A. PRESS STATEMENT BY SECRETARY OF STATE DR. KISSINGER ON THE SOVIET-AMERICAN STATEMENT ON STRATEGIC ARMS LIMITATION. November 1974. Survival. Vol. 17. No. 1. January/February 1975. pp. 33—34

Komer, R.W. TREATING NATO'S SELF-INFLICTED WOUND. Foreign Policy, No. 13. Winter 1973—74. pp. 34—48. (Discusses NATO's conventional capability and the myth of Warsaw Pact superiority)

Kostko, Y. MUTUAL FORCE REDUCTIONS IN EUROPE. Survival. Vol. 14. No. 5. September/October 1972. pp. 236–239. (Reprint from MIROVAYA EKONOMIKA)

Kurth, James R. WHY WE BUY THE WEAPONS WE DO. Foreign Policy. No. 11. Summer 1973. pp. 33–56. (A contribution to the debate on the military-industrial complex)

Lambeth, Benjamin S. THE EVOLVING SOVIET STRATEGIC THREAT. Current History. Vol. 69. No. 409. October 1975. pp. 121–125/152–153

Lambeth, Benjamin S. DETERRENCE IN THE MIRV ERA. World Politics. Vol. 24. No. 2. January 1972. pp. 221–242

Lander, John A. LESSONS OF THE STRATEGIC BOMBING SURVEY FOR CONTEMPORARY DEFENCE POLICY. Orbis. Vol. 18. No. 3. Fall 1974. pp. 770–790

Marriott, John. NATO'S ASW POTENTIAL. Survival. Vol. 12. No. 9. September 1970. pp. 298–303

Marriott, John. NAVAL MISSILES. International Defense Review. Vol. 3. 1969. pp. 245–248

Martin, Lawrence. CHANGES IN AMERICAN STRATEGIC DOCTRINE — AN INITIAL INTERPRETATION. Survival. Vol. 16. No. 4. July/August 1974. pp. 154–164

Martin, Lawrence. THEATRE NUCLEAR WEAPONS AND EUROPE. Survival. Vol. 16. No. 6. November/December 1974. pp. 268–276

MccGuire, Michael. SOVIET NAVAL PROGRAMMES. Survival. Vol. 15. No. 5. September/October 1973. pp. 218–227

Migolotyev, A. THE MILITARY-INDUSTRIAL COMPLEX AND THE ARMS RACE. International Affairs (Moscow). 1975. No. 11. pp. 63–71

Morse, John H. NEW WEAPONS TECHNOLOGIES: IMPLICATIONS FOR NATO. Orbis. Vol. 19. No. 2. Summer 1975. pp. 497–513

Mumford, Lt.-Colonel Jay C. PROBLEMS OF NUCLEAR FREE ZONES — THE NORDIC EXAMPLE. Military Review. March 1976. pp. 3–10

Newhouse, John. U.S. TROOPS IN EUROPE: ISSUES AND ALTERNATIVES. Atlantic Community Quarterly. Vol. 9. No. 4. Winter 1971–72. pp. 460–476

Pierre, Andrew J. LIMITING SOVIET AND AMERICAN CONVENTIONAL FORCES. Survival. Vol. 15. No. 2. March/April 1973. pp. 59–64

Polmar, Norman. ALARMIST *v.* REALIST. Atlantic Community

Quarterly. Vol. 10. No. 3. Fall 1972. pp. 368–378. (An assessment of Soviet naval power and policy)

Proektor, Dimitry. MILITARY DETENTE: A SOVIET VIEW. Survival. Vol. 18. No. 6. November/December 1976. pp. 261–265. (Reprint from INTERNATIONAL AFFAIRS (Moscow). 1976. No. 6)

Ranger, Robin. MBFR: POLITICAL OR TECHNICAL ARMS CONTROL. The World Today. Vol. 30. No. 10. October 1974. pp. 411–418

Rathjens, G.W. FLEXIBLE RESPONSE OPTIONS. Orbis. Vol. 18. No. 3. Fall 1974. pp. 677–688

Rattinger, Hans. ARMAMENTS, DETENTE AND BUREAUCRACY: THE CASE OF THE ARMS RACE IN EUROPE. Journal of Conflict Resolution. Vol. 19. No. 4. December 1975. pp. 571–595

von Raven, Wolfram. NATO'S BIGGEST NORTH ATLANTIC MANOEUVRES. Aussenpolitik. Vol. 23. No. 4. 1972. pp. 406–417

Record, Jeffrey. U.S. TACTICAL NUCLEAR WEAPONS IN EUROPE: 7,000 WARHEADS IN SEARCH OF A RATIONALE. Arms Control Today. Vol. 4. No. 4. 1974. pp. 1–2

Record, Jeffrey. TACTICAL NUCLEAR WEAPONS IN EUROPE: ALTERNATIVE POSTURES. Survival. Vol. 17. No. 2. March/April 1975. pp. 73–80

Record, Jeffrey. THEATRE NUCLEAR WEAPONS: BEGGING THE SOVIET UNION TO PRE-EMPT. Survival. Vol. 19. No. 5. September/October 1977. pp. 208–211

Rudnick, David. THE CASE OF THE LEOPARD TANK. International Affairs. Vol. 52. No. 2. April 1976. pp. 197–207

Russett, Bruce M. COUNTER-COMBATANT DETERRENCE: A PROPOSAL. Survival. Vol. 16. No. 3. May/June 1974. pp. 135–140. (Reprint from PUBLIC POLICY. Vol. 22. No. 2. Spring 1974)

Sandstrom, Anders. MBFR: A NON-STARTER OR A SLOW STARTER? Conciliation and Conflict. 1976. No. 2. pp. 71–94

Schlesinger, James R. FLEXIBLE STRATEGIC OPTIONS AND DETERRENCE. (Press conference 10 January 1974). Survival. Vol. 16. No. 2. March/April 1974. pp. 86–90

Schlesinger, James R. THE THEATRE NUCLEAR FORCE POSTURE IN EUROPE: REPORT TO CONGRESS BY SECRETARY OF DEFENSE SCHLESINGER, 1975. Survival. Vol. 17. No. 5. September/October 1975. pp. 235–241

Schwartz, David N. THE ROLE OF DETERRENCE IN NATO DEFENCE STRATEGY: IMPLICATIONS FOR DOCTRINE AND POWER. World Politics. Vol. 28. No. 1. January 1975. pp. 118–133

Scott, William F. SOVIET MILITARY DOCTRINE AND STRATEGY: REALITIES AND MISUNDERSTANDINGS. Strategic Review. Vol. 3. No. 3. Summer 1975. pp. 57–66

Scoville, Herbert, Jr. BEYOND SALT ONE. Foreign Affairs. Vol. 50. No. 3. April 1972. pp. 488–500

Scoville, Herbert, Jr., *et al.* STRATEGIC FORUM: THE SALT AGREEMENTS. Survival. Vol. 14. No. 5. September/October 1972. pp. 210–216

Scoville, Herbert, Jr. FLEXIBLE MADNESS. Foreign Policy. No. 14. Spring 1974. pp. 164–177. (On Schlesinger's 'flexible strategic response')

Simmons, Henry T. NATO EQUIPMENT STANDARDIZATION AND COMMONALITY – U.S. OPINIONS AND PROPOSALS. International Defence Review. April 1975. Vol. 8. No. 2. pp. 156–157

Smart, Ian. THE STRATEGIC ARMS LIMITATION TALKS. The World Today. Vol. 26. No. 7. July 1970. pp. 296–305

Stanley, Timothy W. MUTUAL FORCE REDUCTIONS. Survival. Vol. 12. No. 5. May 1970. pp. 152–160

Steinbruner, John. BEYOND RATIONAL DETERRENCE: THE STRUGGLE FOR NEW CONCEPTIONS. World Politics. Vol. 28. No. 2. January 1976. pp. 223–245

Svyatov, G. and Kokoshin, A. NAVAL POWER IN THE U.S. STRATEGIC PLANS. International Affairs (Moscow). 1973. No. 4. pp. 56–62

Timofeyev, K. NAVIES IN IMPERIALIST POLICY. Survival. Vol. 12. No. 3. March 1970. pp. 101–104. (Reprint from NEW TIMES (Moscow). 28 November 1969)

Tomilin, Y. PROBLEM OF ARMED FORCES REDUCTIONS IN EUROPE. International Affairs (Moscow). 1973. No. 4. pp. 37–42

Tomilin, Y. THE RESULTS OF THE VIENNA CONSULTATIONS. International Affairs (Moscow). 1973. No. 9. pp. 78–81

Ullman, Richard H. NO FIRST USE OF NUCLEAR WEAPONS. Foreign Affairs. Vol. 50. No. 4. July 1972. pp. 669–683

Unattributed. THE ULTIMATE ARM. (Britain's nuclear deterrent). Survival. Vol. 12. No. 9. September 1970. pp. 290–292. (Reprint from THE TIMES. 6 July 1970)

Unattributed. FOR A MILITARY DETENTE IN EUROPE. International Affairs (Moscow). 1972. No. 1. pp. 64–66

Utkin, A. U.S. TROOPS IN EUROPE: POLICY AND FINANCE. (Review article on: ed. J. Newhouse: 'U.S. troops in Europe: Issues,

Costs and Choices'. Washington: The Brookings Institution, 1971). International Affairs (Moscow). 1972. No. 7. pp. 89–90

Viktorov, V. THE VIENNA TALKS. International Affairs (Moscow). 1974. No. 8. pp. 22–30. (Re. MBFR)

Viktorov, V. VIENNA TALKS: ROUND FIVE. International Affairs (Moscow). 1975. No. 7. pp. 97–103

Weinland, Robert G. THE CHANGING MISSION OF THE SOVIET NAVY. Survival. Vol. 14. No. 3. May/June 1972. pp. 129–133

Weinland, Robert G., et al. ADMIRAL GORSHKOV'S 'NAVIES IN WAR AND PEACE'. Survival. Vol. 17. No. 2. March/April 1975. pp. 54–63

Wieck, Hans-Georg. PERSPECTIVES OF MBFR IN EUROPE. Aussenpolitik. Vol. 23. No. 1. 1972. pp. 36–48

Williams, Alan Lee. IS A EUROPEAN NUCLEAR FORCE DESIRABLE? Atlantic Community Quarterly. Vol. 10. No. 2. Summer 1972. pp. 185–188

Williams, Phil. WHATEVER HAPPENED TO THE MANSFIELD RESOLUTION? Survival. Vol. 18. No. 4. July/August 1976. pp. 146–153. (i.e. on reducing American forces in Europe)

Wohlstetter, Albert. IS THERE A STRATEGIC ARMS RACE? Foreign Policy. No. 15. Summer 1974. pp. 3–20. RIVALS, BUT NO RACE. Foreign Policy No. 16. Fall 1974. pp. 48–81. (For miscellaneous comments, see Foreign Policy. No. 16. Fall 1974. pp. 82–92)

Wohlstetter, Albert. HOW TO CONFUSE OURSELVES. Foreign Policy. No. 20. Fall 1975. (A reply to critics, notably Michael Nacht: 'The delicate balance of error'. Foreign Policy. No. 19. Summer 1975. pp. 163–177; Johann Jurgen Holst: 'A strategic arms race? What is really going on?' Foreign Policy. No. 19. Summer 1975. pp. 155–169)

Woolridge, E.T., Jr. THE GORSHKOV PAPERS: SOVIET NAVAL DOCTRINE FOR THE NUCLEAR AGE. Orbis. Vol. 18. No. 4. Winter 1975. pp. 1153–1175.

Wyle, Frederick S. EUROPEAN SECURITY: BEATING THE NUMBERS GAME. Foreign Policy. No. 10. Spring 1973. pp. 41–54. (A contribution on MBFR)

Yakushkin, D. NATO NUCLEAR PLANS: PAST AND PRESENT. International Affairs (Moscow). 1973. No. 11. pp. 105–106

Yochelson, John N. THE AMERICAN MILITARY PRESENCE IN EUROPE: CURRENT DEBATE IN THE UNITED STATES. Orbis. Vol. 15. No. 3. Fall 1971. pp. 796–802

Yochelson, John N. MBFR – THE SEARCH FOR AN AMERICAN

APPROACH. Survival. Vol. 15. No. 6. November/December 1973. pp. 275–283. Orbis. Vol. 17. No. 1. Spring 1973. pp. 155–175
Zavilov, I. NUCLEAR WEAPONS AND WAR. Survival. Vol. 13. No. 3. March 1971. pp. 90–93. (Reprint from RED STAR. 30 October 1970)

Ref
Z
6464
N65
G67
1978

JUL 17 1979